TOTALLY ORGANIZED

Also by Bonnie McCullough

401 Ways to Get Your Kids to Work at Home
(with Susan Walker Monson)

*Bonnie's Household Organizer: The Essential Guide
for Getting Control of Your Home,* Revised Edition

*Bonnie's Household Budget Book: The Essential Guide
for Getting Control of Your Money,* 4th Revised Edition

TOTALLY ORGANIZED THE BONNIE McCULLOUGH WAY

Written and illustrated by
BONNIE McCULLOUGH

Additional illustrations by
Tom Smith

St. Martin's Press   New York

Acknowledgments

Thanks to Erma Rutherford and Glenna Berg for reading.
Thanks to Barbara Anderson at St. Martin's Press for editing.
Thanks to my husband and kids for enduring.

Any similarity of the examples used in this book to real circumstances is purely coincidental. All names have been either invented or changed, except in the case of certain "good" examples where real names have been used with permission.

Some material in this book has appeared in a different form in *Bonnie's Household Organizer*. Copyright © 1980, 1983 by Bonnie Runyan McCullough.

Design by Beth Tondreau

Library of Congress Cataloging-in-Publication Data

McCullough, Bonnie Runyan.
  Totally organized the Bonnie McCullough way.

  1. Home economics.   2. House wives—Time management.
I. Title.
TX147.M384   1986   640   85–25184
ISBN 0-312-80747-3 (pbk.)

20 19 18 17 16 15 14 13 12

Contents

Introduction

Is your home sometimes out of control? Would you like to get organized? Do you ever feel like a slave in your own home? You can be the master. You can get control—by making the principles of good time management and organization work for you. To be organized is not to be sterile or rigid; it means to give order so people can move, operate, and function without getting tangled in undone things.

Naturally organized people have an inborn instinct that helps them arrange things in an orderly fashion. If something is out of line, they are uneasy until they have taken care of it. They have an urgency to "finish" things. If there is a lot to do, they somehow know what ought to be done first. The unorganized person does not get visual clues or prioritize things in his or her head. It doesn't so much matter that there are two styles of thinking, except that there are some advantages to being at least a little bit organized. You can save time, money, and worry and still leave the fun and spontaneity in your life. A person who has trained herself to put things away and to clean up as she cooks can cut the clean-up time in half. A family with a smooth laundry system will need fewer clothes and will wash fewer loads than the family with haphazard habits. An individual who keeps all financial receipts, bills, and notations together will spend less time figuring income taxes. Good organization habits equal more free time.

If you want to be more organized but don't know where to begin, don't despair. The unorganized person can learn to be more organized. Without taking personal offense, let me parallel disorganization to an individual who cannot walk. Unless the nerves are damaged, leg injury can usually be overcome with physical therapy. Trained professionals work with the patient each day, repeating the same motions, gradually increasing the complexity of the exercises until the patient can walk again. Likewise, people who are not organized can retrain themselves. Work habits are changed by doing the right thing, over and over. It means at first you have to concentrate intensely on the new pattern. You may need to use "crutches" in the form of a calendar and lists. But you can strengthen your body and mind until you start to think and act like a naturally organized person. Let this book be your therapy manual.

Start where you are and work with your problems one step at a time. Because not every home or home manager has the same problems, this book is divided into short chapters so you can quickly find the exact information you need. If you need immediate help with clutter, start with the first chapter, on Minimum Maintenance. Your home will show instant improvement, right now, today. Add to this a simple morning routine of getting dressed, washing dishes, and preparing a daily To Do List and you are well on your way. Then make or buy yourself a calendar notebook and start using basic time management principles to get control of your life. From there, pick and choose whatever you need, perhaps organizing the garage and laundry area, or setting up a filing system. The format of this book is divided into various aspects of your personal and home life, moving from time and motion to things and people. Tailor the principles to fit your life. Do them in a way that feels comfortable to you.

It is possible to rise above clutter and confusion, to create new habits and to change. I did it. I had very poor, self-defeating work habits when I began homemaking. Those poor habits started to get in the way of the things I wanted to do for myself and my family. I decided that if I were going to be in the mothering business for another twenty years and would be cleaning the bathroom until the year 2032, I might as well learn to do it quickly and well. And I did. I even got so organized that we took two more children into our family. There has also been time for education classes, for a mini-career, for arts and crafts, and for church and community service because I was able to get a handle on the routine tasks. As I made transitions from one season of life to another, I used the same principles to meet new challenges. It helped to be organized when I had five children under ten years of age. I was glad the routine was second nature when those little ones grew up and I discovered that teenagers can take as much time as babies. These ideas helped when I went back to school and when I launched my career. Now I am a different person living a different life, but the laws of organization and problem solving have served me well. My house is never perfect—it usually rates 7.5. That's clean enough to allow us to do and be what we want without the clutter getting in our way. I would like a 9.9 house, but I don't want to spend that much time cleaning. Things like a school carnival or helping a child with a term paper seem to be more important. But there is a minimum level of order, and when the house falls below that mark, the mess gets in the way of our progress and affects our moods. Everyone has to decide according to his own needs. May you conquer the mundane things so that you can concentrate on doing and being whatever you choose.

Totally Organized is designed to help you organize your time, your personal life, your house, and everything in it. This book is written so you can read about and try some of the tips even if you don't use the whole system. Some men and women read this type of book, not because they need it, but to see if they can't find "just a little more." It gets to be as fun as going on a treasure hunt. To be in control of a home is a process of constant refinement—being aware of new needs or circumstances, adjusting, changing and problem solving; always watching for new ways to make work easier and placement of things more convenient without being fanatical. Even though this book is written about a house and everything in it, the building is never more important than the people who live in it. There is a delicate balance between people and things, but the reason I spend so much time helping people organize their homelife comes out in my theme:

**People are more important than things,
but the order of things affects people.**

—Bonnie McCullough

GETTING ORGANIZED FOR *FAST* RESULTS

1. Fast Results With Minimum Maintenance

Have you ever had to stay at home, lock the doors, and take the phone off the hook to shovel out after a PTA pancake breakfast? This is the Typical Crash Crisis System of too many busy people, and it's doomed to failure. They let the house go while taking care of a Scout activity or church social. Then they dig out. When more than one outside activity occurs in a week, the house is unlivable. The husband or wife resents the "service" that is given in the name of compassion or career, and tension develops.

There is a better way! You can put an end to frazzled nerves and short tempers by developing your own MM system. I chose to explain this simple process first because it will make the biggest, most immediate, most visible improvement in your home.

There is no such thing as a miracle cure, but MM (minimum maintenance) can set you free by 9:30 in the morning or have you ready to leave for work on time—and that means with breakfast wiped away, children dressed, dinner planned, and the clutter cleared. The MM system is simple to use. It calls for daily, organized house "keeping" rather than weekly or seasonal house-cleaning ordeals. MM will give you more R&R (rest and relaxation) time for you. Here's how to do it:

1. *Begin with the basic plan.* Put on an apron or shirt with pockets, check the time on your watch, and give each room five minutes before leaving for work or starting any major project of the day. You put away, straighten up, and wipe off. Where do you start? There is an art to knowing where to begin. What does a caller at your door see first? Pick up this area and it will not only give your spouse, children, and guests a feeling of neatness, if will also give you a feeling of pride and accomplishment, no matter what the rest of the house looks like. Begin with the biggest items, such as bed, newspapers, or kitchen table. Work your way down to the smallest

objects, which can be collected in your apron pockets. Work with gusto. It's amazing what you can do in only five minutes, but don't stay longer. (You can allow yourself fifteen to twenty minutes in the kitchen if it needs it.)

This is only the basic maintenance. When it is finished, you can begin the day's project, whether it be work, school, or shopping. You can leave the house knowing that when you return, everything will be in order. If your house is in order, it says, "You are successful. You are making progress." If you come back to dirty dishes, unemptied ashtrays, and last night's newspapers, your house says to you, "You're a failure. You'll never catch up!" The pickup process is rewarding and generates success. This positive reinforcement gives you more energy to go on. It's a good feeling to walk into a room and see it in order.

2. *Don't start cleaning too deeply during your morning run-through.* This isn't the time to scrub the whole kitchen floor or clean out the refrigerator. When you see jobs that need doing, jot them down on a project list for later, during cleaning time. If you're thinking you can say good-bye to thorough cleaning forever, remember that MM is no miracle. It is a method for keeping clean what you've spent valuable time and energy to get thoroughly clean.

3. *Don't let the needs of others control your life.* Suppose a friend calls and says, "I'm desperate, can you help me make posters today?" It's for a good cause. This friend has helped you before. *But don't just drop your world.* Do the maintenance first. (Work before pleasure.) A home can run smoothly for a long while on minimum maintenance. Throw the meat and potatoes in a crock pot, dress the children, wipe away breakfast, quickly pick up through the house while a batch of clothes is in the washer, and you can be ready to go by 9:30. Going straight from the breakfast table to posters is asking for a backfire at about five, when you'll be thinking, "I hate this housework; I can't ever do what I want." Anyone who chooses to come back to undone chores *should* hate it. Learn to reward yourself after, rather than before, your MM is finished.

4. *Make the dinner decision early.* The longer you wait, the fewer choices are available. No preparation yet—just get it settled. Five o'clock is too late to discover you need to take something from the freezer or stop at the store.

5. When the enthusiasm strikes to clean, don't make the mistake of starting in the cupboard, closet, or drawer. Start from the outside in. Take care of the clutter scattered around the room before digging into the chest of drawers. Starting with the closet first makes a double mess. You'll get discouraged and quit before either job is finished. Begin from the outside in—clutter before closet.

6. Categorize your household items. You might ask, "If the drawers are messy, where will I put everything?" Put the items in category areas where they will be used or stored: gardening supplies to the garage, arts and crafts to the game room, Cub Scout materials to a closet. The categories that you originally create may not be the most efficient, but start by grouping. Then get more specific. I know one mother of five who is so involved with organizing her cupboards that the "living" parts of her home are stacked with "I'll-get-to-it-someday" items. Putting every bottle, button, and bobbin in its place takes all her time. By practicing MM and taking thirty minutes to do this grouping before she begins the cupboards, she would have her entire home looking neat and tidy—not just the cupboards and closets.

7. Learn to pick up before the mess becomes monstrous. This applies to every member of the family—especially children. After each play period and just before eating or going to bed, allow time to pick up.

8. Make the picking-up process a habit. At first it will take great effort, but it will soon become second nature.

The ideal time to take care of this daily run-through is in the morning. If you could take the first hour of the day to do your MM, that would be perfect, but it isn't possible for everyone. There are many variations, but the important thing is that you give every room, especially the general living areas, some daily attention. This plan is very flexible. The working person can do half in the morning and the other half after work. A parent with lots of interruptions from little children can accomplish the MM in five-minute bites.

When I get up in the morning I make my bed, even before going to the bathroom, so I'm not tempted to go back to sleep. (That room looks better already.) I wipe down the shower and straighten the grooming supplies in the bathroom so that by the time I leave, the bathroom has also received its care and can be checked off my mental list. There is no guarantee that it will stay nice all day, but at least it will be better than if nothing had been done. When I go to the kitchen, I eat something, see that my kids have breakfast and pack lunches, straightening as I go. I put the breakfast dishes in the dishwater or set them neatly by the sink. I put the cereal box back in the cupboard and wipe off the table, leaving the kitchen fairly neat. Three rooms done. By the time your children are off to school or you leave for work, half your MM can be done. If you stay at home, you can take another twenty minutes to finish this daily run-through. If you have to leave, the other rooms can be given their five minutes later in the evening. Try a five-minute pickup in your car, too—it works miracles. Keeping up is easier than catching up.

Never feel so defeated by a tornado-struck room that needs several hours work that you don't do anything at all. Just a few minutes in the room will keep it from getting worse. Mondays will be hardest because there is more "turn over" with the extra activities of the weekend. Do this pickup for several days in succession and you will see how each day you can build on yesterday's progress.

Keeping up with MM means there's hope. Develop the habit of putting things away while they're still in your hand and before going on to something else. One woman wrote to confirm what a miracle this MM work process can be and added, "To motivate me to do my MM early, I fantasize my mother-in-law is on her way over." Remember, though, you are not keeping your house neat because of what someone else may think. This principle applies to family members as well as guests, that feeling upon entry sets the tone. Thus, if your family enters a back door or garage, that may be reason enough to give that area some extra attention.

Minimum Maintenance is based on the First Impressions Principle: When you enter a building, if the first impression is one of neatness, you assume the whole building is clean. Should you walk around the corner and see a mess, the assumption is, "This is temporary." Most people don't see dust or smudges on the windowsill when they walk into a room, they notice clutter. It is clutter that gives the illusion of dirt or mess. Anyone who walks into your home and sees the living room neat will assume, "This is a clean house." Should he or she go around the corner and see the kitchen messy, the conclusion is, "This family is industrious." We are not so much worried about what visitors think about your house, but how it makes you feel. A tidy atmosphere boosts morale.

If there are children in the home, they also can be taught the basic principles of MM in their bedrooms: daily pickup, biggest to smallest, most visible items first, etc. Eventually you may be able to turn this daily pickup in the general living areas over to them and make your MM efforts last longer. Help your children with interim pickups before lunch, dinner, and bedtime. Stop the mess before it becomes a monster. For yourself, take time to straighten up when it's time to stop any project, even if it isn't finished.

If need be, you can put a house on "hold" for a long time by daily allowing for this pickup, keeping up with meals and dishes, tossing in a batch of laundry and perhaps adding one major cleaning project each weekend. Essentially, this is how working women survive. The secret is in knowing what has to be done and what can be put off. You can start today. Just put down this book, try picking up for thirty minutes, and see if it works.

Advantages of the MM Plan:

1. It keeps things from getting worse.
2. You like yourself and your house more.
3. Areas you have already cleaned stay clean longer.
4. You gain freedom to move onto new projects without tangle or clutter.
5. The program is easy to teach and delegate to spouse and kids.

2. Get a Head Start by Doing Daily Have-Tos

If you are busy organizing the church carnival, can you let the dusting go? Sure. Can you let the dishes go? No. There is a division between those who sink at busy times and those who don't. The dividing line is made by knowing what work can be skipped and what must be done. The first place to start organizing a home is not in the cupboards and closets, but with the things that have to be done over and over again. Learn to do those daily things so quickly, so effortlessly, so efficiently that you don't even have to think before you do them. To gain a new habit takes concentration and effort. If you are having trouble, take a careful look because you may be trying to skip these basic necessities. The daily five-minute pickup is part of this, but there is more. Naturally organized people do this by instinct.

To define these needs, write a list of daily have-tos. To start, your list will include things such as: cook, wash a load of clothes, do the dishes. That's a good beginning, but you need to be more specific. Rewrite the list of things that have to be done every day and separate them into details. Instead of just putting down "cook," write each meal separately. Your object is to make a logical plan of daily have-tos and then you will use this plan to reprogram yourself until the work process becomes so natural you don't have to think about doing it. Include personal grooming steps if necessary. As you prepare your list, put each entry under a heading that indicates the best time of day for it to be done at your house. For example, if you pack lunches, is it better to do it in the evening or in the morning? Maybe you don't worry about lunches at all—lucky you. At my house, I make the bed immediately when I get up, but if there is still someone in it, you can't do that. It may be better for you to do the pickup or make a to-do list in the evening. Think it through.

Daily Have-Tos

Morning	**Evening**
Get up: _____A.M.	Prepare dinner
Make bed	Wash dinner dishes
Shower	Kids in pajamas
Teeth and hair	Pick up toys
Fix breakfast	Bedtime story
Pack lunches	
Decide on dinner menu	
Clear away breakfast dishes	
Bobby dressed	
Baby dressed and bathed	
Bobby's bed mad	
Pick up house	
Write to-do list for today	

When I was much younger, not only did I have three children under three, but also I was very disorganized and had many self-defeating work habits. I remember one afternoon about 3:00 P.M. looking up and noticing my toddlers running around in their pajamas. A thought flashed through my mind: I better get these kids dressed, their daddy will be home soon—but why do it now when it's almost bed time again? In those days, I had three occasions each week to leave home by 9:00 A.M. When I returned home I was worn out and the house looked like a tornado had struck. It would take a day and a half to recover, and then it was time to leave early again. I cried a lot because it was important for me to succeed at home and because I loved my children. To top off the guilt, my college major was home economics. I had learned to make ice cream without crystals and tailor a coat, but not how to handle the everyday maintenance. Some women would have given up, taken a job to escape, or stayed home and not gone anywhere at all. But I did not want to give up my pleasures. I was determined to conquer the problem. I decided if I had to leave home three days a week by nine, we would be ready every day by nine—and that meant having the breakfast cleared, beds made, and clothes put away so the return home was pleasant.

My primary goal every day was to do the basics as soon as possible. I made 200 copies of my daily routine, much like the one shown. At that time I needed that boost of seeing the little things I had finished crossed off my list. It took me six months to get control of the morning routine, partly because I had a young baby, but mostly because I was so undisciplined. Once I had this under control, I was the master. For seventeen years, by 9:30 A.M. I have been ready to move on to other things—cleaning a closet, volunteer or church work, writing, family projects, sewing, laundry—whatever the project for the day. There have been some slips caused by a new baby, illness, moving, emergencies, and even burnout. But I always begin working myself back to an early morning deadline until I have it mastered again. Find your own deadline. Mine was 9:00 or 9:30; yours may be 3:00 P.M., before dinner, or bedtime.

Get up on time. That doesn't necessarily mean 5 A.M. (I delayed getting organized for a long time because I thought being organized was synonymous with getting up before the sun.) That's great if you can do it. You decide the best time for you, your physical body, and your family and/or your job. If you are going to leave home, allow an extra ten minutes to pick up after yourself—it's a gift to you for later. Once you determine the best hour to get up, get up at that time every day. To sleep past the appointed time is defeating—you'll be trying to catch up all day. To sleep in when your young children are up can be disastrous and dangerous because they make messes (like spilling cereal all over), they could get hurt, and because children need adult supervision.

Get dressed, even if you are to be home all day. The way you dress dictates how you work, so don't wear slippers! You will work better if you wear your running shoes. Take time to brush your teeth and wash your face. I know a woman who works from home but who puts on her professional clothes before she begins her telephone contacts, as this affects the way she feels and speaks. You don't have to dress up to clean house; in fact, if you did, you probably wouldn't work very hard. Dress for the job.

Decide on dinner early. When do you decide what to serve for dinner? Learn to include it somewhere in your daily routine. It saves so much confusion and unhappiness if you have made that decision early. I recommend the ten o'clock rule: If you will be away from home, decide by 10:00 P.M. what you will serve for dinner tomorrow. If you are to be home during the day, the deadline is 10:00 A.M. The longer you wait each day to decide what to fix, the fewer the choices. This one planning technique can make your day go much better. So much of life revolves around the purchase, preparation, consumption, and cleanup of food. Basic organization can simplify the cycle. Give it a try. Men and women who are caught at 5:30 P.M. wondering "what shall we eat?" often end up going out to eat, not because they want to eat out or like the food, but because they aren't organized. Without thinking, they may be using money they would really rather spend on something else. It isn't the cooking that is difficult (you can bake chicken breasts in twenty minutes), it's the planning. If you are going to eat, wonderful. Get twice the value from it by enjoying the pleasant anticipation all day, rather than deciding at the last minute to get fast food because you are too tired or the kitchen is a mess. More than once I have spent all the money I saved canning my own fruit by running out for a quick dinner. If I had given five seconds of thought in the morning, I could have put barbecue chicken in the crockpot for less than five dollars.

If you are to be away and if you write down those dinner plans, someone else may cook for you. The hardest part of cooking dinner is identifying the possibilities and making the decision. If you put up a note, a child or spouse will not have to guess what you had in mind. They may not recognize that tomato sauce, hamburger, cheese, and noodles from their respective cupboards could be lasagne. Make it easy for others to help you. This policy of making the ten o'clock dinner decision rewards you every time you use it. It can prevent tension and does save money. If you want to take the planning one step further, plan several meals at a time and double the rewards see (pages 173–179).

One of the first steps in organizing your life is to master the daily basics that keep life running smoothly. Just as breathing sustains your body, these things sustain your home. First it's a matter of accepting the reality that they have to be done. Second, learn to do them as effortlessly as breathing. Learn to do them at the right time of day and learn to do them quickly so you can go on to other things. How to help organize and accomplish the "other things" is the subject of the next few chapters.

Organizing
Your Time and
Your Thoughts

3. Get Control of Your Time With a Planning Notebook

P lanning takes time but, in the end, saves time and gets better results. The best tool for good time management is the planning notebook. Writing down your commitments, figuring out a work schedule, keeping track of your ideas, and then putting them all together in one place will make this planning process much easier. Professionals pay up to $1,000 to be instructed in these notebook techniques; you can learn and apply the best of these home-management ideas for as little as $8.50.

The planning notebook that I describe is one that you can make yourself and therefore adapt to your individual needs. It can be divided into sections for monthly and daily planning, and have separate indexes for phone numbers, budget, shopping lists, menus, and so on.

To start your notebook, you will need a pocket calendar or datebook, a small ring notebook (the same size as the calendar), filler paper, and dividers. Total cost: $8.50. Buy the ring notebook at a discount store and the calendar from a stationery supply center (these calendars are often given out free by banks, greeting card companies, etc.).

If your life has a predictable rhythm, you may need only a small calendar on which to note occasional differences. If you coordinate numerous activities, you will need a calendar with more space to accommodate all the details. Almost everyone can benefit from using a calendar in two ways: (1) it will give you a visual image of your time; and (2) it brings abstract thoughts into a concrete realm. It saves embarrassment over forgotten appointments and helps you protect yourself from overscheduling. You can respond immediately to requests on your time, and it will be possible to take more activities into your life and not get them tangled. The notebook will help you correlate details between job and personal life. It can help you plan quiet time and allow time just for you. You deserve it! A calendar can help you get rid of stacks of papers, notes, newsletters, and invitations. If your life is complicated with erratic work hours, meetings, and rehearsals, it will also save your nerves. It can change your status from laborer to professional, even at home.

Once you have chosen a calendar, carefully remove the outer cover of the calendar and punch holes along the inside crease to fit the rings. Put the first few weeks or months of pages behind the first divider in the notebook and you have begun. Now use it! Write down your commitments and a daily to-do list, figure out a work schedule, keep track of your ideas, and put them all together in one place.

CALENDAR SECTION

After you have a calendar, how do you use it? Take it with you everywhere. Keep it by the phone when you are at home. Check it every day. As you learn to use the calendar effectively, it will be like having your own private secretary. Write down engagements as you hear about them. Gather information from work, school, church, and club newsletters. Group leaders are very good about publishing a yearly calendar for meetings and activities. Just because you write down a meeting doesn't mean you have to go. You may decide not to attend, but that is different from forgetting. Use the calendar to jog your memory for details such as when to pay bills and when to return library books.

Record happenings that will affect your family—holidays and half-days at school or work, vacation days, business trips, etc. Knowing these things in advance, you can make arrangements for child care, dog kennel, newspaper stop, and more. You are beginning to visualize your commitments and take charge of your life. As invitations arrive in the mail, note all the details, including address, phone number, directions, and time. When there is a request to bring something, write that down, too. Then you can throw away that stack of reminders that you would probably have forgotten to look through in your unorganized days, anyway.

Do you put something on the calendar, and then forget to look at it? You need to include checking the calendar in your daily routine. Get professional. What would happen if a doctor forgot to look at his/her calendar? It helps to keep your calendar and daily to-do list together in one notebook. In fact, some calendars, such as the time-line, often have enough space so that you can prepare a to-do list on the daily page. For my personal use, I prefer a time-line calendar because it gives an instant visual picture of commitments and I can tell at a glance how much time I have left for other things. However, it you choose this style, be careful not to use the time markings to schedule yourself like an airport runway. Other then commitments for meetings and appointments, the to-do-list will identify small projects and phone calls to be made, as well as a goal-project to be worked on during discretionary time. You will be surprised how many things you can accomplish in one day if you have prepared this reminder list.

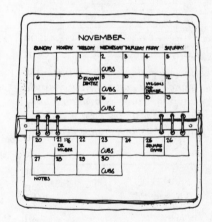

Two examples of box calendars and how they can be set in a planning notebook.

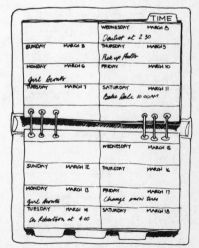

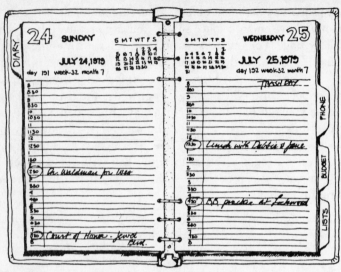

The time-line calendar with a page for every day gives an instant visual explanation of the day. At a glance one can tell how many hours are already committed and how much time is available for other tasks. There is plenty of room on this daily page for a To-Do List, notes, or directions. The priority calendar (below) groups items by category.

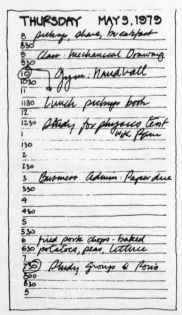

PHONE SECTION

Since you will take your notebook with you wherever you go, you'll find it helpful to have a few basic phone numbers written in it. This shouldn't be the same as the family directory you keep by the phone at home: these are the numbers you may need when you are away from home. For example, I was very glad to have the phone number for our Ralph's 66 Station when the car broke down and the telephone book at the public phone booth was missing. You can make your own index tabs within the phone section by cutting away ¼ inch from the outside edge of several pages of filler paper on which you have written three or four alphabet letters. Avoid using a whole packet of dividers or even a page for every letter of the alphabet because they will make the book too bulky and there are still other important sections to include in your planning notebook.

Make your own index tabs

MONEY SECTION

Use this section to record business expenses and mileage. If you are in charge of car maintenance, this may be the place to keep a log of service and repairs. It all depends on what parts of the family budget you are responsible for. Those who are in charge of household money could use this section for planning food and clothing purchases. Title a new page for the coming month to collect ideas for clothing, groceries, office supplies, toiletries, and household items you need to buy next month. As you become more accurate at predicting your needs, you will save time and money lost to emergency shopping trips.

I like to keep a master shopping list because I have found that I buy just about the same food items every month. As I prepare for the major monthly grocery shopping, I check two lists: (1) this master list and (2) a list, kept in the kitchen, on which we write

down each item as we notice that we will soon run out of it. It might
be to your advantage to also keep a copy of the monthly family
budget in your notebook. You will be happier with your clothing
purchases and save money if you have an overall plan, and this is a
good place to keep track of it. (Later chapters are devoted to explaining a wardrobe plan and saving food money.) If you can get
past "emergency" buying, you can take advantage of seasonal sales.

PEOPLE SECTION

If you are the general purchasing agent for most family clothing or
if you like to buy clothes for your boy or girl friends, you'll find it
helpful to keep track of everyone's latest shoe, shirt, skirt, or pants
size. A "people section," with a separate page for each person, is the
perfect place to keep such information.

Use this section to gather ideas for gift giving, too. Always be on
the lookout for things that might surprise and please others. Listen,
and when someone you care about lets you peek into their heart by
mentioning something he or she wants, write it down—not that
very moment, but at a private time. If a child is shopping with you,
notice the things he or she longs for. If you visit Grandmother, who
lives far away, keep an eye open for clues. When it comes time for a
birthday or holiday, you have an idea list from which to choose and
you will save hours of shopping time. To take it one step further, if I
write a date next to "popcorn popper" under Dad's name, I won't be
giving him another popper next year.

The people section can also be used to record family medical
information. You don't need to carry details about measles and DPT
shots here unless your child is a baby and is going through the
initial series. You might, however, be asked for the date of a child's
last tetanus shot. Keeping track of past physicals, dental visits, or
eye exams can be useful, too, for knowing when to schedule new
appointments.

The people section can also be used to keep a list for yourself. Put
such things as your social security number, your checking and
savings account numbers, and the date of your last physical and/or
pap-smear and chest x-ray. Then start your own want list. Whenever
a thought comes to mind of something you would like to have, write
it down. My want list usually fills both sides of the page, but I've
found it an effective way to manage my wants and desires. I am

convinced that I could spend at least $300 on incidentals and nonessential items. If I am cleaning in the living room, I want new end tables. In fact, I can hardly live without them, even though we've gotten by for ten years with the old ones. If I am working in the office, I want another disk drive for my computer. If I am working in the yard, I need a plum tree. Our wants tend to be associated with what we have been doing. By writing these ideas down, where they are safe, they will not torment you as much. Then, when you have some discretionary money, instead of blowing it on your want-for-the-day, take a second to review your collection. That's called intentional spending. Your purchases can be more rational, you'll be more satisfied, and will have fewer regrets. If you are the type of person who would be offended to get an iron for your birthday, you ought to make two separate lists—one for household needs and another for personal wants. You might as well learn to live with your unfulfilled wants because they will always be there. It's human nature to want more than we have. Studies show that even if some magical windfall would grant your wants today, in a few weeks you would have a new, more expensive list of desires.

Another occasion when this want list comes in handy is when someone says to you, "What would you like for your birthday?" Do

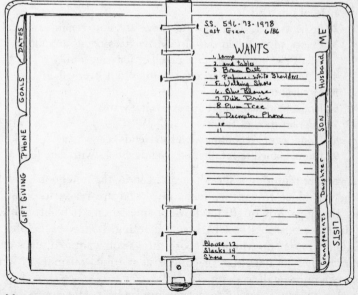

Manage your wants and collect ideas for gifts by gathering gift-giving ideas all year long and writing them in your planning notebook.

not hand them the page in your notebook because some of those things you don't care about anymore. If that person is serious about wanting some suggestions, take out a blank piece of paper and look over your want list. Write down a few practical, inexpensive ideas; list a couple frivolities; and include a dream item (trip to Mexico), just for a glimpse into your heart.

LIST OF LISTS SECTION

This is a file of ideas—thoughts and plans that come to mind that you may not remember when they can be best used. If you are just beginning a notebook, I would suggest that you take nine blank pages and allow one page for each of the following topics. When a good idea surfaces, file it under the appropriate title. Work with them for awhile and see if these are the areas in which you need to collect information. Add pages for the categories that you may need in addition to the following. If you find you're starting too many lists, *don't stop making them!* You may need to learn to write smaller to help keep the number of pages to a minimum. If you want to succeed, you can't afford to forget things. As ideas pop into mind, jot them down. It's a waste of memory ability to remember what you could just as easily write down.

1. Books to read
2. Projects to be done (sewing, home and auto repair, hobbies)
3. Places to go when out-of-town visitors come to your city or when you have a day to yourself or for your family
4. Problem areas and/or tension times to be worked on
5. Movies to rent
6. Household needs and/or decorating wants
7. Current movies to see
8. Restaurants recommended by friends
9. Items loaned to family and friends; books with date loaned

If you are planning a speech or an agenda, the notebook can be a gathering place to capture ideas until you are ready to organize your thoughts. You might jot down business items to be brought up at the next business or PTA board meeting. It may be helpful to designate a page on which to record things you want to discuss with your mother or daughter in college next time you make a long-distance phone call to them.

Learn to use a pencil to gather information and compare the issues whenever you have a decision to make. For example, suppose you are shopping for a new apartment or house. First, write down the features you want or need and the pitfalls to look out for. Then, as you walk through each new place, take a clipboard to list likes and dislikes of each house. Later, as you review your options, compare the want list with what you saw. You don't have to rely on memory or emotional impression alone, you can deal with the facts. Most choices are not absolutely right or wrong, and you usually have to compromise one feature over another. You will be more satisfied with your decisions if you use this system of written comparison, whether you are buying a new freezer or deciding which job offer to take.

THE FAMILY CALENDAR

Homes where the adults and children are involved in several activities will find it helpful to correlate dates on a central family calendar, the bigger the better. A desk pad calendar, 17 inches by 22 inches, with plenty of room to write in the boxes, can be purchased for less than $5 in an office supply department. Tear off one sheet at a time and post it on the refrigerator or tack it to a bulletin board in a high-traffic area, probably in the kitchen. There are five advantages to the family calendar:

1. It cuts back on those unplanned surprises.
2. Each family member will know where others are in case of emergency.
3. You can coordinate rides, responsibilities, car privileges, babysitter needs, and dinner plans.
4. As adults, you know when you are free to plan your own things; you do not have to be on duty all the time.
5. The children can begin to learn how to manage their time, how to plan, and how to compromise.

After Sunday dinner, my family takes fifteen minutes to coordinate the upcoming week with such a calendar. It saves surprises. For me, it means keeping both a personal and family calendar, but living in a home with four teenagers requires big-business management, and it certainly pays off. We cover details of babysitters, rides, who gets which car, making cupcakes for Cub Scouts, and when we will find time to buy a birthday present. By careful coordination, we can each pursue career, volunteer projects, sports, fun, school, and be a family, too. Make more time by taking time to plan.

4. Develop the List Habit

W hile watching a football game, I was interested as the commentator raved about how well prepared the home team was, coming into the game with their first twenty-five plays memorized. They knew where they wanted to go and who was going to do it and within the first few seconds they scored. Like the ball players, if you go into the day with specific goals of what you would like to accomplish, you are more likely to win. Having a plan gives you more control. You can score accomplishments early in the day while others are still trying to decide what to do. The plan may need to be revised, altered, or totally abandoned, but to have a goal and get half finished is better than to have no goal at all. Don't define your day as win or lose; consider that some days you make more progress than others. At times, all you can do are the necessities, on other days you catch up or even get ahead. But you can get better at the game by applying time management principles.

In addition to establishing a routine pattern for daily basics, you will want to use several types of lists to facilitate personal business and family projects. A written list makes it easier to set priorities and serves as an external reminder as the day wears on and you get tired. Prepare your daily plan first thing in the morning or after work or at night before you go to bed, whichever serves you best. One of the problems with this technique is that when a person starts a to-do list, they put too much on it. The novice writes out a list that would take a year to accomplish and then is discouraged when it does not all get done. Thus, it is helpful to separate items into two types of to-do lists—one for today and a running project list.

THE RUNNING PROJECT LIST

Write down all the things you have to do on the project list, whenever they come to mind. That means you'll need to take it with you. Keep it with your calendar or on a 3 × 5 card in your wallet. Get in the habit of writing down your ideas as soon as they occur. For one thing, those promptings are more likely to come to you when you are at a high energy peak, already into another project, or when you are depressed (when they bombard you like a sinner being stoned). Writing them down tells your brain the ideas will not be forgotten and your mind does not need to bring them up over and over again. Running-list projects should not be the routine things such as dishwashing, but the extras such as stopping at the shoe repair shop, writing a letter, or trimming the trees. Don't feel defeated if you never get to the end of this list. It is always "running," catching more as the days go by. List things and forget them until you can make time. Every Sunday evening I prepare a project list as a reminder of things I need to, or would like to get done in the coming week. Some items are new thoughts, others are carryovers from the week before. After an item has been on the list several weeks, I decide to either do it quickly or cross it off, because it is legal to decide not to do a project. After all, who is in charge?

TODAY'S LIST

Besides the running project list, stuck neatly in the front page of my planning calendar (I love those self-stick note pads), I also take a few seconds to scribble a to-do list each morning. To prepare this, I gather information from several sources: (1) I look at my calendar to check for appointments, meetings, or social engagements; (2) I jot down small projects that ought to be done such as buying bread or making a phone call; (3) I evaluate routine household chores such as laundry or vacuuming that this day may dictate; and (4) if it's a day with discretionary time, I glance at the running list to see if I can add one of those projects. From these four categories, I set daily goals. If you make the dinner decision early, you can work or play with gusto on your main project right up to the minute it is time to start dinner. Thus, a daily to-do list will have three types of entries:

1. **Minute projects** such as water plants, wipe off toaster, take out trash, and phone calls that can be tucked in between other things. It can be a reminder to buy stamps and stop at the cleaner on the way home from work. Write down these little things as you think of them so they aren't forgotten.

Prepare a To-Do List every day to make better use of your time.

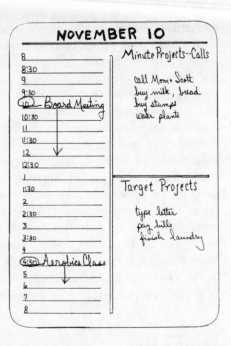

NOVEMBER 10

8
8:30
9
9:30
10 — Board Meeting
10:30
11
11:30
12
12:30
1
1:30
2
2:30
3
3:30
4
4:30 Aerobics Class
5
6
7
8

Minute Projects··Calls

call Mom· Scott
buy milk, bread
buy stamps
water plants

Target Projects

type letter
pay bills
finish laundry

2. **Deadlines** are things that have to be finished today, or appointments, meetings, or social engagements. A day filled with too many deadlines is deadly, especially if you have young children or an unpredictable lifestyle.

3. **Direction goals** are projects you will work on or activities you will take part in when you have time available during the day. These are the things to be done if you can and when you can, after the have-to projects are completed. (Have-tos include child care, basic routine, appointments, and deadlines.) Define which task you will start on and proceed as far as possible during the time allowed. Number them 1, 2, 3 or A, B, C to show which you will start first. Don't overschedule your life with too many extra projects as general living takes up more time than you think. Some people who work full time feel that when they leave work they are finished with have-to things. That attitude will lead to guilt, anger, and frustration. There are other parts of life that also need attention. Use the same professional time management skills you use on the job to prepare a plan for off-work hours, to aid in completing the essential and in allowing time for personal projects.

Once we get going, some of us don't know when to stop. If you have small children, trying to work into feeding or child-care time is harmful to family life and defeating to the manager. You cannot skip dinnertime when you have a family. It will be faster to stop and feed them. If you don't get everything on your list done, some of it may be carried over to tomorrow. Some of it may be skipped, part of it may be put on hold for later. Since work at home is never totally done, be sure to have a quitting time. If you want to take charge of your life, if you want to get more accomplished, start this technique of making a daily list and keeping a project list. Your lists will help you make better decisions about what to do rather than doing just what your eyes happen to see. Lists keep your mind freer. The only way to find out if these to-do lists work for you is to try using them for at least two weeks. Try it; you'll like it.

Long-term Projects

So far we have been discussing how to use the calendar and how to set goals for everyday work and living. These principles can also be used to accomplish big projects such as moving, preparing for a vacation, putting on a wedding, planning a city-wide parade, gathering research for a dissertation, or making it through the holidays. Basically, no matter what the project, the process is about the same. First you set the goal, chop it into small steps, and then chart them backwards on the calendar, setting intermittent deadlines until the whole thing is mapped out. Lists are essential to govern so many details. If you don't know enough about organizing this project, find someone with experience to help you set up the format. When the project involves other people, you need to take time to brainstorm with them, set up commitments, make assignments, and then define responsibilities *in writing*, with a copy for yourself and another copy for them. In the back of this book in the chapter Handling Major Holidays is a sample of a November–December calendar with simple deadlines for getting Christmas projects finished before the big holiday arrives. A wedding would need the same type of plan-ahead calendar with early deadlines.

Let's suppose you are moving. If ever there is a time to get organized, this is it. First you would begin a new section in your planning notebook or start a totally new workbook to keep track of all the details about the move. You will need to prepare a list of repairs and cleaning projects that need to be done to be eligible for a return of your rent deposit or to get the house ready for sale. Booklets that give instructions on preparing for a move or for planning a wedding set up a time-line list of things to do three months ahead, two months ahead, six weeks, four weeks, two weeks, and on down to what should be done the morning of the occasion. You can do this, too.

5. How to Set Priorities and Goals

Over and over you are told to "set" your priorities. The assumption is made that you know what it means. Maybe so, maybe not. To "set" means to determine, write out, or identify. Several times a year you should evaluate how you are spending your time and whether that is truly what you want. Sometimes we drift with the tide or stay with a course that no longer suits our needs. Take a good look at your life whenever a major change takes place: move, new baby, school starting, or new year. Try the following four-step process to help set priorities and goals.

1. Collect goal ideas. To begin the goal-setting process, start gathering ideas of things you would like to do. Write down all those things that have been running around in your head. Divide a paper into sections and title them for the various categories of your life: personal, spouse, children, career, house, hobby, physical (exercise, diet), spiritual, and recreational. Brainstorm for ideas of what you would like to accomplish in each area—including everything from catching up on the scrapbooks to carpeting the living room. Include projects for helping your children such as improving their spelling, earning a Scout award, or strengthening a relationship. Add to this list often and keep it where you can review it, preferably in your planning notebook.

2. Rank your goals. Since none of us will have enough time, energy, or money to do everything on the list, select the ones you will concentrate on first. Basically, your brainstorm list will have three types of goals: (1) short-term projects that are easy to accomplish and where progress is easily measured; (2) long-term goals that take time and must be accomplished in stages; and (3) "dream" goals that must be postponed for sometime in the future.

3. Set your course of action. Especially with long-term goals, it is important to decide how each goal will be accomplished. For example, if your long-term goal is to lose weight, you must define specifics—how much and how will it be accomplished. The major goal needs to be broken down until the task can be measured in daily or weekly progress. A realistic breakdown might be to lose one pound a week, eat three hundred calories less every day, or exercise four times each week. If one of your career goals is to earn more money, what can you do to accomplish it? Take more classes, learn more about marketing, improve your image, join a professional group, change jobs? If your goal is to be better organized at home, where will you begin? With daily MM? By keeping a calendar? By organizing the laundry?

4. Follow through on your progress. If you want this process to work, you need to write down your immediate goals in some designated place. Then you need to set aside a regular time to review each category, to consider your available time, and to decide what you will try to accomplish, within reason.

I take a few minutes the first Sunday of each month to review my goals, set directions for that month, and then write them in my personal notebook. Let me explain a few more of the specifics by showing how I do it.

Suppose it is the first Sunday of February. While my husband is watching football, I take a few minutes to think about next week and next month. Self-talk can be very therapeutic. I pull out my brainstorm goal list and quickly review each category. Am I making progress? How am I doing physically? Not bad—I went to exercise class three times every week in January. I feel better, and even though it took up so much of my time, I will set it again as a goal for February. I ask myself, how are my relationships? Maybe it is time to take my daughter to lunch next week.

My major career goal at this time is to write a bestselling book. But I decide to mail at least one query letter each week to see if I can get a response to another of my goals, which is to get my weekly column in more newspapers. As I take stock of another category, personal life, I know immediately that "catch up on the scrapbooks" is one of those dream goals that will have to wait. Setting priorities means selecting one goal over another. I must set aside other desires, but at the same time these new goals do not rank above the basic responsibilities of home, spouse, and children that I chose long ago.

USE SPARE TIME TO ACCOMPLISH SHORT-TERM GOALS

By setting priorities for my long-term goals, I have a direction and a focus for my large blocks of time. But what about the dozens of times during the week when we have five or ten or even fifteen "unclaimed" minutes—when we sit down to watch the news, while we're waiting for the dentist or hairdresser, while we're waiting for the cookies to bake? Naturally, there are times when we should simply relax and take things easy, but these golden minutes can be ideal times for accomplishing your short-term goals.

Take a close look at your brainstorm list. Are there mini-goals that you could work on during these spare minutes? Needlework or other hobby projects that can be carried in your purse or car? A book that you could have handy to help increase your vocabulary or brush up on a foreign language? Without becoming obsessed with filling every free moment, it's easy to make great strides in accomplishing your goals. All it takes is a little planning.

KEEP A VICTORY LIST

I keep a victory list right next to my goals to give me a quick boost. A radio commentator on a religious station stated that we write our blessings in the sand and carve our burdens in granite. It is the same at home. We feel guilty about the things we don't get done, and don't recognize what we have accomplished. Last year my first entry read, "Read one magazine from cover to cover." It may sound trivial, but I had a subscription for two years and never read a single issue. Every time I looked at that entry, I thought, At least I've done one thing. Glance back to see that you have already reached some of your goals. If it is good for you to write down a to-do list, you can also make a list of things you have done. Start a victory list for yourself. Today, take a few minutes to write down what you have done since the first of the year. List small things as well as large projects.

WHAT IF IT DOESN'T WORK?

Many people abandon their goals after a few weeks because the goals are either too lofty or because they are not well enough defined. Sometimes the target is lost because they don't write out the goal or stop to evaluate progress every week or two. If things aren't happening the way you hoped, ask yourself why. Maybe it is time for new strategy or a change of goal. It is perfectly acceptable to change your mind or alter direction. Build in a safety feature when setting goals by defining what you will do if this effort does not succeed. Have an alternative plan, a new strategy. For example: If this plan doesn't work to help my son stop wetting his bed, I will then try . . . or, Should I get all negative answers from job applications, then I will do . . . to get a job.

Don't work on too many self-improvement objectives at once. Good and bad habits are developed over time. To redirect oneself will take concentration and effort. Just pick one or two at a time and move onto other goals only after you are satisfied that the desired change is well established. This can work for you. The nice thing about writing down all your goals is that you know they are recorded, and when the time is right, you will choose another one to focus on. Sometimes, when we want to do new things, we are not willing to let go of the old ways and make room for the new. For example, when I was a full-time homemaker, I was able to do a great deal of sewing. When I wanted to try writing and teaching, I had to make a choice. I chose to write but still found myself buying fabric as in the old days. As you become more organized, you can fit more into your life, but this world has too many possibilities, too many opportunities to do everything.

WHERE DOES THE TIME GO?

If you suspect you are wasting part of your time, or if you can't account for it, try keeping a time log for several days. Tuck a pad and pencil in your pocket, set your watch-alarm for thirty-minute intervals, and each time it rings, write down what you have been doing. This exercise will reveal miscalculations and time leaks. Perhaps you are trying to fit too much into your life. A second technique is to calculate just how much discretionary time you have, taking a good look at reality. Suppose you allow yourself seven hours of sleep, and begin the day with seventeen hours. Obviously, for most of us, that time is not totally ours to do whatever we want. If we work an eight-hour job, that leaves nine hours. But then we have to subtract time for personal hygiene, travel, and eating. Now we are down to four or five discretionary hours. That isn't much when you consider we still have to do the household chores and shopping, and need to provide for child care and personal recreation. On the weekend those discretionary hours increase, but they are precious. You can see how easily those few hours can slip away. Calculating them on paper will help you realize the value of your free time.

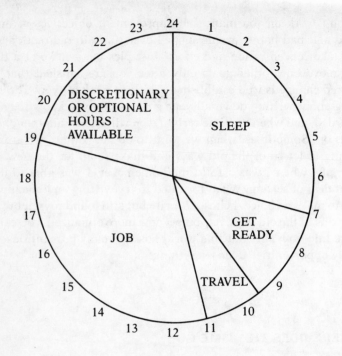

EVALUATION

Each season of your life will find you using your time a little differently. Be patient with the season you are living in now. If you have small children, you can't expect to accomplish as many things as someone whose children are in school full time. Likewise, if you work full time, don't try to keep up with the projects a full-time homemaker can take part in. A change in routine or job is a good time to think through and determine how you allocate your time and which responsibilities and activities get what percent of your life. Once your aims are defined, it is easier to apply the "yes-no" theory. That is, when you give into someone else's request, you are saying "no" to any other possibility with that time. On the other side, it is sometimes necessary to say "no" to others so you can say "yes" to yourself or your family. You will see more growth in yourself—more accomplishment, more satisfaction, and more self-esteem—if you make rational choices. Some people don't make choices, they just let things "happen" and then they wonder why they don't get lucky breaks. Another word that goes along with goals is sacrifice. To set your course on a goal means you must set aside other desires; you must choose one over the other. When you set goals, you are taking the first step toward time management. Take control of your life, be actively accountable for your decisions and how you use your spare time. Take time this week to write out your goals and chose one to start on.

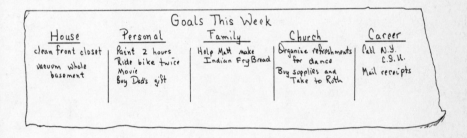

Goals This Week

House	Personal	Family	Church	Career
clean front closet	Paint 2 hours	Help Matt make	Organize refreshments	Call N.Y.
vacuum whole	Ride bike twice	Indian Fry Bread	for dance	C.S.U.
basement	Movie		Buy supplies and	Mail receipts
	Buy Dad's gift		Take to Ruth	

ORGANIZING YOUR HOUSEWORK

6. Create a Pattern for Housework That Really Works!

I f you were looking for Grandma, fifty years ago at ten o'clock on Monday morning, she probably would have been washing the clothes. She, and every other housewife, had a well-defined weekly routine. Everyone knew when the bread would be baked and when to expect clean clothes. Activities, jobs, modern appliances, and convenience foods have moved us away from such a formal routine. None of us wants to go back to outhouses, wood stoves, and scrub boards, but there are some lessons to be learned from Grandmother's method of handling the weekly necessities.

If you set up a reasonable routine, not with the hourly expectations of a timeclock, but with enough structure to carry the basic necessities of home life, you can concentrate on the extra projects. It is like trying to get children to practice the piano. If you have to "find" the time every day to get them to practice, every single day you have to concentrate on that effort until it is done. But if you and the child agree that practice will be at four o'clock every afternoon, you don't have to deliberate all day. Yes, you have to capture the child at four, but the rest of the day you are free of that concern. If you set Wednesday or Friday aside to do the wash, and you take care of it then, you won't have to fret about it at any other time; you are free for six days. What time do you have dinner? If you have a fairly reliable routine say, between five-thirty and six-thirty, everyone knows when to be home, when they should have evening chores done, and when to break from homework or TV. An established dinner hour gives a focus to the evening hours.

The same is true with most other weekly needs. It helps to have a simple structure and not to leave everything "on demand". The problem with the "demand" system of housekeeping is that all the needs surface at the same time. A general routine can give strength to your life.

Consider the minimum weekly needs of your household. Such a realization is helpful in understanding the ups and downs of your home. For example, at my home we have to find time to do the following every week:

Work activity	required time
Bake	2 hours
Clean kitchen	2 hours
Clean bathrooms once thoroughly	1½ hours
Laundry, pressing, mending	5 hours
Deep-clean one room	2 hours
Cook meals, wash dishes	9 hours
Daily MM	7 hours

That averages out to four hours per day. Since we don't work on Sunday, it means we need to put in four and a half hours a day. The total was twice that high when my children were little. One day just after our last baby was born, I kept a log and was surprised that baby required eight and a half hours of care all by himself. The minimum amount of time needed is relative to the number of people in the household, their ages, their pickup habits, the size of your apartment or house, and its age. I cannot tell you how much work you need to do in your home, you need to calculate that for yourself, but the average is one hour per person per day. You know you are working below mininum when undoneness keeps getting in your way. If you are working below your minimum, you are setting a time bomb that can be triggered at the least bit of agitation and usually at an inopportune time. Notice this average does not include shopping, child care, or yard work. To look at the above list on Monday is depressing, but you don't have to deal with it all at once if you divide it up, assign those tasks to specific times in the week, and get other people to help. Over the years, the distribution of the housework will change with each season of your life. Two or three times a year, usually January, June and September, when our routine shifts, I draw up a seven-day chart and take a look at the whole picture. I set aside a time for laundry, for baking, and for cleaning. If I am trying to do a special volunteer job or am working, I figure out how it will all fit into my life. This paper exercise gives me a great deal of insight and control. In the following pages, I will show how a working parent or an "at-home Mom" can organize their work.

SAMPLE SCHEDULE: PERSON WITH FULL-TIME JOB

	Monday	Tuesday	Wednesday	Thursday	Friday	Saturday/ Sunday
6	Get up, dress, personal grooming.					
6:30	Breakfast, wash dishes, wipe off counters.					
7	Pick up throughout the house, put one load of clothes in washer.					
7:30						
8						
8:30						Pick up
9						Vacuum, dust
9:30						Clean one room
10						thoroughly
10:30						Plan menus
11						Shop
11:30			Work			Errands
12						
12:30			and			
1						
1:30			School			Individual
2						
2:30			(time committed to someone else)			and family
3						
3:30						fun
4						
4:30						
5						
5:30	Dinner preparations, wash dishes.					
6	Dry morning wash and start another load of clothes.					
6:30	One small cleaning task.					
7–9:30	Flexible time for family needs and activities—meetings, personal projects, homework, etc.					

Look at your overall weekly pattern: Try making a seven-day work chart. Fill in your fixed commitments and the basic family happenings for a week: departure, meals, arrivals. From these, a general horizontal time schedule will emerge, showing the structure of your routine, and revealing the best and worst times for different types of work and activities. There will be busy getting-ready times and there will be other times during the day when certain jobs seem to fit in better. Households with school-age children will find time more horizontally structured than those with no children. Although it seems confining, you'll notice that people with built-in time structures (because of school children or jobs) do seem to get more done. People who don't face a forced schedule and still reach accomplishments have learned to create their own deadlines.

Review outside commitments. One time when I was a full-time homemaker, I prepared a chart and discovered my family had twenty-six activities and commitments every week besides school and work. No wonder I was harried. Normally, as an unsaid rule, our children have a limit of two outside activities at a time, such as Cub Scouts and basketball. After the above revelation, we rearranged lessons and cut down activities. How does your skeleton chart look? Sometimes you have to get off the merry-go-round and take a look at the pattern your life is following.

Set aside a time for fun. Treat it like an important appointment. If you don't set aside a specific time for relaxation, your work and other commitments will take over and life will pass by while you're thinking, "We'll go on a picnic soon." The first time I tried to build a schedule for myself, I drew the seven-day chart and filled in every cleaning job recommended by typical organization teachers of the day. When I got all the work put in the calendar, there was no space left. I took out a clean piece of paper and started over by first designating a time for me, for me to be with my children, and for my husband and me alone, but together. One respected woman's leader said she takes a SID day (Self-Improvement Day) each week, on which she builds friendships, has fun, and often takes a class, either academic or fun, to keep her mind alert. She uses Sunday to nourish spiritual roots, rest, and strengthen family relationships.

SAMPLE SCHEDULE: FULL-TIME HOMEMAKER

Monday	Tuesday	Wednesday	Thursday	Friday	Saturday	Sunday
		Family up and off.	Daily pickup (MM)			
Major pickup	Wash	Special projects or needs	Clean one room thoroughly: Two weeks of month will be kitchen.	Day off	Projects	Day of rest
Bake	Iron	Piano lessons	Rotate:	Date night	Yard work	Church
Bathroom rugs wash towels	Mend		wax floor cupboards windows walls furniture stove refrigerator		Help kids w/ rooms	Family time
					Vacuum basement	Plan next week
Family night at home			Cub Scouts		Baths	
					Plan Sunday dinner	

Make time for housework in your weekly schedule. In the beginning I thought I had to create a work outline that listed trivia, e.g., empty dishwasher at 9:00 P.M., etc. I found I do better by categorizing in general areas. For example, in my schedule I do one thorough cleaning job a week, rotating rooms, doing the kitchen twice as often as the bedrooms. It takes about three months to make the cycle—not that I have such a big house, but other needs come up. When a room has been targeted, I include everything that needs to be done within those four walls, such as the light cover, walls, and windows. The old method read, "Clean all light fixtures on the first fifth Thursday of the year." It was too hard to follow. The bathroom and kitchen are exceptions. When I give the bathroom its weekly cleaning, I try to do one little part of it extra well: shower plants or wash curtains or clean out cupboard or wipe walls. The same holds for the kitchen, rotating the thorough cleaning of the various appliances so I don't have to do them all in one week. Natural organizers and reformed organizers get their clues for housework from what their eyes see "needs to be done," and then they automatically "find" a time to take care of that job soon. Those of us whose brain waves do not follow those channels need to use a schedule to guide us.

It doesn't matter so much when you do housework as that you reserve a time for it and do it then. One full-time homemaker works on the house every morning until noon and then uses the afternoon for other types of projects. Another woman arranges her time to stay home three days a week and works like crazy to get everything done—Monday to do general cleaning and recover from the weekend, Tuesday to do all clothing and linens, and a third day for deep cleaning or redecorating. That gives her four days of light housework to take care of the special needs that seem to come every week. Each of these full-time homemakers has a different time set aside to work and is successful in this area of life.

What about men and women who work full time—how do they handle housework? They would like to be free of "have-tos" when they get off, but such is not life. The reality is the working person has two choices: do a little every day or marathon on the weekend. One woman concentrates on getting all the basics done on week nights so she can relax on the weekend. You'll find others who chose just the opposite, doing most of the work on Saturday and Sunday or whichever days they have off. A family near me sets Saturday morning aside as work time. They all pitch in for three hours and the rest of the weekend is for other projects. If you can afford it, hire some help. If you take time to plan, there can be more time for you, but I can't promise it will get rid of all the work. To juggle home and career, the rules are primary:

1. **Correlate** a calendar with others so you are free of unexpected responsibilities.
2. **Keep life simple,** taking on very few time-consuming aspects of home life: baking, gourmet cooking, redecorating, hobbies, sewing, or gardening. The number of these things that you can do when compared to a full-time homemaker is minuscule. The woman who moves from full-time home life to wage-earner finds it especially hard to let go of these types of projects, but seasoned workers aren't so tempted. They know how to keep life simple.
3. **Be strict about keeping up** with the basics: daily pickup, meals, dishes, and laundry. You can't afford to fall behind. Avoid anything that will break the rhythm of your routine, especially the first year you go back to work. Don't get involved in big volunteer, school, or remodeling projects.
4. **Get other people's cooperation.** Share the work. You don't have to do it all unless you live alone. Every member of the household should carry part of the load. As manager, you can set up the system. Others will work better if they understand the system and feel like they have had a say in it. Theoretically, the working parent should have less housework to do. While he or she is away at work, the house stays as is and there won't be as many messes made. This is true only when no one else is home. If the children leave for school after you depart and arrive home before you do, work multiplies. It is not the nature of children to notice things that need to be done or to carry out chores without adult supervision. The parent is likely to feel like a martyr who is slaving away to put bread on the table while the "ungrateful" kids loaf at home. There is a more detailed discussion later under Organizing Kids.

If your commitments are unpredictable, you can still get organized, but in a different way. One substitute teacher wrote, "If I am to teach school, I get a call by 5:30 A.M. I wake up about 5:15 and lie in bed waiting to know whether it's a day at school or at home." She has two plans. If she gets a call, she hops out of bed and initiates the rush routine for work days. When there is no ring, she turns over and goes back to sleep for an hour. My friend, whose husband is a fireman, also has two schedules. Not that she bows to any masculine pressure, but the circumstances of his being home change the things she does and alter the balance of delegation and authority. When husband is home, she adjusts her life to accommodate his sleeping. They go out to lunch, they work on special projects, and they eat dinner family style. When husband is at the firehouse, she works on her volunteer projects with no worry about a big dinner—just soup and sandwiches. When I call, I ask, "Are you 'on' or 'off' duty today?" Another woman, who is on call for the family business, has no schedule at all, but she does have a list of the necessary things that have to be done every week (much like the list on page 40). She first starts the laundry, then does some general cleaning, and, whenever time permits, moves down the list until all the necessities are finished. She cannot assign specific tasks to certain days of the week because she never knows when she will have to work. During some seasons the business is less demanding, and she has extra time to deep clean and even take part in community affairs. Likewise, I have two styles of living: one when everyone is away at work and school, and a second style for group living on weekends, at Christmas, and during summer vacation.

When it's work time, work! Pretend you are paying yourself a professional wage; after all, this is a highly technical occupation. Guard against interruptions. Some of them can't be helped, but often we interrupt ourselves. Once you stop, it takes extra time to warm up to the job again and get to full speed. Every Monday morning I want to run away—watch TV, sew, go shopping. But I know if I do not do my appointed work on Monday, I lose my freedom for Thursday, Friday, and Saturday. Be true to yourself; go to work when you say you will. Group the same types of work—errands, phone calls, or baking—together in your schedule as much as possible. A friend who has a home-based candy business says she can get much more done if she sets aside one day each week to do all the errands, to buy supplies, and to take care of all the family details, than if she takes a side trip everyday.

Two schedules are included in this chapter as samples, but you must decide on what suits your lifestyle. You are the executive manager and should be able to make changes to fit special opportunities as they occur. Only in extreme emergencies does the organized person abandon the basics. Certainly, they can be altered or amended, but not dumped. Just because you are busy getting things ready for a YWCA convention, or decorating a birthday cake, doesn't mean the laundry and dishes won't pile up. And when you, the manager, are extra pressured, other family members tend to think they can take off. When you postpone basics for long periods of time, as one "event" happens after another, it takes a long time to dig out and recover. Such extreme highs and lows will wear you out. Rather, learn to manage your extra-curricular activities without letting the basics get far behind.

7. Identify and Avoid Time Robbers

Interruptions are a roadblock to work, but they come all day long in the form of babies, friends, and personal and household emergencies. Life involves learning to accomplish things in spite of interruptions. Don't wait to organize yourself until all the interruptions are gone. You have three strategies: (1) work around them, (2) eliminate some, and (3) manage others. When you are stopped for one reason or another, train yourself to go right back to the job you were doing. When the task is well defined, it is easy. For example, if your first housekeeping goal for the day is to clean a bathroom, when an interruption comes, it's easy to go back to the original chore. Otherwise, you may waste time or risk being sidetracked. You can learn to work with direction and purpose. Think of how a receptionist at the front desk of an office operates. She takes care of each request as it comes, but goes back to typing a letter whenever she gets a chance. Do not let an imperfect situation be an excuse to do nothing.

Eliminate some of the hassle by taking a good look at your life. If you are really serious about this, keep a log for two days. Make a brief entry of what is happening every fifteen minutes. Efficiency experts do this analysis in businesses to pinpoint time leaks and problem times. Who is the offender? When? Is one time worse than others? What was needed when they interrupted you? With this insight, you can start improvement. Some interruptions are caused by lack of order: runs to the dryer for socks, trips to the store for forgotten ingredients, or shoe hunts. Devise a way for kids to get their own drinks of water. Install a pet door so your animals can get in and out without your help. As one father has said, "Instead of putting out fires all day, catch the guy with the matches." A little organization can save a lot of hassle.

Sometimes we interrupt ourselves. Perhaps you are not very dedicated to the task and can be easily distracted. You might think

48

of a phone call that needs to be made, remember to take something out of the freezer, or get an urge for a snack. There is a difference between a break and an interruption. To stop in the middle of a job with an unnecessary interruption is a defeating work habit. It takes time after each interruption to start up and build momentum again. Next time you are tempted to jump from what you are doing, ask yourself if you could wait a little longer until you finish this project or until you get to a better stopping point. Plan periodic breaks to refresh yourself and take care of such needs. A paid secretary gets "coffee" breaks. You can, too. This is self-control.

PHONE MANAGEMENT

The biggest interrupter is probably the phone. There are people who think the solution is to take it off the hook. I don't care for that option myself because then I forfeit the advantage of being available should someone I care for need me. An answering machine might be the answer to help screen your calls. I prefer to answer the phone and manage the caller. If it's a salesperson, I tell them "no" right off. Almost any of my calls for business, church, or volunteer work can be handled within five or ten minutes. If it requires more time, I request that the call (meeting) be rescheduled. I can't give up my work time or I also lose my fun time. For a friend, I can always take out ten minutes, but during high-priority work hours, I don't allow myself the luxury of a lengthy chat. Another secret: Don't wait for them to phone back. Initiate the call yourself because the one who makes the call has more control over the conversation.

Once in a while a friend calls with a real problem. I like to be helpful, but some people with problems are phone-a-holics and seem to live soap-opera lives. They are always looking for a listener to share the intimate details of the saga. I don't waste my time watching it on TV, and I don't waste time listening to it, either. There is a difference between being a caring and loving person and being used. When you give in to such an interruption and allow that person unlimited phone time, you are saying "no" to your work or whatever you might choose to do—take a bath or nap, work on a project, read, or help your child. You are the manager. Tell them, "I am busy right now. Is there another time we can talk?" Or lie: "I have an appointment (with the typewriter) and must run." The

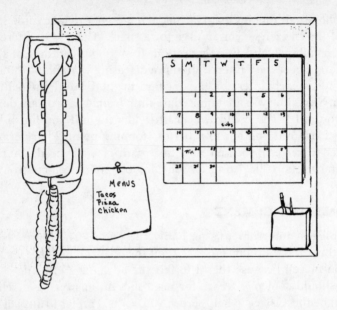

telephone is a wonderful invention. It helps keep friendships alive and saves hours of shopping and working on service projects, but it can gobble up work time. You can't get much done with the receiver propped on your shoulder. By all means, have a long cord on the kitchen phone. If you can polish the refrigerator or clean out a drawer while talking on the phone, fine, but count it as recreation, not efficient work time.

CHILDREN'S INTERRUPTIONS

If you have young children, stay flexible and expect interruptions because it's all part of parenting. Look at children's requests as opportunities, not intrusions. Even so, a child's needs can be managed somewhat. For example, taking care of a child's physical needs early in the day—bathing, feeding, and dressing—can eliminate intrusions later. Start the day your way. Get up on time and fix breakfast. When you sleep in, the kids are likely to get up on their own, get out the cereal and milk (with a few spills), and start watching TV. It will take time to clean up the mess, a hassle about turning off the TV once they are into their show, and a battle to get them started on their grooming and chores.

One single parent, Dave, found that if he took the first twenty minutes with his child after he picked her up from the day-care center, she felt content and then he could get more of his own projects done. When he gave the child his undivided attention for a few minutes after they arrived home, she did quite well. But if he put her off, she was unsettled and afraid Daddy didn't notice her. She sensed she would not get "her time" and interruptions became more frequent. He also found this true at bedtime. Dave needed to stop at the appointed hour and take enough time to go through the standard routine—pajamas, drink, brush teeth, story, prayers, and tuck-in. When he tried to shortcut the routine, it took much longer for the child to settle down.

There are good and bad times to work. Think back on yesterday. At what time did most interruptions occur? Maybe you are trying to work at an inappropriate time. Do not try to work too long into child-care time, particularly eating times or bedtime routine. A parent of young children probably cannot do anything for more than thirty or forty-five minutes without attending to the child in some way. Face it. You do not have the same freedom as an adult without children or with an older family. Babies and toddlers need almost constant adult supervision. Save those adult-only projects for nap time, or for when someone is around to supervise the child, or wait until they grow up. Discover and accept your limitations.

8. Take Action Against Procrastination

W hy do we procrastinate? There are little things we hate to do, so we keep delaying, often making them worse. For some people it's emptying the dishwasher, for others it's putting away the clean clothes or vacuuming the car. Why do you put it off? Do you hate the job? Perhaps you aren't sure how to do it. Sometimes it's such a big project you don't know where to start. Other times it's too boring and mundane. Is it a matter of time? Can you never find time to sort the socks but go to the dryer fifteen times to get a pair? Do you have no time to empty the dishwasher and let the dirty dishes stack up on the counter waiting?

Focus on the problem. Pick it apart, and explore your emotions. Under what circumstances do you procrastinate? All the time or just once in a while? When are you most likely to put something off? Sometimes the hard part is breaking into a project. There are times when you have to use an outside nudge to get you going. Is it too big or overwhelming? Have you had an unpleasant experience in this area before? Maybe you delay because you don't know how. Each cause has a different answer. But without self-evaluation, you won't initiate a program to overcome. At home, we all have projects that are harder for us to tackle. There are those who think pulling weeds is wonderful therapy and others who feel it's torture. Most of us hate to clean the oven and toilet. The slowdown is different for each of us. How do we conquer? David Burns, who wrote the book *Feeling Good*, explains it this way: "Motivation does not come first, action does! You have to prime the pump. Then you will begin to get motivated, and the fluids will flow spontaneously. . . . Individuals who procrastinate frequently confuse motivation and action. You foolishly wait until you feel in the mood to do something. Since you don't feel like doing it, you automatically put it off."

Kick yourself into it. Offer yourself an incentive. Get that action started. Play beat the clock. Turn on the timer for five minutes and see if you can get the clean dishes put away. Make yourself work for thirty minutes at the task, perhaps cleaning out the car, and then reevaluate whether you want to keep going or not. Sometimes it's getting started that's hard, not the work. After you are into the chore, you will probably say to yourself, "I am half finished, I might as well go on. This wasn't so bad after all. Why did I wait so long?"

Years ago, as a young, "born-again" organizer, I set a goal to do one thing each day that I didn't want to do. Each day that I completed one, I felt great power and deep satisfaction, even over small things. It was the beginning of changing some of those bad habits that got in my way at home. For example, it seemed to be easier to wash clothes than to fold them. I initiated a rule of discipline: not more than one load of clean clothes could be stacked on the dryer at any time. This often meant that I had to stop before loading the washer to fold the clothes on the dryer. I changed the bad habit of not taking time to fold the clean clothes. This hint may work for you. You can train yourself to be a self-starter.

Sometimes we put things off because the job seems overwhelming or hopeless. If a job is too big, break it down into manageable parts. Either divide the project into time segments or into physical dimensions. If the kitchen is a mess, work at cleaning it one square foot at a time. Or work on it for forty minutes and take off twenty, then go back again. Don't leave the job in the realm of "I need to get to that soon." Set a definite time to begin. Maybe you can offer yourself a bribe. One way or another, force yourself to get started. No matter who you are, you can divide a job and conquer. If you can overcome procrastination, you can get ahead instead of constantly catching up. Finishing a job is wonderful therapy; behaviorists call it a self-reinforcing action. It is fuel for another successful task.

There are times when the causes for procrastination have to do with thought processes. We can't control thoughts that pop into our mind, but we can decide whether or not to let them stay. I met a woman who makes herself depressed as she works because she allows herself to think of all the things she still has to do, all the things she would like to fix but can't, and all the things she would like to buy but doesn't have enough money. She torments herself the entire time with undoneness. The experience is unpleasant, and she puts off doing it again. She should isolate the task at hand. For example, if she were scrubbing the kitchen floor, she should concentrate on making the floor as nice as possible; not dwell on the fact she can't have new flooring yet. She should be content with what she has chosen to do.

Look for causes and possible solutions. Sometimes there are external things that affect us that are so obvious that we don't think of them. One mother found it was the lid that kept her daughter from putting dirty clothes in the hamper so she got rid of the lid. Another woman hated to get up in the morning because she couldn't think of anything to fix for breakfast. A trash bag in the car can help keep the floor clean. One man found his lack of energy was due to a nutritional deficiency. Identify your problem and give it some deep thought to find answers. Some problems can be taken care of in one big effort, others are irritations for a lifetime that we just have to learn to live with. Maturity is learning which is which and solving those you can.

When wishing won't make it happen, try work. Yes, one answer is to work yourself out of the mess. Some men and women feel justified in putting off housework because they "hate it." Who doesn't? No more procrastination. And don't coddle yourself thinking it's easier for "other people." Yes, you can eliminate the unnecessary and organize for more efficiency, but in the end there is no substitute for *work*. If you are in a mess, start with the MM pickup plan for a little instant improvement. And while you're doing this recovery pickup, it won't do any good to get angry at those who caused the mess. The miracle of the MM is that after about thirty minutes, you feel better and can get a more rational perspective. By then you will have caught that intrinsic motivation David Burns talks about, which comes after you get into an activity.

9. Getting Your Partner to Help

In every household, one partner emerges as the home manager. The position of manager does not mean having to do it all; it means you are the organizer of this area of family life. If you are primary manager over house chores, the other partner will not notice things to do because it is not his or her "territory." A big part of the manager's job is awareness training. Some of it is verbal, some is visual. One woman, in order to get her husband's attention, nailed his clothes to the floor: "If that's where you're going to put your clothes, I'll put a hook there." I do not recommend this action.

First of all, explain your efforts to get organized and **ask for your partner's help and support.** Most people, when they see a spouse's renewed efforts also try harder. You may need to discuss your level of expectation for cleanliness. Environment affects people differently. If your child were allergic to strawberries, would you serve them at every meal? No! But if a man is negatively affected by a messy house, we interpret it as unfair sexism against the woman. Whether it be man or woman that is more sensitive to the order of the environment, the other partner should be understanding. It should not be all one person's responsibility to take care of everything in the house. There is a lot the non-home manager can do to help keep things neat. In most cases, all he or she needs is to be given some direction.

As an organizer, you will need to **set up a system that's easy to follow and then explain it.** This sets the stage for success. Put a clothes hamper near the place your partner undresses. Label shelves and boxes so others can find supplies and put things away easily. If you want family members to scour the tub when they finish a bath, see that a sponge and cleanser are handy. I painted arrows on the washing machine dial so they know which way to turn it and can start a batch of laundry. If you are the one who does the grocery shopping, others will not know what you bought for meals unless you tell them. There will be the obvious things like hot dogs, frozen pizza, and steak, but they probably won't recognize several ingredients (broccoli, canned chicken, cream soup, bread crumbs, and cheese) as a meal unless you give them the message. Post a list of meals for which you purchased ingredients. The object is to create programs so others can easily do the job. After you organize the job so that it is easy to do, then you have to tell them about the plan and how it works.

Do not nag (say it over and over) or hint: "I wish someone would clean this room." Talk to your spouse in a straightforward, specific manner. "Will you vacuum the floor today?" When you come right out and ask, you may get a no, or you might get a definite commitment. Then, after the floor has been vacuumed, acknowledge it in a positive way and you'll get far better results.

If you want help, you have to **be flexible.** You cannot dictate every little motion of every job. The longer you have been manager, the more you have refined your system and the harder it is to let go; your partner's ways will not be your ways. When my husband finishes with the dishes, he drapes the dishtowels over the drainer. That drives me crazy. I hang the towels on a rack under the sink. My logic is that the dishes don't dry with a towel on top of them. His logic is that the towels will dry better if they're stretched out. And you are saying, why should I complain? I should be grateful that he helps at all. That's the point. You can discourage someone's efforts or give reason not to help at all if you're too fussy. If you always have to have it done your way, you'll probably have to do it yourself.

It seems reasonable that if both partners are working at paying jobs, both should help with chores. In this case, write out all the responsibilities and divide them. It is assumed that a partner who is at home all day will perform a larger share of household chores. If someone should get lazy and not carry a fair share of the responsibilities, you have a better chance of coming to a mutually acceptable solution if you both discuss it. Some couples divide responsibilities by literally sitting down and writing out an agreement. They appreciate knowing where they stand and what is expected.

Most of the time, responsibilities are decided by tradition: woman's work (home) and man's work (job). But there are many small responsibilities that aren't gender related. For example, who puts out the cat and locks the door at night? Does that job fall to you because when you were a child your mother did it? Does it really matter? Assignments often come from logical arrangement: the last one home locks the door or the last person to go to bed turns out the lights. Many little jobs are thus assigned and stay that way forever. Who pays the bills, fills the car with gas, cooks Sunday breakfast, writes letters, or packs the suitcase? One man, a social worker, said he resented having to be the one to put the Christmas lights on the tree every year. The first year he did it out of innocent love when his new bride handed him the boxes, assuming he would do it because, at her home, her father always did it. The point here is, if you are not happy with the arrangements, say something. Don't talk it over with your friend or your mother, discuss it with your partner and family. Get it out in the open. It doesn't matter so much who does what as it matters that the couple have discussed the division of responsibility, have come to specific agreements, and keep up his/her share of the bargain.

Communication and assumption may be your problem. Your work plans may not match your partner's, and if you don't take a minute to talk about it there will be unhappy feelings. For example, my husband may have in mind to "wash and clean the cars on Saturday," and I have in mind to go treasure hunting at garage sales. If we make assumptions and don't discuss them, we might both become angry. We have finally learned to ask, "What do you have in mind for Saturday?" before we get our hearts set on personal projects. By asking beforehand, the topic is open for discussion and compromise. I have learned to accept the fact that when the children are home I have less free time for myself, and when my husband is also home, the "line of authority" changes and I no longer have absolute control because another adult is involved and because goals are a joint rather than a single decision. I go into the weekend with two alternative plans: one plan is to do family projects and the second is a personal goal if everyone else is involved elsewhere. You must communicate about household chores, repairs, and redecorating, and not simply assume that your partner agrees with you.

How do you answer a child who asks, "Why should I pick up my shoes if daddy never does?" You can tell your child it was grandma's job to train father, not yours. "But, dear child, you are mine, and since it is my job to train you, go pick up your shoes and put them away." It isn't wise to treat your spouse like one of your children.

Once you explain the difference in relationships, you have license for different house rules. And partners don't need to have identical parenting techniques to succeed. The secret is that when one parent takes a stand, the other parent supports the decision even if it is not exactly the way he would do it himself—as long as it is not an abusive form of discipline.

Sometimes it's good to **stop and look for the causes** of trouble or discord. It might be the relationship. It might be thoughtlessness. Sometimes one member of the partnership is having an especially hard time. If the other member of the partnership puts forth extra effort to do his or her own part better when the partner is troubled or depressed, it will often lift the other's emotions and give added strength. Nothing will be done any better or faster if both partners give up because one person is having trouble with his or her share of the responsibility.

When one partner has been away from home for a while, whether on business or vacation, it takes time to acclimatize to the change in environment before facing decisions, home crises, naughty children, undone chores, or social engagements. If one adult has remained at home, he or she can consciously smooth the waters and thus avoid the resentments and arguments that typically ignite at this critical time. Put that person in a decompression chamber for a few minutes when he or she returns home. You'll notice that a child returning home from Grandma's house, school, or even a birthday party needs this same readjustment time. One mother says "It takes as long to 'get back' as it took to get ready to go."

If you have tried all these methods with love, patience, and kindness, and serious problems still remain, perhaps you need outside help. (Help is available from church, state, or county social services.) There may be a compassionate friend or family member, a doctor, lawyer, or marriage counselor you can talk with. You may also find answers in how-to books or selected classes. Don't forget paid professionals who are often referred by any of those listed above.

P.S. There isn't a man or woman in the world who doesn't have at least one fault that bothers her or his partner—but be glad it isn't worse. (It's frequently that very quality that attracted us to them in the first place.)

ORGANIZING YOUR WORK MOTIONS

10. Get "The Habit"

WORK SMARTER

When I first started my study of home management, over and over again I read, "Work smarter, not harder." To me, it was an ambiguous statement, with no real meaning. Now, with a few years experience, I understand. To work smarter means to work so that your efforts show, so that your accomplishments last longer, and so that your work takes less time. You want to smooth out those peaks and valleys between tidy and messy so recovery won't be so hard. Working smarter has to do with how you tackle a job, how you decide what to do first; concentrating on improving pickup and do-it-now habits. These are not just helpful hints, they are work patterns that carry big benefits. The next few chapters cover details of work motions that will retrain disorganized people into bona fide organizers.

THE PICKUP HABIT

You either have it or you don't—that is, the habit of picking things up. If you don't, it's worth cultivating. In my disorganized days I read in an article, "A good homemaker picks up the house before she goes to bed." I had pre-schoolers at the time and by eight o'clock at night I was ready for the sack. To think that I would have to summon enough energy to go through the house again was overwhelming. I could not do it and I felt like a failure. Then one night, after watching the ten o'clock news, I thought to myself, "I don't have enough energy to pick up the whole house, but maybe I could make this one room a little better by picking up just five things on my way out." I did, and it really didn't hurt since I was on my way out anyway. Thus, I created for myself a new policy: I will give the last room I am in before I go to bed a little pickup. I could handle that much, and I did it almost every night. I straightened the afghans and pillows, tossed the newspaper in the trash, and took the shoes and socks with me. About ten years later, I was lying in bed one night, thinking over the day, and realized that I had picked up the whole house before I went to bed. Somewhere, between the time my children were babies and now, I have acquired the pickup habit.

Whenever we try to initiate a new habit, it takes great effort and concentration. Eventually, though, it moves from the side of the brain that creates thought patterns to the other side of the brain, which directs unconscious effort. It happened to me and it paid off. Whenever I go into a room, if I see something out of place, I put it back. If it belongs elsewhere, and I am going that way, I take it with me. I can enjoy this silent helper the rest of my life. While I'm brushing my teeth, I put away the hair equipment with my other hand. (A waitress's first rule of success: Never go anywhere empty handed.) If I'm going downstairs, I pause before descending to see if there is something sitting there that needs to be taken down. If so, I pick it up and deliver it. I don't just toss it in the room, I take a few extra seconds to put it exactly where it belongs so as not to make one room worse while making another room better. What are the benefits? The house looks better, it's easier to find things, and I spend half as much time cleaning.

Yes, there is danger in the pickup habit. You might start picking up things for other people when they should be doing it themselves. In fact, you might get so good at it that everyone else becomes lazy. Yes, there is a time for training spouse and children, a time to set up a system of assignments, a time for discipline; but if this is *not* their training hour, do your work without getting upset. It may help to turn on happy music. There are times when you pick up things for your own reasons. To get angry every time you pick up a towel or shoe will give you an ulcer and turn you into a nag. Anger leaves you out of control. One of the hardest things in the world is to get children to "see," for themselves, things that need to be done. They probably will not have that intrinsic motivation until they have a home of their own. However, you can do some incentive training that will make life livable until they move out. In the meantime, work on getting the pickup habit for yourself.

Pause now and then to put your work area in order whether you are at the desk, sewing machine, or workbench. When it's time to stop, take a second to "wrap it up." If you insist on this, more than one person can use that desk or machine or shop. For many years my husband and I shared a desk. I used it in the daytime and he used it in the evening for lesson plans. It worked only because we put our papers away when our turn was over. I remember in sewing class at school we put all our supplies into tote-trays. Would anyone have been able to sew if ninety-three girls had left their sewing out because they were coming back to it tomorrow? In a day when many homes are small, most of us don't have the luxury of a separate room for each hobby and activity. The pickup habit could help you use your space for dual purposes. This is especially true in the kitchen, where we have continual projects. As you cook, put away each ingredient after you get what you need from the container. Apply the rubber band theory: pretend there is a giant elastic band attached to each bottle or box or can that snaps it right back into place. Wash (or at least soak) each utensil, bowl, or pan. If you do it as you go, cleanup will be faster.

THE DO-IT-NOW HABIT

There are two battlefronts to beating clutter: one, as we have discussed, is acquiring the pickup habit; the other is the do-it-now or put-it-away-now habit. Dropsy, the habit of setting things down before they are where they belong, is a rationalization, a self-defeating thought pattern. That is, I will set this down just for a while because I don't have the time or energy to put it away now. Very seldom do you save time putting things down in temporary spots. Let's compare. Suppose you and your twin walk into the house with a box full of books that are to go to the basement. You take the box directly to the basement and set it on the shelf. Your twin, however, is in a hurry, and sets the box on the chair by the front door because there is no time to put it away. The next day your twin moves the box to the stairs, hoping someone will take it down when they go. Several days pass. No one thinks to carry down the box, even though it is passed by twenty-six times. On the weekend, or just before company comes and there is a push to clean house, the box is hustled downstairs and set by the shelf to wait again. The rubber band habit that makes you put things away as soon as possible is so much more rewarding than the I'll-do-it-later theory.

The "closure principle" is a psychological term that has to do with a person's intrinsic drive to finish things. It's the urgency to get the library books back and the promptings to finish the ironing or balance the checkbook. It's a desire to get the dishes done or to keep a room tidy. Why? Because people like to be done with something; it makes them feel relieved to check it off. Organized people have this trait; disorganized people can learn it. Setting goals and working with a to-do list can help you finish things until you feel that compulsion on your own.

Do it now. Don't save anything for later that you can do now. Every time you go into a room, make it a tiny bit better. Put the lid on the toothpaste or straighten a towel. You not only need to learn to pick it up and put it away where it belongs, you can learn to do it now. If you see a smudge on the wall, wipe it; crumbs in the drawer, dump it; newspapers spread, pile them; coat out, hang it; dirt on the floor, sweep it; mirror smudged, polish it. Put things away from a project as soon as you can. Why leave the sled in the car for six weeks? Make yourself put the gear away after an outing whether it be a sledding trip or a picnic. My husband I have a mutual agreement that when we get home from a trip we spend the first hour putting things away. Kids help, too. Yes, the dirty clothes are piled in the laundry room, the sleeping bags may be airing on the clothesline, but there are no other clues left out to show we have been away. Compare this to the young man who didn't finish unpacking from his spring band trip to Hawaii until he needed the suitcase for summer camp. Use that closure principle to your advantage and simplify your life.

The question is not how much time it takes to put something away where it belongs. Rather, it's the emotional and mental effort that has to be exerted each time you must deal with the same item. Some of us don't do things until we've given ourself many reminders. In the example above, Twin had to psych himself four times into picking up the box. If we multiply that example over and over by the number of things we use each day and don't put away, you can imagine the clutter and stress. There would be coats everywhere, books, shoes and socks, empty dishes and glasses, pop cans, dirty clothes, towels, boots, gloves—everything that is used. It's not unusual for a home to have 300,000 items. In any one day you get out, use, and handle hundreds of things. If you don't cultivate the do-it-now habit, your house will always be a mess. Clutter causes confusion; it gets in the way of doing things; it destroys self-esteem. Make what you have look as nice as possible—that is working smarter.

ELIMINATE HALFWAY SPOTS

Halfway spots make your house look messy. Keep them to a minimum. You may not realize how many piles you have, so try this exercise. Stand at your front door, pretend you are a visitor, and look with new eyes without making excuses for each and every pile. When you've pinpointed the problem areas, take action. Whenever possible, keep those areas covered—for example, use an end table with cupboard doors for magazines. Gradually work at eliminating those collection spots. Any flat surface, such as a coffee table, is likely to be a catchall; people use the kitchen window and file things behind the toaster at the breakfast nook. What about the top of the refrigerator? Some things that could just as easily be put away take up permanent residence in open areas. The first difference between neatness and clutter is that the neat person puts things *in* cupboards, closets, containers, shelves, and drawers whereas the clutter person fills every available surface—counters, tables, desk, chairs, anything horizontal. They leave things *out* for reminders. A tidy person moves those daily necessities inward one phase, saving surfaces for work or decoration. At home or at work, we think, I'll leave this letter out so I will remember to answer it soon; or, If I leave the tulip bulbs on the counter, I'll be reminded to plant them. Do you write? Do you plant? The advantage of effectively using a running project list is that you can put something away and not worry about forgetting it. If you're one of those people who forgets about them if they are on a list, at least move your reminder piles where they cannot be seen from the front door. This is not a moral issue. Neatness and clutter do not parallel good and evil. But deep clutter can get in the way of things you want to do and be. Remember: People are more important than things, but the order of things affects people.

How can you get The Habit? A few years ago, a friend named Donna vowed to get organized. She set only one goal: "Since I am working, I don't have time to rearrange my whole house, but at least I can keep it from getting worse. From now on, when I have something in my hand, I will put it away, exactly where it belongs, even if I have to go all the way upstairs to the back bathroom." She had decided that even if it took a few extra steps at the time, eventually she would be ahead, and she was. She had to make a concerted effort for a whole year to conquer her dropsy habit. She won. No more piles—the atmosphere is clutter-free and has given her peace of mind and less housework. Think of the benefits she has already gathered, and if she lives to be eighty, she still has another thirty-seven years to reap rewards. It's one of those investments in yourself that pays dividends forever.

EIGHT O'CLOCK PICKUP

One of the most difficult family problems is training children to pick up their things. The solution is difficult but not impossible. For toddlers and preschoolers, the answer is to train yourself to allow five minutes before lunch, nap, dinner, and bedtime to go with the child and help them "wrap it up" regularly. If you have giant messes time after time, the answer is to cut down the number of things available to dump by putting some of the toys and books out of reach and rotating them. After a child is five or six, you can use other tactics. At first we tried standing guard. As soon as the kid lay something down, we'd grab it and they'd have to pay a fine to get it back. That meant we were always on duty and that we were asking them to live a law of perfection that we, as parents, did not follow. We did not mind that things were temporarily laid down, but it angered us when those temporary spots became permanent. For example, one of our sons had three coats. He would go to the closet everytime he needed a coat and only when there was not another one in the closet would he think about where he might have laid one of the others. (Part of the solution to that problem was to only have one coat to keep track of and put the extras away.)

We decided to compromise. Every day we went through the house at eight o'clock and impounded anything left out. To redeem the item, the child had to do a chore. (Redemption chores were simple and required less than five minutes' time—wiping off the TV screen, shaking the rugs, gathering newspapers, or emptying the trash.) The collection box was titled the Extra-Service Box because the children had to perform an extra service to get the item back. Children were not allowed fun time on Saturday until all their belongings in the box were earned back just in case there were some things in there that they did not feel were worth working for. Along with the discipline, we tried to make positive comments whenever we noticed good behavior: "Becky is saving herself a chore by picking up her shoes, hurrah!" An important ingredient for changing a habit is giving positive recognition for the desired action. We made the eight o'clock rounds in the morning and at night. The box was conspicuously left on top of the refrigerator as a reminder. If the children found Mom or Dad's stuff out at eight o'clock, they could also put it in the box. After several weeks the box was put away because the children had improved. (Please notice, I did not use the word perfect.) Three months later, we used it again for a few days to reinforce the principle. Why did it work?

1. The children were mature enough (over six) to understand. Mom and Dad took care of baby's things.
2. The eight o'clock rounds were easier to enforce than the all-the-time rule.
3. The Extra-Service Box was left in plain sight.
4. Redemption chores were kept very, very simple.
5. Special efforts were made to give positive attention when the children picked up and put things away at other times.
6. A gentle, one-time reminder was often given before the eight o'clock rounds were started.
7. Things left out in the child's bedroom did not count in this program.

11. Ready, Set, Go!

E very home has a runway, either natural or designed, which is used for landing and quick take-off, and it is usually about five steps from the front door. It's where everyone drops his briefcase, purse, books, mail, and other pending material. Landing pads are fine so long as the whole family agrees on one place and you recognize the extra effort it will take to manage that area. Decide on a place that is acceptable, where you won't ruin a good piece of furniture, and where it can't be seen from the front door. Any flat surface is an inviting target, but hold the line. As manager, you have to enforce the rules. Train family members that this is only for temporary parking. At my house, we have to work at clearing off our landing zone three or four times a day. If I am not careful, we find ourselves just moving the stack from the kitchen table to the counter when it's time to set the table for dinner; afterwards, we shuffle it back to the table again when we clean off the counter. When I notice this nonproductive shuffle, I have to be more insistent about putting things where they belong and making some resolution to the pending items.

That landing spot also naturally becomes a launching pad, a place to collect necessary supplies as you are preparing to leave for work or school so they are all together and they can be picked up in one motion as you rush out of the house. It's a good habit to cultivate and can help train family members to think through their responsibilities before they leave home. It will help kids remember their homework and lunch or tennis shoes. Many people set aside a "get ready" corner in which to gather things they need to take with them if they are going on a trip. That eliminates a rush at the last minute and prevents forgetting things.

Families can build on this technique to train children to be responsible. One such family put a bookcase by the back door. Each child has a shelf on which to gather lunch, homework, gym clothes, etc. In the morning, they assemble these supplies until they are ready to leave. Part of being a good student is getting organized, and parents can help their children get these details in order. The kids in this family are getting better grades because they don't forget essays and math papers. When they arrive home, they are allowed to set their school books on the shelf instead of having to take them downstairs to their bedrooms. It was easier to make a place for these things at the natural landing spot than to create a new habit of taking them to the bedroom each time. On occasion, it is easier to go with the flow.

For every problem, there is more than one solution. In some homes, this runway technique is also used for coats, boots, hats, and gloves. If the family enters through a back door, hooks and tote baskets can be installed for quick deposit of outerwear. In homes

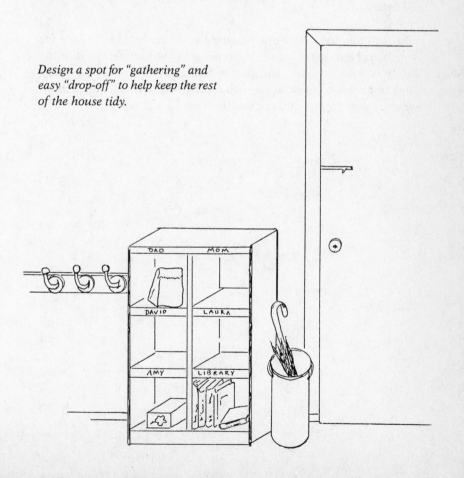

Design a spot for "gathering" and easy "drop-off" to help keep the rest of the house tidy.

where everyone enters by the front door, there is a dilemma: Is practical more important than pretty? Depending on the age and circumstance of your family, find the best possible answer that is likely to succeed. It may take several tries to find just the right spot that is convenient but at the same time out of the way enough so as not to make the house look cluttered. One family with three young children installed coat hooks in the front entry. Because they live in Colorado where you may need a sweater, jacket, and coat all in the same day, they chose practical over pretty and saved a lot of hassle. In some cases, the house has a closet near the front that can be remodeled to contain coats and/or drop-off shelves. This area will need to be monitored, however, or things will take up permanent residency.

To sum up, just about every home has a runway that is used for launch and landing. Find the right place in your home, one that the family is willing to use and that is also away from the front door "first impression" view. With such a program, you can better manage the many things that constantly come in and out.

12. No More Dirty Dishes

D ishes are something you do every day—even if you have a dishwasher. By handling this task efficiently and automatically, you can spend your energies on other goals and responsibilities. Here are some hints:

Put away the clean dishes as soon as you walk into the kitchen. Get them out of the way to give yourself a larger and clearer work area and to allow space for the next batch of dishes. Bypassing this obvious detail can cause a big backlog.

Deal with the mess. If the kitchen is in such a mess that you don't know where to begin, start by putting away any clean dishes, making a place for the next batch of clean dishes, then clear off tables and counters, one item at a time, one area at a time, either clockwise or counterclockwise, depending on your kitchen arrangement. If you have an automatic dishwasher, scrape off the food particles and store the dishes inside the washer until you have enough to justify running a full cycle. You will probably still have some utensils, pans, or plastic containers that cannot go into the dishwasher. Take care of them right away. When the washing is delayed, stack the dishes neatly near the sink to clear the table and counters. Since dishes must be washed often, teach yourself to do it quickly and without anger.

Clear off the counters and work areas before beginning any kitchen job. Give yourself a fighting chance. Don't try to fix dinner on top of the lunch mess. It will take longer, and cleanup is harder. Before you start, take five or ten minutes to clear off drinking glasses and snacks. There is more satisfaction in creating a meal in a tidy kitchen.

Wash utensils, bowls, and pans as you use them. This is an especially good trick if you have an apartment or home with a small kitchen. Consider the cleanup as part of the meal—just like the preparation or eating. Saving dirty dishes is not like saving money. You don't earn interest. Rather, you pay a penalty because it takes extra time when you finally get around to it. Play a game with yourself. See how much of the preparation mess you can clean up before it's time to serve dinner. Your reward is more free time after dinner.

Design your kitchen to be an efficient work area. The more you have in the kitchen, the harder it is to keep clean. Reserve prime space for a few frequently used appliances and supplies in cannisters. Then take a close look at your other equipment. Keep the inventory simple by getting rid of the items you use least often. If you still want to keep them, put them in a long-term storage area. If you can live without them, pack those seldom-used items in a box and put them in the garage for a few weeks to test whether you can cook without such a large inventory of pans, bowls, and appliances. If so, give them to the next charity that calls.

Store things near where they will be used first. Kitchen cleanup is easier if placement of things is well defined. Don't be afraid to label a few shelves if many people use the kitchen.

All family members should help with the dishes. For the first ten years of our family life, we used the system where everyone helps in the kitchen until the cleanup is finished. It worked for nine and a half years, and then it didn't. We called the kids together, presented the problem, and asked how they thought we should solve it. They voted on each doing the dishes one night a week. Interestingly, that was the system I hated as a youth, and I had avoided using it during my parenting years. With the once-a-week system, each child chooses the best day for him or her, and writes it in the calendar. We have followed this program for five years and it has worked quite well. (Younger children need adult assistance.) We use the "good neighbor policy," where each person takes his or her own dishes to the sink, scrapes and rinses them, and puts them in the dishwasher to help the person assigned.

There are several other successful systems. In one household, each person does the dishes for the entire week and is accountable for a thorough kitchen inspection on Saturday night before the job

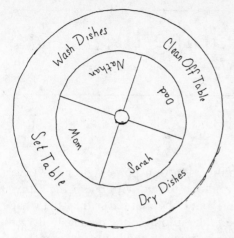

One way to organize dishwashing is to create a circular chore chart to assign after-dinner chores.

is turned over to the next person. One family works in pairs; another uses a circular chart where each person has a small assigned part of the cleanup—clean off table, wash pans, sweep floor, etc.

Complications arise when teens work evening hours or deliver newspapers or if there are sibling arguments over responsibilities. As circumstances change, adjustments must be made. You will know when it's time. I can't guarantee there won't be hassles, but with a program you are more likely to keep things running smoothly.

13. Deep Cleaning the Organized Way

W hat is the level of cleanliness in your home right now? Give your house a rating from one to ten, with one being filthy-dirty and ten being sterile. (Be honest, but not too critical.) At what level would you like it to be? Take into account the feasibility of your goal: the number of people living in the house, their pickup habits, their ages, the size of the house, the age of the house and its furnishings and equipment, all affect how much time it takes to keep a neat atmosphere. You decide: "I want to be at #____ level." You can't jump from arithmetic to calculus; don't try to jump from a cluttered house to immaculate in one easy step. It takes time to change habits, and its easier to concentrate on one habit at a time.

In order to keep a clean house, you have to have a good reason. Why do you want it clean? One of the most compelling reasons is it makes you feel better about yourself. When company comes, it saves embarrassment. There are fewer arguments and fewer accidents in a clutter-free home, and you save time looking for things. You will also save money because the things you have will look nice longer.

There are three degrees of cleaning: pickup, surface, and deep. You already know what a pickup means from our discussion of Minimum Maintenance. This is your front line. When you do it you have immediate improvement, and it serves to make what you've deep cleaned stay clean longer. Surface cleaning is done between the pickup and the complete job—when you pull out the furniture to vacuum but might not go so far as to shampoo carpet or clean drapes. Deep cleaning includes cleaning all surfaces (walls, drapes, floors, furniture), and involves sorting and maybe some redecorating. There are different strategies for each degree of cleaning. It helps to identify which kind of job you are doing so you stay on target. Housework survivors take care of the surface and deep cleaning in one of two ways: marathon or small bites.

MARATHON CLEANING

Great-Grandma used a marathon system of spring and fall house-cleaning. Sometimes a deadline such as house guests or a party initiates a cleaning marathon. School teachers are typical mara-thoners. They keep up with the basics during the school year, then catch up with deep cleaning and redecorating projects during time off. The ideal time for an annual cleaning is October, after the busy summer and dust. If you use this system, set a specific date and then keep it. In the old days. Grandma would take everything out of the house onto the lawn, clean the rooms, wash the curtains, beat the rugs, and polish each item before it went back into the house. When it was finished, the house was sparkling, but the family was dead tired. That isn't a very logical way to clean in our day, because we don't have enough time to do it all at once.

ONE ROOM AT A TIME

A modification is to "spring clean" one room at a time. Do it completely, but don't upset the whole house. You can learn to work without making a giant mess if you pay attention to what you are doing. One day as I stopped to pick up an item at a woman's house, she made her apologies for the confusion and explained her daughters were cleaning their rooms. The mother had instructed them to take everything out of the bedroom and toss it into the hall. Other things came up and the project was delayed and so it stayed in the hallway all that night. (Everyone tromping on it as they made their way to the bathroom.) In the end, all the stuff was put back and the bedroom looked nice, but the "processing" time was terrible. Even from the front door you can tell something was happening. Suppose there are ten rooms in your house, and it takes you three days to deep-clean each one—that would be thirty days of total confusion. Some homes never look good because they are always "into a project." The solution is not to cut out the activity, but to contain it. The reason Great-Grandma emptied the whole room was because the rugs had to be taken outside and beaten to remove the dirt. Now we have powerful vacuums so we don't have to tear out a whole room to clean the floor. Keep the mess within that room if possible. Straighten up after work sessions and *do not* neglect MM. Just because you are busy in one room doesn't mean you can totally

neglect other areas or you'll never make any progress. Work so
progress shows, without making a bigger mess in the process.
Should you be painting or need to empty a room, designate a
second area for "storage" to hold everything while you are working,
but try to disturb only one more room. Don't let it take over the
whole house. How will you choose which room to clean next? I tend
to go by "need," which means I use visual clues to prioritize.
Another possibility is to make a list of rooms, putting the kitchen in
the list twice and then follow it through. One woman spotlights a
"room for the month" (like ice cream flavor of the month). It reads:
January and September: kitchen; February and October: family
room and laundry; March and November: bedrooms. Summer
months are for yard work, redecorating projects, the garage and
canning.

It may help before you start to deep-clean a room to go in with a
pencil and paper on a clipboard and survey the room. Check the
walls, the drapes, the carpet, and the light fixtures and list everything that might need your attention. If you have written cleaning
specifications for your rooms, most of this list will be ready. Cross
off each cleaning task as it is done, so you'll know where you stand.
Work on the target room *until it's finished*. When the room is done,
designate another area to concentrate on. You can accomplish this

deep cleaning in one of two ways: (1) thirty minutes a day or (2) one three-hour block.

I have been assuming here that you will be using the physical wall-boundaries to designate where to clean. Some workers prefer to group similar jobs—windows, light fixtures—at the same time. They like to go through the house and do all the dusting, vacuuming, or emptying of trash in one go-round. It does not matter whether you set up the cleaning routine according to activity or by room. Decide which cleaning pattern suits you and then *start*. Problems arise when people don't follow through or wait too long between cleanings. Treat your home as a business: "I have an appointment to clean the attic." So often we figure we can do domestic chores anytime—there is no hurry. Procrastinating or dragging it out just makes the job take longer. It doesn't matter whether you choose to work a half hour every evening or all day Saturday, but put in your time, one way or the other. Most career women use the thirty-minute-a-day system. When a deep cleaning is necessary, they focus on one job and come back to it again and again until it is finished.

PROFESSIONAL HELP

One full-time home manager can keep house for four people, including him or herself. Those who work outside the home or who have more people in the house need an "ace in the hole." Those who are succeeding have either cut back the work or have gotten help. Some who manage both job and home don't have any children and/or live in a condo with no yard work. They have cut back the work.

If you need help, there are two possible sources: One, get spouse and children to pitch in. They may not do it because of commitment, obligation, or shame. Two secrets to getting their cooperation: (1) Have a specific work time, such as fifteen minutes before dinner each day or two hours on Saturday morning; and (2) design a system of written delegation—chore chart, job jar, or to-do lists. Work won't happen without a personnel manager.

A second form of getting help today is hiring out some of the work, but not necessarily in the old live-in servant style. The popular trend today is to have a crew of workers from a domestic cleaning service come once a week. Specialized and efficient, they aren't slowed by guilt or confused about priorities. They just come in, clean, and leave. Hiring a cleaning service still requires organization and good management. Just like learning to use a new appliance you can learn to use paid help effectively. I was married twenty years and forty-three weeks before I hired someone to do part of my house cleaning, not that I didn't need the help before, but I felt I couldn't afford it. The first time they came I was so nervous, I felt like I was going to court. When they left, it was so wonderful to have everything looking nice at the same time. Once I learned what my two workers would do, I had to learn to leave it for them to do. What good does it do to have someone help with cleaning if you clean to save embarrassment before they come. One homemaker saves a half a day to work along with her helpers. It forces her to keep her "cleaning" appointment and they get a tremendous amount of work done together, whereas before she would never get around to it. A bonus that I have greatly appreciated is the weekly deadline to "get ready" for them by putting away projects and picking up when I might otherwise put it off a few more days. The reaction from my teens was interesting. I had not intended to tell them about my helpers for fear they would relinquish what little responsibility they felt. But just the opposite happened. When my helpers went into the children's bedrooms to vacuum, they also did things that I wouldn't dare do because the kids would take offense. One time they cleaned off my daughter's dressing table (makeup), put everything in a box, polished the dressers, and put a clean scarf on top. (That was the day my kids came home early for lunch and discovered my secret.) The next Saturday my daughter cleaned out her drawers to make room for the stuff that used to be on top, and I hadn't said a thing. You never know whether your family will react to cleaning help by caring more, or by doing less. Over the weeks, my cleaning personnel and I came to an agreement as to what would be done. It was a wonderful boost, but alas, the arrangement was only temporary until I completed my latest writing project.

With most cleaning services, you sign a contract in the beginning, agreeing on exactly what will be done each week so there are no misunderstandings. If not, and you need to design the cleaning schedule, write it out. How many hours will they be working? Make a list of the routine things that have to be done every week (general cleaning, dusting, vacuuming, trash, front door, etc.), just like the specification cards suggested in the chapter on room priorities. Put the other things on an alternating schedule. For example, in the kitchen it may run first week cupboards, second week stove, third week floors, fourth week refrigerator. If you learn to "manage" your cleaning service in this way, the arrangement will be happier for all concerned.

14. The Right Supplies and Equipment

The right supplies and appliances will improve your efficiency at home. Every business needs the proper tools and equipment to deliver good service. How long would it take a carpenter to build a house without a power saw? Who could afford to hire that carpenter? We should apply the same principles of efficiency to our homes as we do to a paying job. The president of a large women's service group told me she waited eight years before getting a long telephone cord. She lost hundreds of hours because she couldn't get more than five feet from her phone. She could not turn down the burner, wipe the counter, or empty the dishwasher. What office worker would put up with such conditions? But at home, efficiency isn't as obvious and doesn't seem so necessary.

Very few homes have a budget that will allow unlimited spending for supplies and equipment. Besides, in this era of smaller living space, we have to be very selective. You'll need to manage this fund and carefully weigh the cost, time savings, and actual need for each proposed investment. Before buying, ask: Do I have to have it? How much time will it save? Will something I already have do instead? With careful managing, you select just what you need at a price you can afford.

When you do get new equipment, it will be necessary to adapt your work habits. When I got my first dishwasher, it took longer to load and empty it than to wash the dishes by hand. Give yourself a "learning time." Anything new or different that you do, whether it's trying a new recipe or using a food processor, will take longer in the beginning. I was afraid I had been unwise in my dishwasher investment, but after mastering the motions, I considered it my most valuable appliance, next to the washing machine.

Many businesses go bankrupt every year because of mismanagement. Home managers can go bankrupt, too, if they buy more equipment and appliances than they really need. Nevertheless, you wouldn't expect a secretary to use a manual typewriter, but sometimes at home we use dumpy equipment. Take a tour of your local housewares store once or twice a year to see what's new. Without breaking the budget, keep your household equipment fairly professional. Good tools and equipment are as essential to the home manager as they are to an auto mechanic, carpenter, or doctor. Set aside a reasonable monthly allowance to upgrade or replace things. Buy a new throw rug or dishtowels, or replace the bent cookie sheets. Getting new things once in a while gives the housekeeper a boost.

VACUUM CLEANERS

Every household needs a good vacuum cleaner. There are two types: (1) tank with a hose, and (2) uprights with a beater brush. Both are good, but not good for the same things. To maintain carpets, traffic areas need to be vacuumed everyday with a vacuum that has both good suction and a beater brush that combs and beats at the same time, loosening and drawing up the dirt before it gets to the carpet backing. Tank vacuums are wonderful for dusting corners, cobwebs, stairs, drapes, edges, and the car, but not for carpet. You'll work yourself harder than necessary and wonder why your carpet doesn't look nice. If you live in a small place, I would choose an upright that comes with hose and simple attachments. Those maintaining a house would benefit by having both. And, if you're really into family (large house, garage, yard, or lots of do-it-yourself projects) you will need a wet/dry vacuum that will also help when the basement floods, toilets clog, hot water heater breaks, or if you want to shampoo your own carpets and upholstery.

An investment in a vacuum that preserves your carpet will be a savings in the long run. Bags need to be changed regularly. If you go over the floors with a full bag, you might as well have taken a nap. Be ready with extra pulley belts, and have the vacuum checked periodically to see if the brushes need replacing or if the fan has been damaged by pennies, nails, or paper clips.

CLEANING SOLUTIONS

If a professional custodian had to return to the supply closet every time he or she needed a dust cloth, a sponge, or a can of disinfectant, he/she would never be able to provide necessary services. To save time, steps, and money, professional cleaners always carry their supplies with them in a basket or bucket or cart. This same rule can be applied to cleaning at home. Over a period of a month or a year, a cleaning basket can save countless hours and will put an end to those unnecessary trips up and down the stairs, and to and from the utility closet. (A duplicate set of supplies may be left permanently where you clean daily in kitchen and bathrooms.) As you work in other rooms, having the supplies with you in the maidbasket will encourage you to do a better job. If the proper cleaner is right there, you are more likely to take a second and wipe the smudges off the lightswitch or polish the mirror.

Your cleaning basket can be anything from a wicker basket to a rubber or plastic pail, but it makes your work easier if the basket is wide, with low sides and a flat bottom so each bottle, can, or brush can be seen and easily reached. Keep the inventory of cleaning supplies simple and evaluate each product's effectiveness periodically. If your children are doing part of the cleaning, include only supplies that are safe for them to use and fill their containers less than half full. The following is a list of the basics to have in your maidbasket:

> General cleaner
> Glass cleaner
> Disinfectant
> Furniture polish
> Sponge with mild abrasive pad on one side
> Cleanser
> Several soft cloths
> Paper towels
> Old toothbrush
> Plastic bag to collect trash
> Rubber gloves for tough scouring jobs

SUPPLIES

It is important to have the proper equipment and supplies readily available. Benjamin Franklin wrote in *Poor Richard's Almanac*, "A little neglect may breed great mischief . . . for want of a nail the shoe was lost; for want of a shoe the horse was lost; and for want of a horse the rider was lost." Plan ahead. Have basic supplies on hand so you can make repairs before an item is damaged beyond use.

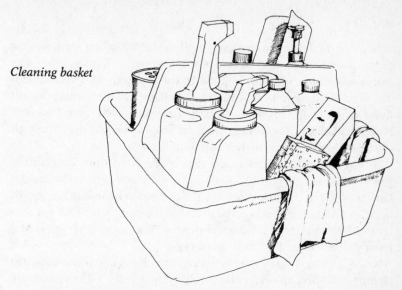

Cleaning basket

If you have a supply of various colors of thread, a small hole in a knit shirt can be stitched before it becomes a long run. With a screwdriver close by, the knob on a chest of drawers can be screwed back in before it is lost. If the equipment is handy, repairs are much easier. Here's a list of other basics you should have on hand in the house. The garage will probably have additional tools for more extensive repairs.

- A variety of glues for glass, paper, metal, and wood (one glue won't do)
- Heavy-duty strapping tape for mailing packages or mending the backs of books, a roll of good transparent tape for mending book pages
- A permanent magic marker, liquid embroidery-paint tube, and printed cloth name tags to put your name on all items likely to leave the house, even the broom
- A hammer, an assortment of screwdrivers, and a pair of pliers (an extra set kept in the kitchen will save many steps to the garage)
- A plunger and length of wire or coat hanger to free clogged drains
- An assortment of nails, screws, washers, and bolts
- Clear nail polish, that old standby, to stop runs in nylons
- Extra light bulbs and fuses
- A flashlight and batteries

RAGS

As a child, I can remember my grandmother's rag bag, which hung in her kitchen for ready access. Grandmother, a Kansas farm wife transplanted to Colorado because of the drought, tore up old bedding and clothing in preparation for their second life. Grandpa used those rags to wipe his greasy hands; Grandma used them for every household chore. Those rags were recycled over and over through the wash, until they vanished into nothingness.

In days gone by, people used rags more often than we do now, partly because disposable paper products are readily available. However, there is still a place for the common rag in our homes. To be a "good rag," it needs to be made of the right stuff and cut to a convenient size. Modern-day fabrics, such as nylon, acrylics, and most polyesters do not make good rags.

At my house, I have two types of rags. First are those used for cleaning, appropriately called "cleaning cloths." They come in handy for polishing the shower, scrubbing the kitchen floor, cleaning mirrors and windows, wiping up spills, and dusting. They have to be absorbent. Terrycloth fabric makes fantastic rags. Use those old washcloths and handtowels for cleaning. If you don't have enough of your own, watch for them at rummage sales. Cloth diapers make the best possible rags, for the same reason they are good for baby. Professional cleaning services often buy diapers for use in their business, paying more than a dollar each because they clean so well and wash easily. The right equipment, even a rag, makes the job easier and is as important as the cleaning solution. (If a cloth, by the way, has been used for cleaning the toilet, it cannot be used on the sink without spreading disease organisms. And it should not be washed with the face cloths and hand towels.)

The second classification for rags is the disposable kind that are used for messy jobs such as polishing the car, changing oil, or painting and then thrown out, since it would cost more than they are worth to wash them. Old sheets are great, as are polo shirts, given several snips to separate front from back. (Cutting up the shirt also signals that it is a rag and keeps it from getting back into the drawer.) Take off buttons, rough seams, zippers and grommets so as not to mar the surface on which the rag is used. Flannel makes great wiping cloths; mechanics pay top dollar for the red flannel squares they use in the shop.

I keep this supply of work rags in a bag, formerly used for diaper storage, and it looks very much like the one grandmother had in her kitchen. When the rag supply gets low and I don't have enough to meet the demand, I buy sheets at a garage sale and tear them into eighteen-inch squares. At some thrift stores you can purchase them by the bag.

I am glad that we have some wonderful paper products, for example, tissues. But maybe we have gone too far with disposables. If you are interested in saving a little money, you might consider using rags to wipe up kitchen spills. The average family spends close to forty dollars a year on paper towels. You could probably cut that in half by keeping a wipe-up cloth handy. We keep ours on a hook under the kitchen sink, but occasionally I still see someone reaching for the dishtowel to wipe up a spill and I have to remind him or her. If the towel is used on the floor, it goes into the laundry, so as not to be used on clean dishes.

RAG BAG

15. How to Clean and Where to Start

With your cleaning supplies in hand, you're ready to start—but professionally, with direction—*clockwise*. Starting at the supply closet and ending there, go through your house or apartment one room at a time. The basic idea of the clockwise system is to start at the back and bring the dirt to the front so you are never moving from a dirty area into a clean one.

Dusting is the first step in cleaning. Dusting also has a movement technique: *Always follow your hand*. If you are right-handed, start at the right and dust to the left; if you're left-handed, start at the left and dust to the right. By following your hand, you won't spread dust over places you've already wiped. Professionals also use the technique of dusting high places (picture frames, door jambs, etc.) first, and then moving to lower areas to prevent dust from dropping all over cleaned areas.

After dusting, use a general cleaner for metal or tough plastic finishes, and use furniture polish on wood furniture (moving with the grain). Be careful to use the right cleaner for each surface (try using a different color or type of cloth with each cleaner to prevent such mixups as wiping your mirror with the oily furniture-polish cloth).

As you work around the room, pay special attention to finger-marks on doors, light switches, and door handles. Then stop and look. Are things like the chairs and pictures straightened? The room not only has to be clean, it needs to *look* clean. Leaving the vacuum or some other supplies out in the middle of the room gives it that not-yet-done look no matter how long you have worked in it.

Now vacuum the room, starting at the back of the room and working toward the door. Carpet spots should be sprayed with carpet cleaner and blotted carefully. Heavy traffic areas, such as halls and entrances, need to be vacuumed daily, but rooms with very little use may need a thorough vacuuming only every week or two.

BATHROOM

What about the restroom? It calls for special, daily care, but can be done in a very few minutes. Here, again, you'll move clockwise, bringing the dust and debris from the back to the front in order to go from a cleaned area into a dirty one. Always clean from high places to low places.

Professionals get a fresh, pleasant smell from cleanliness, not scents. Spray the entire outside surface of the toilet with disinfectant and let it stand a moment while you lift the seat, flush the toilet and clean the bowl, being sure to swab the inside and under the lip of the bowl. (A sponge brush works better in the toilet bowl than a bristle brush.) Starting at the top and working down, wipe down all the outside surfaces of the toilet with paper towels, polishing the metal fixtures and wiping behind the toilet and around the bottom of the bowl. (I choose to use paper towels here to eliminate any chance the rag will be used again and spread germs.)

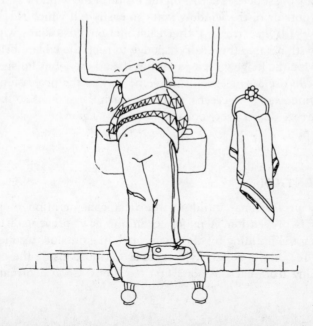

Sinks and tubs should be lightly scoured with a dab of cleanser, rinsed, and then the fixtures polished. Replace the toilet tissue. Custodians suggest the paper unroll toward the person, not toward the wall, but this is really a personal preference. The cardboard tube can be flattened so it doesn't unroll too easily and thus waste paper. Dust door and mirror edges, cleaning any spots on the walls, door, and light switch. Don't forget to sanitize the door handle! Wipe the floor, catching the corners and behind the door.

WINDOWS

How do custodians clean windows? Watch them. They don't use squirt bottles or newspapers. They use a squeegee with a good rubber edge that extends beyond the metal edges of the squeegee frame. (You can buy one in your hardware department.) They put a couple of drops of dishwashing liquid in a bucket of warm water as a wetting agent and wet the window with a sponge. They wipe the squeegee across the top and side edges of the window to prevent drips and cut the water bead that adheres to the edge. They pull the squeegee either down or across the wet portions of the window. (If you draw the squeegee across on the inside of the window and down on the outside of the window, you can easily tell which side of the window still has streaks.) After each motion, custodians wipe the blade with a *damp* (never dry) sponge to keep the edge lubricated. They wipe the ledge with a paper towel, and the job is finished.

You can use a squeegee in the same way as the professionals. If your windows have screens, brush or wash the screens so the first little breeze doesn't get your windows dirty again.

PREVENTION

In any professional building, the first consideration in saving money is prevention. A major technique is to prevent dirt from entering the building by placing a rough mat outside to collect the heavy dirt, and a softer, nylon-rubber mat just inside the door to catch dirt from each person's first few steps. Good doormats will

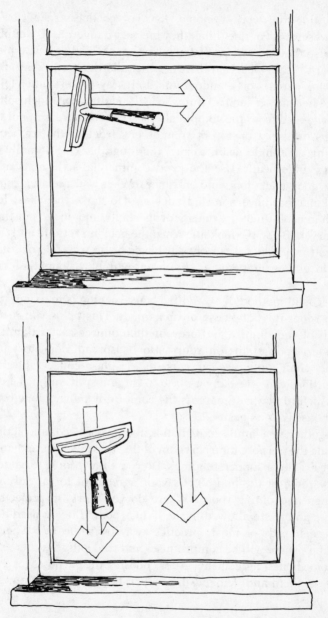

Wipe across top edge to cut bead of water. Then pull either down or across to wipe off the rest of water.

save time and work at home, too. For goodness sake, don't use carpet scraps. For one thing, they are very dangerous. Older people, because they are especially frugal, are more likely to use a piece of carpet to "save wear" on their new installation. Don't do it. Do not let your parents or grandparents do it. My grandmother fell and broke her hip on such a "throw" rug. It caused her much suffering and she died from the complications. The second reason not to use scraps of carpet on top of your other carpet, is that rather than "saving" the underneath carpet, the rough backing actually *wears* what's underneath. Use the good commercial-style mats at your front door, back door, and entrances. When you use area rugs, get the kind that have non-skid backing. (To make them last longer, wash in cool water, use detergent sparingly, and do *not* put them in the dryer.) Be on the lookout. When the backing gets old and the rug starts to slide, get it out of your house before you fall, or someone you love trips on it. You are better off with bare floors than broken bones.

A second method of preventive housekeeping is to assign uses to each room in your house or apartment. This helps you meet the needs of your family, and prevent such unnecessary calamities as raspberry-pop stains on your satin bedspread, dog hairs on the velvet chair, and race-car ruts on the glass coffee table. Room definitions can give baby a place to eat and spill, siblings a corner in which to play, and parents the comfort of knowing one room in the house is at its best.

Together, in a family council, talk about your needs and activities. Decide the purpose for each room of the house. Write them down so there are no misunderstandings. Do you allow people to eat food in every room of the house or is your agreement to eat only in the kitchen and dining room? Where do you work on projects? Are paints and paste allowed in the living room? Do you need a place for quiet study or music practice away from the TV? Where will that be? There will be compromises and tradeoffs, but there should be some honest agreements. After choosing the purposes for a room, stick to them and demand the cooperation of all family members and pets.

ROOM PRIORITIES	Entry	Front room	Kitchen	Dining room	Family room	Bathroom	Bedroom	Laundry area	Garage	Outside
Eating			✓	✓						
Allow pets to sleep									✓	
Reading		✓			✓		✓			
Music practice		✓								
Homework			✓				✓			
Craft projects			✓					✓		
Sewing								✓		
Watch TV					✓		✓			
Drop off coats and school books	✓						✓			
Dressing						✓	✓			
Playing					✓					✓
Wrestling										✓
Other										
Other										

Define the purposes for each room. Check if yes.
Review together in family meeting.

ROOM SPECIFICATIONS

Here is a one-time work tactic you can use to organize housecleaning whether you do it yourself, assign it to your children, or hire a maid. Write a job description for each room in your home. Divide it into two parts: what you expect for a daily pickup, and your expectations for a weekly cleaning. To prepare such a list will initially take less than twenty minutes and may require a little updating after the first time through. Why take time to write it out? Because it defines your expectations. If you do your own housekeeping, and you are keeping up, you probably have such a plan in your head. But for the home manager who is having a hard time, writing it down will help get control. If part of the housework is assigned to children, writing out a specification sheet for each room will help them understand what you intend to be done. If they do not clean it correctly, when you go for inspection, they will probably try, "You didn't tell me I had to do that," in which case you can refer them to the posted list. It takes you out of the bad-guy spot and puts the responsibility on the child for self-inspection. Post the spec sheet somewhere in the room (in closet, behind drape, in medicine cabinet), to be readily available but not conspicuous.

If you hire someone to do your housework, organizing such a cleaning strategy helps you maintain control and get the results you desire. The worker will know what to expect, and it will take less time to make the assignment and run through the instructions. Usually a professional cleaning service will review every detail to be performed. You agree upon the details and sign a contract before any service is begun. There are no misunderstandings on what is to be done each week. Some tasks need to be done every day, others weekly, and still others can be rotated. Put this professionalism in your home. It takes only a few minutes for the initial investment. For starters, look at the sample cleaning specifications in the following chart.

**CLEANING SPECIFICATIONS
(TO BE POSTED IN EACH AREA):**

Front Room

Daily:
Put away books and toys
Close piano; put bench
    under
Straighten cushions
Put newspapers neatly
    under table in far corner
Vacuum traffic areas

Bedrooms

Daily:
Make bed
Pick up clothes
Fold and put away pajamas
Keep top of bed and chest
    neat

CLEANING SPECIFICATIONS
(TO BE POSTED IN EACH AREA):

Front Room
Weekly: (Saturday)
Vacuum carpet
Dust all furniture
Take newspapers to garage
Damp-wipe around door
Shake rugs
Sweep porch

Bathroom

Daily:
Pick up all hair equipment
  and straighten counter
Pick up toys and clothes
Straighten towels
Scour sink and polish
  chrome
Wipe off back of toilet
Shake rug

Weekly:
Scour toilet bowl
Wash towels
Wash brushes and combs
Polish mirrors
Sweep and mop floor

Yard
Weekly:
Pick up trash
Sweep porch
Wipe entry
Mow lawn

Monthly:
Rinse trash barrels
Sweep sidewalks
Weed
Trim shrubs

Bedrooms
Weekly:
Dust
Vacuum
Straighten drawers
Change bed sheets
Damp-wipe around door

Kitchen

Daily:
Rinse and put dishes in
  dishwasher
Refill cold drinking water
  (if necessary)
Cover leftovers and put in
  refrigerator
Wash pans and serving
  bowls
Dry pans and serving
  bowls
Shake rugs
Sweep floor
Scour and polish sink
Wipe off counters and table
Put away chairs
Fold down table

Weekly:
Scrub floor
Clean one cupboard
Wipe out microwave
Rotate cleaning one:
  stove
  refrigerator
  dishwasher

SEMI-ANNUAL CHORES

How do you keep track of those jobs that need to be done only once or twice a year? Do you wait for a visual reminder? Does the change of season give you a clue? Most of us in Colorado don't think about having our snow tires put on the car until after the first snowstorm and then there is a mad rush. One solution is to make a list of household items that need to be done once or twice a year. Tack it up in the garage above the workbench or keep it in your planning notebook. Likewise, you will probably need some sort of system to keep track of car maintenance and repair. Sometimes mechanics put a self-sticking form on the inside edge of the car door on which to record lube and oil changes. You could keep such a record in the glove box of the car or in your personal financial file. The point is, if you faithfully maintain your household equipment and vehicles, they will last longer. Set up some sort of a program according to the equipment you own and the climate you live in. Consider the following sample:

Semi-annual House Maintenance

Replace furnace or air-conditioner filters
Trim bushes and trees
Wash windows
Clean out gutters
Check chimney
Winterize swamp cooler, humidifier, or dehumidifer
Clean and lube lawnmower, snow blower, etc.
Put up or take down storm doors and windows

Car or Truck Maintenance

Tuneup
Lube
Change oil every 3,000 miles
Rotate tires every 4–5,000 miles
Change air filters at least once a year
Wax exterior every 90 days
Shampoo upholstery
Thoroughly clean interior

16. Licking the Laundry

N o wonder the laundry is such a big job. The average family of four will have 224 items of clothing to wash in a week (not including linens), and each article is handled at least six times before it goes back to the closet. Add to this sheets, towels, and special needs if you have a baby, a bedwetter, or an invalid at home, and you can see that setting up an efficient laundry program is a must.

Martha is twenty-eight and has four children aged two to ten. She lives in a small home with three little bedrooms, no garage, and no basement. Mom and Dad share one bedroom, two little boys have one room, the older girls share another. Because of the size of her house, Martha is likely to have problems. When you have a small house, the quantity of things you keep has to be kept in proportion. Martha is fighting hard at this point, and feels she is losing the battle. She needs to work smarter. As Martha and I talked about her laundry, she said she did twenty loads of washing a week. (The wheels in my head began to spin as I quickly calculated that it is twice the laundry I do, and I have five children.) It seemed to me she was doing more than was required. I asked her whether, if all the clothes in the house were clean and folded at once, she would have space in the closets and drawers for them. Her answer: "Well, no, but I stack them *on* the children's chest of drawers." I suspected that, and in my mind I could see a little child picking out a pair of pants in the middle of the stack and the whole pile toppling to the floor. Then I imagined the little kids walking on those clean clothes and, a few days later, Mom insisting on a pickup and tossing them into the hamper to be washed again.

Martha has multiple laundry problems. But there are many possible solutions, as I will outline below. No one solution fits everyone, but as I discuss Martha's problems, watch for possible refinements to apply to your own system.

Problem 1: Martha has too many clothes, especially for the size home she has. Because she is washing so often, she could get by with three or four days' worth, but certainly no more than could comfortably fit into the closets and chests. For example, her ten-year-old daughter has twenty pairs of jeans. At my suggestion, Martha replied: "But I am working, I just don't have time to go through everything." That old hangup, the Big Job, was blocking her progress. If you can't do it all at once, do it in little parts— maybe one drawer at a time. Also, Martha could start a gradual system of sorting to catch things as they come through the wash. All she would have to do is set an open bag or box near the washer in which to put things that need to be moved out. In two or three weeks, much of the sorting would be done. Then, twice a year, she will need to go through the drawers and closets for a more thorough sorting. It helps to tackle only one closet at a time. Any clothing that does not fit or that belongs to another season should be stored elsewhere, out of circulation where the children cannot get into it, so they do not have to manage it.

Problem 2: There were no towel rods in the bathroom, so that each time a towel was used, it was tossed on the floor to be washed. If you want to simplify the laundry, you must have enough towel rods so that each person has a spot for his or her own towel. You need a rod in the kitchen, too. I live in Colorado, where the air is dry and we can use the same bath towel more than once if we choose. Even if you live where it is humid, if you have a place to hang the towel, it will air better than in a heap on the floor. You could use it to wipe your hands, which you wouldn't do if it has been on the floor. One woman, with the same size family but with teenagers, said she washes fifteen towels a day. Think of the cost of soap and hot water, not to mention the time. There is no excuse for not having towel rods. To find space for the extras, you may have to put some rods high and low or on the back of the door or maybe use hooks instead of rods. If you don't know how to install them, go to the hardware store and ask. They have simple, easy-to-read packages of molly screws that anyone can put up, even me. It will cost you more to wash one batch of towels than to buy those long screws that won't pull through the wall. This is a one time effort that will pay off over and over.

Problem 3: No deadline; no beginning; no end. Martha never has a time during the week when she can say, "My wash is caught up." How is it possible to be caught up when the clothes on your back will be in the hamper tonight? You can set a dividing time. This week's deadline is "anything dirty before 9:00 P.M. on Sunday." Anything worn after that hour is part of next week's laundry. The home manager then washes, folds, presses, and puts away every piece of that quota. Couples or singles may have a dividing time every two or three weeks. If it is possible to do that laundry (at least the clothing if not the linens) in one day without overworking the washing machine or yourself, do it. With all the clothing back in the closets and drawers, the clutter problem is greatly reduced. Wipe off the machines, sweep the floor, and enjoy that finished feeling for a whole week. (Naturally, exceptions will need to be made for diapers, baby clothes, a bedwetter, or athletic clothes. But at my house, I have never made it a habit to entertain requests for "a favorite shirt," etc.

One busy woman washes one load a day: Monday, whites; Tuesday, denims; Wednesday, perma-press; Thursday, towels; Friday, sheets. It takes her a little extra time to gather up the clothes every time, but she feels it is worth it since she is not home long enough to put in one batch after another. However, you need to be on the lookout for inefficiencies that creep in. The person who takes several days to finish the laundry is tempted to gather up "new" dirty clothes, increasing the number of pieces in circulation and decreasing the possibility of total completion. There is a temptation to overwash items that don't really need to be washed or to mix the wrong articles together just to get enough for a full load. The cycle can become endless and expensive. In homes where there is a perpetual system, more clothes per person are required. The first secret to laundry management is to have a recognizable beginning and end. Otherwise, with a continuous conveyer of clothes from bedroom to laundry and back again, some items get sidetracked, especially those that need a little special attention. Instead of eight days worth of clothing, each person may need fourteen or twenty-one outfits per person per season. Thus, you always have 50 percent of the clothes in circulation: on the floor, in the washer, or piled on the dryer. All this complicates housekeeping, makes the home look messy, and creates more work. Reap the rewards of order, especially in this area, as it affects so much of your homelife.

Problem 4: Martha does not have an organized sorting system. Her washer and dryer are in the kitchen. There are always piles all over the floor waiting to be washed. As the children walk through, they tromp on them, mix them up, and drag them around on their feet. This young mother thinks that washing clothes means picking up an armload and stuffing them in the washer. There are three important steps before that: careful sorting, pretreating, and checking pockets and zippers.

You can create a sorting system. Spread out boxes or baskets and put one batch of dirty clothes in each container. Just getting those piles off the floor and into containers will do wonders. (If need be, the boxes can then be stacked one on top of the other to save space.) Carefully sort the dirty clothes by color, fabric, and soil. Wash whites, especially nylon or polyester, only with other whites, as they absorb other colors. Wash denim only with denims. Proper sorting is a very important step in keeping your clothing looking nice. Each article should be "meeting" the same friends each week. Putting lightweight garments with heavy items, even if they are the same color, will wear them out faster. Extremely dirty work clothes or greasy coveralls should be washed separately, even stored separately until wash day. When you acquire something new, don't put it in with an established load until you have washed it once by hand to check for fading. You could ruin several hundred dollars' worth of clothing if a red flannel nightshirt gets in with your blouses or shirts by mistake. Check your washer and dryer and follow the manufacturer's instructions for weight and size of wash load. Too many clothes in the tub prevents adequate circulation and clothes will not wash or rinse well. Following is a list of the categories I have found to work for sorting my family wash. Perhaps I am more specific than your needs in this area:

> Delicate whites
> Dress shirts and blouses
> Colored play clothes
> Dark slacks and dark socks and nylon pantyhose (in mesh bag)
> Towels and/or sheets
> Socks and underwear to be pre-soaked
> Delicates: sweaters and wool skirts, etc.
> Denim jeans

Soiled clothing, at my home, is kept in a hamper in each person's bedroom until laundry day, when they take it to the washroom.

Another family has bins in the laundry area and each family member sorts his or her things as they drop them off. When a bin is full, the batch is washed. Still another family washes by room: everything for the people in that room is washed and then taken back, saving sorting. I do not choose this system for myself because the kids don't have enough of one kind of clothes to justify a whole load. Thus, it costs more for partial batches, or even worse, they mix things together that aren't meant to be washed together. Perhaps because I have gained such control and refined my system to the max, I don't want to let go. But many people tell me their teenagers wash and care for all their own clothes. Sometimes each is assigned a specific day to use the wash area. You have to weigh the advantages and disadvantages. If I used this system at my house, my children would leave their unfinished wash in or on the appliances, they would operate on emergency from the laundry room, rendering my room unusable for any other project or purpose. So much of family life is dependent on having clothes ready that I still choose to do it myself.

Scooping up an armload of clothes and stuffing them in the machine spells trouble. Take some extra time here. Put one item in

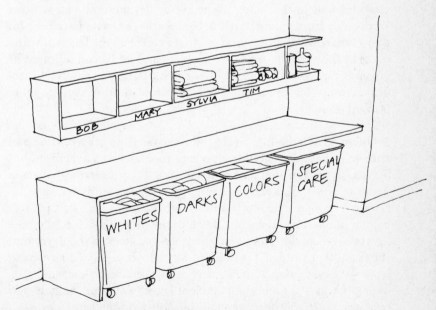

It is as beneficial for a family to have a well-organized laundry center as it is to have an efficient kitchen.

at a time, checking it over. Take a second to close zippers and other
fasteners, tie draw strings loosely together. Put small items or
things that might tangle, such as pantyhose, belts, and scarfs, into a
mesh bag. Turn everything right side out unless directions specify
otherwise. Check pockets for surprises. Treat stains now or the heat
from the water and dryer will set them forever. (Whenever possible,
rinse a spot when it is fresh. If it comes out, hang the garment to
dry until wash day.) If the spot is stubborn, put it to soak as soon as
possible. On wash day, pre-spot collars, cuffs, perspiration or any
other stains. Use commercial pre-spotting products or a concentration of detergent. You will learn with experience what works
best for you. If you suspect a stain will not come out in the normal
cycle, put it to soak in a nearby sink or dishpan. Use a toothbrush or
fingernail brush to gently rub in the liquid soap or a soap paste on
collars, perspiration stains, or other hard-to-clean areas.

Careful sorting and spotting will help clothes stay nice longer.
Whenever possible, soak out a stain rather than bleach it out.
Liquid bleach is not meant for most modern fabrics and colors. Use
it sparingly. Soaking is good not only for problems, but also for
removing regular soil. If you stop the machine and let a normal
wash load sit in the soapy water five or ten minutes, you will get
extra value from your detergent. (But we don't always have time for
that.) I plan my washing order so that I can start the batch of white
socks in the evening, stop the machine, and let it soak all night. (I
also put powdered bleach in this batch.) Detergent and other ad-
ditives must be dissolved in water before putting clothes in to
prevent damage.

Problem 5: Martha has no rhythm. She needs to set a routine and
stick to it. Laundry should be done as regularly as a heartbeat, but
not as often. You don't have to be caught up everyday—that's a
waste of effort. You can save time by grouping similar chores together. A mother who works full time may find it best to wash two
batches a day. She starts one batch in the morning before she goes
to work. When she gets home she puts that load in the dryer and
starts another until she is finished for the week. It is dangerous to
leave the dryer going while you are away because if something goes
wrong it may start a fire. An efficient laundry system can help you
save money. If you do your wash faithfully on the same day each

week, you need only eight or nine pairs of socks. If you wash every other week, you need fifteen pairs, which is all right if you live alone, but for a large family that can be expensive.

For many years I used the "all in one day" method. It took five hours to sort, mend, wash, press, fold, and put away everything for seven people, but I was free the rest of the week except for a few linens. It helps the house look clean to have all 350 pieces of clothing put away. When I work a job, I sort the dirty clothes on Saturday and wash as many batches as the activities of the day will allow. By Monday or Tuesday evening I finish the ironing, call everyone to put their things away, and count myself finished for a few days. When your quota is done you can have a celebration.

Problem 6: Martha has trouble with folding. Why is it so much easier to wash and dry clothes than to fold them? I made a rule for myself, "Never get behind more than one batch." It takes only five or ten minutes. Waiting until you have ten loads to fold creates a major job. I don't allow myself to wash another batch of clothes until I have folded the one on top of the dryer. It is especially helpful to have a table on which to fold clothes, and shelves or baskets in which to separate items by person or room. If you can't have a table there permanently, set up a card table on washday. Martha does not hang up the shirts, blouses, and pants when the buzzer goes off and they get wrinkled. Sometimes she throws them back into the washer on the rinse cycle and tries again and even again. Catching the shirts at the right moment saves ironing. Obviously you need a place (rod, rack, rope, or hooks on the wall) to hang the permanent-press items in your laundry area.

Problem 7: Martha never has all the clean clothes put away. If this is a problem for you, make yourself do it. Offer yourself an incentive if you need a boost. For the first ten years I put away all the clean clothes myself. I could keep the drawers fairly neat, and I was aware of the kids' clothing needs. Best of all, I could count the laundry all finished. One year I decided it was time for my children to put away their own clean clothes. I tried everything—games, treats, and bribery—to get them to do it on their own. It was on my goal list for three years. They wanted to use the laundry room as an annex to their chests of drawers. Whenever they needed clean socks, they went to the washroom to get them. (One family solved this problem by moving all the children's chests to the laundry room. The children (young) dressed and undressed right there by the washer. The rest of the house stayed free of clothing, solving lots of problems and saving energy.) I have not found a solution for getting my kids to put away their clean clothes, but they are better than they used to be. If it bothers me, I put their clothes away myself. If it doesn't, I just leave them until they come for them. I do have one little trick that works: On Tuesday afternoon, they find me sitting in the living room chair casually eating M&M candies when they get home from school. "Can I have some?" I don't even have to answer anymore— they rush right to the laundry room, put everything away, and come back for their treat. It's called incentive.

Problem 8: Martha does not have control of the mending. When something needs to be fixed, unless they "have to have it," it stays in the mending basket for as long as eighteen months. It would be better for her to discard it right away than to take up precious space for that much time in her little house. One mother of a large family claims to have been caught up on her mending for the last twelve years. Each week she mends the two or three items that are damaged that week while the first load of wash is going. If she ever gets behind, she forces herself to make a separate mending time before the new month arrives.

LAUNDROMATS

If you get hopelessly behind on the washing, take it to the laundromat in an all-out effort to catch up. Then put everything away immediately when you get home and you will be clutter free and ready to start fresh the next laundry day.

If you live alone or with one other person, keeping clean clothes is not the same kind of problem it is when you are dealing with hundreds of pieces of clothing and linens every week. The single person usually does his or her laundry in a public area. One man, a construction worker, found that loading up dirty clothing and going to the laundromat takes almost the same amount of time whether he washes three or six loads. His solution was to buy a few more clothes and do the wash every second week. A single person, or even a couple, has more flexibility than a family and they can wash every two or three weeks when they run out of clothing. For them, maintaining a washing machine at home may be a matter of convenience, while washing at a laundromat might actually cost less than buying a machine and heating the water. Some public laundries have a service where an attendant will wash, dry, and fold or hang your clothes. You drop them off on the way to work and pick them up on your way home.

You will need to arrange some way for gathering dirty clothes—box, pillowcase, or duffel bag. One young mother has a series of hooks on which she hangs duffle bags to presort soiled things—linens, denims, colored clothes, and baby clothes. A tote tray is loaded to carry detergent, fabric softener, spotter, a brush to treat spots, and a jar for coins. Everything is ready when she has time for the laundry. The bags are tossed in with the wash load, the clothes are folded back into the bag, and carried home. A primary principle when you use the laundromat is to immediately do any touch-up pressing and put away all clean clothes as soon as you get home. Take good care of your clothing—it's a big investment.

MATCHING SOCKS

Socks present a unique laundry problem. The most helpful trick to simplify sock sorting is to do it after each batch of wash. It's so much easier to match seven pairs than to save them for a week and dig through twenty-seven. (I roll them up and use a rubberband to hold the two together so as not to stretch out the tops.) People living alone and doing their own laundry know to whom every sock belongs. They may choose to toss the bunch into a drawer and rummage through it each morning to get a matched pair. Or, they might be more meticulous and decide to separate the socks and roll them into pairs. No problem. Complications arise when a batch of wash contains clothing for more than one person. Then the problem is not only matching the pair, but also determining which is whose. Let's peek in a few windows and see how different people handle the problem.

The first question is, Do you prefer sorting before the socks are washed, or after? Those who sort before swear that it saves great amounts of time and frustration. They use large safety pins, or rubber bands, or plastic sock-rings (purchased at the discount store) to secure each pair, keeping them together during the wash and dry cycles. The drawback with this method is that you must train your family and/or yourself to take the time to connect the dirty socks. A second prewash method is to have each individual collect his/her socks in a mesh laundry bag and then toss the whole bag into the washer and dryer and send it back to the owner's room.

How do people who prefer to sort socks after they have been washed get them back to the right owner? Some families solve this dilemma by assigning each family member a different style or color of socks: Mom has all whites, Dad white with blue stripes, the first son gets white with green, second son has yellow stripes, and daughter has knee-highs. This is good theory, but it has some weaknesses. What if Grandmother sends new socks for Christmas that don't fit the formula? What if your assigned style or color doesn't match everything you wear? What if number one son needs to have socks with blue stripes for his basketball uniform? Another family with four teenage boys doesn't even bother with sorting. They buy several dozen of the same style sock at a time. The clean socks are tossed into a communal basket and they pick out two each morning.

A system with more options is to identify ownership by stitching a short piece of colored thread into the toe of every sock. (A permanent marker could be used for light colors.) It gives you the choice of having any color or style of sock you desire, maintains personal ownership, and makes it possible for anyone to sort and match. Each member of the family is assigned a color. Whenever a new pair of socks comes into the house, the rule is it cannot be worn until it is marked (wonderful incentive), taking less than thirty seconds. Long ago, to expedite this system, I went to the store and bought seven packets of embroidery floss: red, yellow, blue, orange, green, purple, brown. I put them in a little box with a packet of large-eyed needles and a small pair of scissors. Whenever I need to mark a pair of socks, I get out my box, pick out a needle (usually still threaded from last time) and take a couple of stitches in the toe to signal who is the owner. (I use this same color coding when applicable for toothbrushes, drinking cups, bath towels, and sheets.)

What about unmatched socks? Give them three strikes. Keep them in a specific area (drawer, box, basket)—but, please, not on top of dryer—and hope the missing mate will show up next week (first chance). After a few weeks, tie the mateless socks together in a bundle (second chance). When your kids want to earn a quarter, let them go through this pile and find matches. If the mates still don't show up in another month, consider them lost and toss out the whole bundle. I actually know a family that has kept every mismatched sock for twenty years, hoping someday the mate would show up. Such hope complicates housework.

When pantyhose are new, secure a small safety-pin to the waistband to show they are in top shape and to save the hassle of searching for a good pair without runs every morning. If they get a snag, but are still good enough to wear with slacks, remove the pin; otherwise, throw them out. If you use old nylons for craft projects, tie them in a knot (sending an "attention" signal), put them through the wash and toss them in the craft box. If you have more than one person wearing pantyhose, how do you keep them separate? Either make an embroidery stitch or pin a small piece of colored fabric, naturally from the assigned code color, into the elastic band.

SETTING UP A LAUNDRY CENTER

Caring for clothing and linens is the second biggest process in a home; preparation of food and cleanup being the first. So give thought to your setup and make it as easy as possible to take care of the laundry. If you have a choice, pick a place for your machines that can easily accommodate the processing of hundreds of pieces of clothing—a work-room where you can close the door when needed. Some people prefer to have the laundry center close to the kitchen so they can easily deal with cooking and laundry at the same time; others choose to have it near the bedrooms to save steps collecting and re-distributing clothing. Just as a kitchen is more than a stove and a sink, a laundry room is more than a washer and a dryer. If you are one of the unfortunate ones with appliances parked in a hallway closet, it is important that you get the wash done and put away as quickly as possible so that the process does not take over the whole house. You can design a portable system with a table and baskets that are set up on wash day and then tucked away the rest of the week. As you organize your laundry center, consider the following:

- You need a good washing machine with: (1) adjustable water levels to take care of large and small loads; (2) a water temperature gauge giving you the option of washing and rinsing in

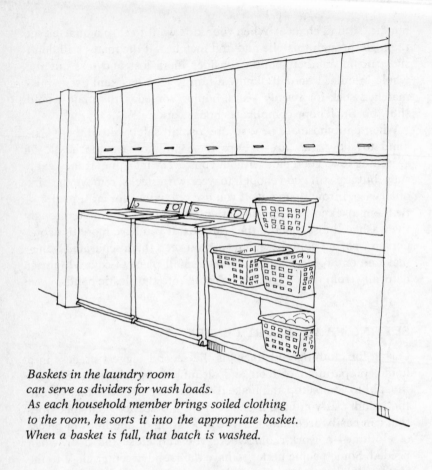

Baskets in the laundry room
can serve as dividers for wash loads.
As each household member brings soiled clothing
to the room, he sorts it into the appropriate basket.
When a basket is full, that batch is washed.

warm or cold water to save energy heating water and safeguard delicate clothes; and (3) a choice of regular or gentle cycles that regulate the agitation. Such a machine will give you many options for special care and keep your clothing looking nice and lasting longer. A middle-of-the-line machine will usually have all of these features.

• You will want a dryer with a few special features so that everything isn't put through the same high intensity heat, which weakens the fabric fibers. It's nice to have the cool-down feature that reduces the temperature before the drum quits turning. A sensor, rather than just a timer, can tell when the clothes are dry and turn off the action automatically. Empty the lint filter often for energy efficiency.

- You should have some type of container in which to sort dirty clothes to keep them off the floor. This one strategy can make a big difference and it doesn't have to cost anything. Plastic laundry baskets are nice, but boxes work just as well. If you pay attention, you can acquire a set of boxes that will nestle inside each other and take up very little space when wash day is over.

- It is very helpful to have a drying rack on which to drape damp items. Many homes have a portable one made with wooden dowels. Another option is to string up a clothesline in your washroom, but place it out of the walkway and high enough to avoid strangulation. This gives a convenient place for drying pantyhose, a swimsuit, or a pleated skirt. One homemaker said she briefly runs shirts and blouses in the dryer to remove wrinkles, then puts them on plastic tube hangers on her indoor clothesline to let them air-dry during the night. Some homes still have clotheslines outside. You have to decide for yourself. In Denver, you can save between 50 cents and $1.50 per load drying on the line. Some homemakers still use the lines exclusively, a few more use the lines for big things such as sheets and blankets and heavy jeans.

- You need a shelf or cabinet to hold laundry supplies: detergent, spot pretreatment, bleach, etc. Keep your inventory simple or it can take up too much space. One of the neatest tricks I ever learned was to use a paper-towel holder for static–free sheets. I sawed off the end of a broom handle (11½ inches) to serve as the center dowel and slipped the roll of dryer sheets on the rod and snapped it into the holder that was mounted near the dryer.

Install a paper towel holder for dryer sheets.

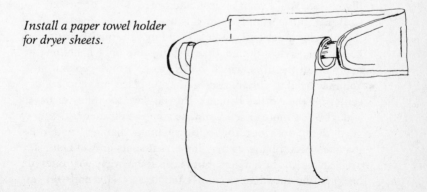

- It will be most helpful to have a table on which to fold and sort clean clothes. You need a set of smaller boxes, dishpans, or baskets in which to put clean clothes by room and/or individual. Then it is easy to pick up the whole container full of clean clothes, take them to the room where they belong, and put them away. Depending on your space, this set up could be permanent or temporary. One family likes a set of vinyl-covered mesh baskets on rollers. Another system is to build cubbyholes (like the ones at a post office only larger), or to set a series of small plastic baskets on utility shelves in which to put clean clothing as it is sorted.

- Since not all clothing will be folded, you need a place to hang clean clothes until the laundry is finished or while it waits to be ironed. A rod in the laundry room would be ideal, but often there is not enough space. Most of us have to work within certain space limitations, and thus a rolling rack or a suspension rod in a doorway may help. A heavy rope across the ceiling might work. What about installing large hooks on the wall like the ones used in a garage?

- Obviously, you will want a wastebasket. Could you also use a ragbag? Would it help to have a container for clothing on its way to charity?

- Designate a basket, box, or drawer for unmatched socks, but please—don't put it on top of the dryer. Don't mix last week's unmatched socks with this week's wash until you have taken out the matches. One woman hung a wire vegetable basket above the dryer in which to toss the extra socks.

- Everyone needs a junk box for stuff left in pockets or found in the bottom of the washer. Money goes to the laundry person.

- If you iron, you'll want an iron and board in this area.

- Optional, but certainly handy, is a sewing machine set up in this area for quick and painless mending. One busy homemaker keeps clear-nylon thread (like fishing line only finer) on the machine all the time, which works great for most repairs.

- You may need to designate a "gathering place" in your laundry center for the clothes hangers. Do you have too many or never enough? Buy more or send some to your dry cleaner. Unless you need them, toss out those flimsy metal hangers and mismatches. Metal hangers may leave rust spots on wet clothes. I prefer plastic tube hangers, but I keep some heavy wire ones for backup. The tube hangers don't tangle as easily, and you can hang damp items on them and they are often cheap at dollar-day sales. But they take up a lot of space if you have to move them. The smaller tube hangers, found in the infant department, are terrific for hanging slacks; they have a shorter rod (thirteen inches as compared to seventeen inches on a regular hanger), which saves the pants from tipping sideways, bunching up, and wrinkling at the knee. Ideally, the small hangers will be a different color than the larger ones for instant recognition.

How do you get the hangers back to the laundry center? One man puts empty hangers on the far right side of his closet so he can just pick them up in one motion when it's collection time. At another house, the family members drop the basket used to carry clean clothes to their rooms on their closet floor and use it to collect hangers until next wash day. Better yet, have one of your children collect all the empty hangers for you (either for pay, privilege, or as punishment).

ORGANIZING YOUR CUPBOARDS AND CLOSETS

17. A Place for Everything

W hat does that mean—
a place for everything?

1. It means to define a logical niche for every single item in your household.
2. It means to make it as easy as possible to return the item to its home base.
3. It means to design the arrangement so that other people can understand and use the program.
4. It means to prioritize positions for things according to how often they are needed.

To get everything in your house organized is not a quick and easy goal. It may take several months or even a year if you have a large home. Once you get things settled, however, you have to make only minor refinements and then you can reap the rewards for a long time. Before you dive in, you need to understand the theory and make an overall plan whether your home is big or small.

MAKE IT DEFINITE

You want no question as to what belongs where. Use dividers of various sorts to create cubbyholes, fences, or boundaries. Your house is somewhat like a giant filing system where everything has an assigned slot. If it doesn't have a place, how can it be put away? Who will be able to find it? Don't let things stay where they happen to land as they come into your house. To start with, where do you keep the newspaper until everyone has read it? Then where does it go? Is the daily newspaper allowed to dominate a room? Make your decision and follow through. At my house the newspaper is kept at the breakfast nook and then it goes in the firewood cupboard until trash day. Why not directly to trash? Sometimes it is needed to start a fire, or someone may want to look at the grocery ads, or a student

might have a current events assignment. It's so much easier to keep
house when placement decisions are well defined. Where do you
keep this book? And after you have finished reading it, where will it
go?

KEEP IT SIMPLE

You will want to make boundaries and assignments that are not so
difficult that they discourage tidiness. Each item must be easy to
put back. For example, at my home, visitors are sometimes disappointed that my cupboards and closets don't look like a showcase.
My clothes, towels, fabric, and spools of thread are not arranged in
rainbow order. I am doing great to separate my good clothes from
my work things. The silverware is separated by big dividers, but the
forks aren't nestled together. Shoe boxes serve as drawer dividers
for underwear and socks, but they are not lined up with "smily
faces" as a military inspection might require. Each bedroom has a
dishpan in which to toss winter hats and gloves (when dry) and a
hook for the coat. Organization does not mean meticulousness; it
means you can find things without too much delay; it means your
system is easy to restore. You will want to create definite boundaries, but too much detail can keep people from putting things back
where they belong.

A room can serve as a general boundary, dictating what kinds of
things go between those walls, and there are several ways to categorize things. When our children were toddlers, we chose to have all
the toys together in the playroom. Absolutely no toys in the bedrooms except for a few books. It worked well for quite some time,
but as the children grew older and possessive identity became
stronger, there was a natural changeover to each child keeping all of
his/her own possessions in the bedroom. The question: Do you keep
all the games together in one cabinet or do they stay with the
owner? What about books? Sporting equipment? Coats? Raingear
or boots? School supplies? Remember the family I told you about in
which all the children dressed in the laundry room? Every problem
has several possible solutions. You could either group similar things
together or divide by owner. Chances are you will use a combination. At our home, after the child uses a game or reads a book, it
tends to go into the family collection. School supplies are commu-

nal unless the child bought them with his or her own money; camping, fishing, and sporting equipment are pooled in the garage. It takes only a little thought to decide for yourself.

Create a system that everyone can use and understand. Don't be afraid to label shelves or boxes to help give things a territory. We McCulloughs have a box (with open top) that identifies the spot for the plastic grocery bags that will be used as trash liners, and there are separate boxes for shoelaces, extra lightbulbs, rags, hats and gloves, bills, jar lids, etc. Naturally, you will need to do some awareness training. Open your eyes to your needs and then look for a way to satisfy them. Determine why an item is repeatedly left out. Is it too hard to put away? Should it be stored closer to where it is used? In some cases the answer is to get duplicates—scissors, tape, screwdrivers, cleansers, and window spray.

SET INNER SPACE PRIORITIES

Decide where things will go logically and by priority. Base your decision on your answers to two questions:

1. How often is this item used?
2. Where is it used?

A true manager doesn't just use cupboards, cabinets, and closets to put things in, he organizes by rank, by earned privilege, by need, or by worth. Before you move into a new place or reorganize your present habitat, make a plan. Take time to prioritize your storage areas. Then, when you start putting things away or are rearranging, you can easily decide where to put them. Rank all inner spaces, (cupboards, cabinets, closets, shelves, and drawers) into three categories: prime storage, secondary storage, and long-term storage.

Prime storage is reserved for things you use every day. Where are your prime storage spots? In the kitchen or other work areas, prime space is nearest the most frequented counters, between neck and waist level. At your desk, sewing cabinet, or work bench, the drawers within arm's length are prime and should contain supplies used most often. Ideally you can pick them up in one motion, without moving other items and without unstacking.

My family bathroom is an example. Because of limited storage space, the medicine cabinet and cupboard under the sink are reserved for everyday needs (including extra toilet paper). This is prime territory. Products that we are not currently using or that we don't need every day are stored outside the bathroom in a nearby hall closet. (Secondary storage area). As manager, I have to be on the lookout for once-in-a-while items that park themselves in the Prime Spot.

Secondary storage space is for things you use, but not every day. These areas are usually high or low or in the rear or under. An example would be keeping best china, silver, and serving pieces in a china cupboard in the dining room. You certainly wouldn't want to have to walk into another room every time you needed daily tableware, but for special occasions you make the extra effort. Because I am a short person, upper shelves in my kitchen are for seldom-used ingredients, supplies, and baking pans, but peanut butter is in the most prime location.

Long-term storage is for things you still have good reason to keep, but don't use very often. This storage area is often in the basement, attic, garage, pantry, or shed. You may need to build or buy shelving to facilitate long-term storage needs. This is where you keep the Halloween costumes and holiday decorations. It's the spot for camping gear, ice chest, turkey roaster, large water jugs, pressure canner, and steamer. If you have more decorations or tableware than you use, store it here until you have need for it. A house is much easier to live in if it has adequate storage. Apartment dwellers often make a set of portable shelves, even putting them against a bedroom wall to accommodate storage needs.

An example of prioritizing inner space at our house is that we have several bookcases on which to put books and magazines. We allow some in current use to be on bedstands for night-time reading. If we did not review them every few weeks, the bookshelf would be empty and the nightstand six feet deep. Bookshelves are secondary storage; the bedstand is prime. We also have a long-term bookcase in the basement for books not used very often, such as game books, primary readers, and picture books that I am saving until I am a grandmother and can read them to my grandchildren. Hope shelf!

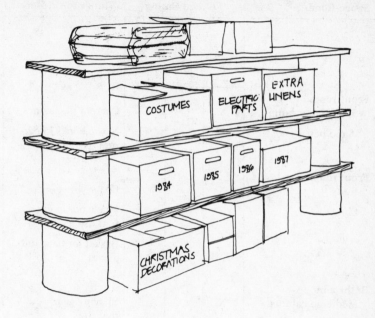

Another example: I have long-term storage cupboards for bottled fruit, vegetables, and staples that I buy in quantity. The small pantry cupboard in my kitchen (secondary) is supposed to be for items we will need within the month: cream of mushroom soup, cake mix, evaporated milk, extra dish soap, etc. Periodically, I have to go through these pantry shelves because they get loaded with supplies brought up from the long-term storage by mistake and there isn't room for my new groceries. Deciding where things should go, and making them stay there, is all a part of managing things.

JUST FOR YOU

Draw a simple floor plan of your house or make a list of the spaces and briefly describe the contents of each. This is an exercise you have to do only once for each house or apartment you live in. If I were classifying storage facilities at my house, it might look like this:

PRIORITIZING SPACES

Space-Room	Prime	Secondary	Long-term	Things to Go Here
Front room:				
Shelf under lamp	X			Current magazines
Piano bench	X			Music books in current use
Front room closet:				
Rod	X			Coats
Shelf		X		Music not in current use
				Basket for hats and gloves
Bathroom:				
Medicine cabinet	X			Shaving gear, makeup
Cupboard under sink	X			Toilet paper, wash cloths, shampoo, cleanser, mirror spray, bar soap, feminine supplies, blow dryer, curling iron
Counter top	X			Cotton balls, toothbrushes, toothpaste
Hall closet:				
1st shelf			X	Permanent rods
2nd shelf			X	Scrapbooks
3rd shelf		X		Backup bathroom supplies: suntan lotion, extra toothbrushes, shampoo, nail polish remover, thermometer, Band-Aids, adhesive, tape, etc.

18. Keeping Your Inner Space Organized

SORTING

In everyday living, things get shuffled around, left out, or put in the wrong places. Part of housekeeping is going through those inner spaces and reorganizing. Plan on going through every cupboard, closet, and drawer at least once a year; work centers will need it more often. When you are ready to clean, make it easy. Arrange four baskets, boxes, or bags near your targeted space. As you take out each item, ask those agonizing questions: Do I use it? What does it do for me? The issue is not whether there is value or wear left to the item. The issue is whether you use it and whether this is the place for it. Put back into the space only those things that truly belong there—the things you love and use. The reason for having four containers near the cleaning sight is to (1) immediately categorize those things that do not go back onto the shelf so you don't have to sort through them again, saving time and energy, and (2) to keep down the mess. It's easier to feel like you are making progress when there is a visual improvement. I recommend the following categories:

1. A large container for trash.
2. A transition box for items that need to be put somewhere else. In the process of everyday life, things land in the wrong place. It happens to everyone. The secret is to leave enough time toward the end of your sorting session to put these items away where they belong.
3. A container for ambiguous things you don't know what to do with. Do not waste your cleaning time on indecision. Put back only those items that belong to this inner space. Take out all the unnecessary, questionable paraphernalia. When you read the chapter The Art of Throwing It Out, perhaps you will have enough courage to take action. After you finish de-junking one room, look through this box again. Some decisions will have already been made; some of this may be sent to long-term

storage. If you come across items that you have borrowed, return them to the rightful owners as soon as possible. Put it on your immediate to-do list. For the rest of the stuff in this box: "If in doubt, throw it out."

4. A container for charity. Send things that still have value back into circulation, not the trash. It is easier to let go if you think someone else can use it. To trash everything when you are in the pitching mood violates the law of resource conservation. It may be best to select only one charity rather than dividing everything into little piles for one group or another. Trying to "place" each item as though adopting out a pet is too burdensome.

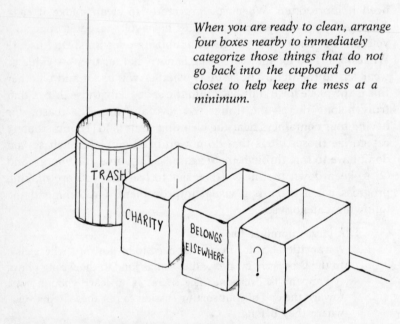

When you are ready to clean, arrange four boxes nearby to immediately categorize those things that do not go back into the cupboard or closet to help keep the mess at a minimum.

RECYCLE COLLECTION CENTER (RCC)

Designate a corner or shelf as the "holding pond" to gather things you are cycling out until it's time to send them to your favorite thrift shop or have a garage sale. You probably already have a spot for your trash until pickup day; likewise, you can have a recycle shelf. You will gather things in two ways: one at a time and marathon. When you pull things out during the annual sorting of drawers, closets, and cupboards, put them in this RCC pile. Secondly, whenever you run across an item you are ready to part with, just put it on the "good-bye" shelf. Learn to pluck things out of circulation when you are in the mood. The "recycle corner" gives you a testing period to see if you can really do without it. I always have an open box in the basement to put things into as they come to my attention and also a basket in the laundry area for clothing. I get rid of as much with the gradual system as I do with the drastic sweep.

19. The Art of Throwing It Out

I n high school chemistry class, we performed a simple experiment with sugar and water. The question was, How much of the element (sugar) will the water take? The water would hold only a certain amount of sugar in suspension; then, when we added more, it just fell (precipitated) to the bottom. Our houses are like that. They can hold only so much, and when they reach saturation point things begin to "fall out." When a house gets to that point, you have four options for easing the squeeze:

1. Get rid of some of the "things"
2. Improve your shelving habits
3. Buy or make more space (new shelves, cupboards, chests, closets)
4. Move

The first step is to get rid of unnecessary items. People often try to solve the problem in reverse by first buying new space. But the new space quickly becomes as cluttered as the old if they don't evaluate why they are keeping things. Eventually you will run out of places to put new shelves and chests or the money to buy them. All of us have the same problem in varying degrees. We keep things without knowing why or how to stop collecting. We tuck it here, stash it there, stack and crowd until the house is hard to clean. With every payday, sale, birthday, and holiday, we crowd in more—the overcrowding breeds clutter.

It's hard to throw things out. In days gone by, when you got something you kept it for life or until it was worn out. But now we live in a world of mass production and marketing, and to survive you either have to build a warehouse or learn to sort and let go. We often keep things, not because of an active decision to keep them but because we have not made a decision to get rid of them. On average, people keep things five years after their usefulness has passed. This happens for several reasons:

1. Sometimes we overbuy and have supplies, materials, and tools left over, and they mount up over the years.
2. There are times we save things hoping to "use it someday."
3. There is a natural progression of our interests from one season of life to another. The things we enjoyed ten years ago are not the things we enjoy today, but we hang on to supplies and equipment from those past hobbies and interests.
4. For some people, saving is an emotional reaction from the depression years. They habitually keep things to satisfy this anxiety. But I find that most compulsive savers have far more things than they could wear out in a lifetime.
5. Other people are burdened with items accumulated during the course of raising a family. Parents whose children have moved out may need a pep talk to gain the courage to relieve themselves of this accumulation.

COURAGE TO PITCH IT!

When it comes time to face the task of streamlining your possessions, ask yourself the following:

- How long has it been since I used this item? Did I use it last year? Do I have good reason to keep it? Have I outgrown my use for it? Is this an unfinished project that I'll never do? Why didn't I finish it? Have I moved on to other interests and projects? So often we keep things long after we should and our attachment is an emotional obligation. After all, you made sacrifices to get these "things." You paid money or invested time. Remember, you no longer live in the era where you have to wear out everything. If it has served your purpose, move it out.
- Is this item an irreplaceable treasure? If it is, how many treasures can you afford to store? Allow yourself connections with the past, but do you have room to keep it all? Choose just a few momentos. I love to collect doll patterns. Other people collect tools or fabric or even beer cans. To treasure too many things, whether valuable or not, can make a mess of your house. If you are in your golden years, your children or grandchildren may treasure some of the things you are thinking of giving away. Ask

them. It is fine to keep things if they still have meaning to you and aren't a roadblock to everyday living.

- If you got rid of this item and should need it again, could you replace it? For example, as you hesitate over the trash can with the thought, "Will I need this?" ask, "Could I get another?" Should you throw out the school newsletter and then need to know who is on the refreshment committee, you could make a call to the president. Do not keep "maybes" that are easily replaced.

- Two more rationalizations for keeping things are that your kids could use this when they get their own apartment and that you will save it for your grandchildren (but you don't have any yet). Unless you expect such within the next two years, don't keep it. Remember, I am discussing daily needs here, not heirlooms. When our youngest child moved to a bed from the crib, my husband said, "That's not going in my garage, you can put it in your laundry room if you want to keep it." My laundry room was small and full. I just hated to get rid of the crib because it was the nicest one we had owned. On the other hand, our oldest child was only twelve, meaning I couldn't justify saving it for grandchildren. Recognizing that as children grow they will progressively collect more and more, I could not accommodate the mushroom growth of their belongings and begin saving furniture for the season of grandparenting. The crib sat in my living room for two weeks until I had the nerve to give it away. I have not been sorry. Hopefully, when I need a crib again, someone else will be ready to part with theirs. Think of it as a cycle of sharing.

- How much is it costing you to keep this item? Storage space is valuable. What would you put on a shelf that cost you twenty-five dollars a year to rent? Not your ninth-grade algebra book. After you've been on your own for a few years, these leftover things can crowd you out. Do you need this space for something you want to keep more than this questionable item? If you were moving and had to pay $1.25 per pound, would you take this? A pending move is often motivation to reevaluate your possessions.

- Will getting rid of this make housekeeping easier and faster? Don't overcomplicate your life. Everything has a maintenance price (time and/or money). A new end table is one more thing to dust and polish. A plant needs watering, feeding, spading, and a monthly shower. (Plants can add color and life to the decor, but when they get scraggly, move them out of the living room to a "nursing station," or send them away.) We continue taking more into our lives, each requiring a few more moments of care until we are slaves to our belongings. Does the pleasure of owning outweigh the care price? We all occasionally have to power-rake our homes, just like getting the dead grass out of the lawn in the spring to allow for new growth.

Magazines and books seem to be particularly hard to part with, especially those with colored pictures. How many people do you know who can't get rid of their *National Geographic* magazines? They are wonderful! Unless you have a good use for them, pass them on to your local school or health clinic for the waiting room. And don't tell me how valuable they are. Our local library sells them for twenty-five cents at their annual fund raiser, and they always have more than they can sell.

Share. When you are in the mood to throw it out, don't do it literally. As a commitment to conserve our national resources, if the item still has some good in it, send it to a charity. It kills me to drive down the street and see wonderful things on the sidewalk for the trashman to haul away. Throwing it out includes giving it to a lucky friend or in-law, but don't make your remedy their problem. If they can use your castoffs, fine, but if they already have a hard time managing things, don't lay more junk on them. In most cities, there are agencies that will pick things up at your door if you just give them a call. Get a double blessing: make your house easier to clean and be generous in sharing. Send things back into circulation before they're too old to be of use to anyone.

It hurts. Parting is a deeper emotional experience than keeping, and you will remember the things you've thrown out better than the things you've kept. Surely, in a few days, you'll think of something you could have used that item for. Look at it this way: If you hadn't given it away, you probably wouldn't have remembered you had it. That's what you risk, but the rewards are terrific—more space without paying for it, a house that's easier to keep clean, fewer "lost" things, and more time for you.

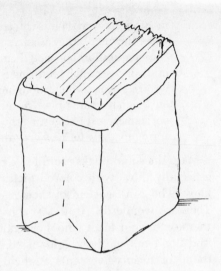

Open one large grocery sack and use it as the container for other bags.

Set limits. It is defeating to save every butter tub, aluminum pie tin, plastic bag, pickle jar, and paper sack. How many do you really use anyway? It takes a conscious effort to keep old things moving out of the house as fast as new things are coming in, but that saves overcrowding, piling, and stuffing. My first success at getting control at home came when a friend showed me I could open a grocery sack and line the others up in it. The technique was a boundary and a limit, too. Don't forget to set limits for clothing. We wear the clothes we like 80 percent of the time. Why keep so many others? The discovery of plastic in the forties was a miracle. To some of us, it is now a millstone. We fill our cupboards with containers in which to store leftovers. Cake keepers and pie savers are piled on top of the refrigerator. We fight to find the right lids. Our dishwashers melt and flip the plastics around so they have to be pampered and washed by hand. I prefer to use wide-mouth mayonnaise jars for leftovers. I can see what's in them and use the food before it grows hair, and the jars can be put in the dishwasher. I was liberated the day I packed up the plastics and gave them to the Goodwill.

Stabilize. After your home has reached optimum capacity—with the cupboards and closets full but with clutter at a minimum—the trick is to equalize the incoming with the outgoing, and that doesn't mean outgoing to the garage. (Some garages are used for cars, some for workshops, but most are "halfway-out" spots.) Should you get a new robe for your birthday, don't keep the old one to use "after the new one wears out." If you get three new pairs of socks, throw out the worst three and keep the inventory stable. This applies to tools, appliances and everything. When you feel the squeeze in your house, send the castouts all the way out.

Cut down and eliminate duplication. If you live in a small space or if you are newly married and are running into problems trying to merge two households, you must take control and make decisions. Which of the two electric mixers and eight mixing bowls should you keep in the cupboard? In a permanent merger such as marriage or the inheritance of your grandmother's household, you might decide to put things in permanent storage or to get rid of part of it. If the merger is tentative—a divorcee moving in with parents or singles teaming up as roommates—store the unnecessary items out of the way, cutting back until you fit comfortably into the new space.

Unload It. Every time you complete a project or activity, what do you do with the leftover supplies? A typical department store gets rid of seasonal inventory as quickly as possible. In early spring, they sell out the winter hats and gloves. Next year, the store will order a whole new selection of hats and gloves. In the store there is a distinct difference between special seasonal items and basic staples that are always on hand. At home, you would do well to make the same distinction between things you acquire for short-term use and things you always keep in stock. Be willing to unload past hobbies, interests, and projects and to walk into a new era without extra baggage. For permanent inventory, you need enough to cover emergencies, to be prepared, to be independent, but not so much that it crowds you out. Such a balance is hard to maintain.

Don't Store It for Others. As we reach midlife, in addition to managing our own accumulations, we have to deal with another complication—adult children. They move away from home but leave their possessions—some of which are important, but much of which they haven't taken time to sort. As Erma Bombeck said, "If the nest is truly empty, who owns all this junk?" How are you going to handle this problem? You can do some early managing. Give your teens warning. Insist that they go through everything, keeping only the necessary and packing it into storage boxes before leaving for college, etc. This does not mean they are not welcome to come back; you may even keep a bedroom for them. However, you need to insist that they make time for a major sorting session. Set a limit on how much you will keep and how long you will store it. I often hear women say their wedding dress and high school formals are still at Mom's, even after twenty years. If you are the mother and it doesn't bother you, what does it matter? But if you have to move it around the country, or want the space for your own things, then give your children fair warning, move it to a commercial storage garage, and send them the bill.

Caution!!! Do not throw out someone else's things unless they ask you to do so. Make suggestions and encourage, but do not take over. Do not throw out things for your parents, your husband or wife, or your children over age six. It won't work; it will only make them angry; it will not teach them the art of parting. They need to be in on the decision. As our parents age, it often falls to us to help them sort through things as they need to move to a smaller place, or after the death of a partner. Be understanding. It is a taxing, emotional experience for them, and difficult for them to do alone. There are social service agencies that can offer suggestions for helping the elderly and commercial companies that will buy out households if that is the only workable solution.

Disclaimer: I am not legally responsible for anything you throw out. Keep what you need, of the rest be freed.

20. Creating a Kitchen of Convenience

You spend a lot of time in the kitchen. Make it efficient. Make it convenient. Make it suit you. Just because you know where everything is doesn't mean your kitchen is as efficient as it could be. Three simple rules govern the placement of things in your kitchen.

1. Put things where first used.
2. Keep only as many items as you need.
3. Allow only the necessities to occupy prime work areas.

You complicate work in the kitchen if you have too much in it. Can you get something out of the cupboard without unstacking a whole pile? Ideally, you can get out the things you use every day in one reach. You may need to relieve crowding and simplify your inventory. How many burners do you have on your stove? Can you cook with more than four pans at once? Then why do you have so many pans? Yes, some are for specialties, but think of the space they take. Could you do with less? Last time you got a new pan, did you get rid of an old one or did you just make the stack higher. When you got a new microwave and started gathering glass and plastic cookware for it, did you get rid of any of the old utensils? I once consulted a woman who had twelve frying pans. When considering items such as pans, ask yourself, Does this particular one do something important which another does not? How many knives do you need? Can you use more than one at a time? What about mixing bowls? An overcrowded cupboard is aggravating. One woman, Marilyn, took drastic measures to pinpoint her self-defeating habits by hauling everything in the kitchen out to the porch. Every time she needed something, she went out and got it, and then put it away near the place it was used. After two weeks, more than half the kitchen equipment was still on the porch, exposing her true needs. Marilyn found she could easily get by with five basic pans if she washed the ones soaking in the sink rather than reaching for a new one, and she never used more than two mixing bowls at once. You might try this experiment with your pans and bowls. Put them in a box far enough away from your kitchen so that it requires effort to get them and see how well you can get by. Appliances and specialty gadgets can take up more room than they are worth. As you review your kitchen, ask yourself how often you use the deep fryer, waffle iron, cookie press, noodle maker, and egg poacher.

DEFINE WORK CENTERS

Look at your movement patterns and organize your kitchen into work centers so you can get your work done easier and faster. This is one place where an investment of time now can pay dividends of more time later on. Work centers should be at waist level and they qualify as "prime" space, with upper and lower spaces counting as "secondary" space. Everything placed in each work center should be necessary for that activity. Start by labeling your counters and cupboards into three work centers (mixing, cooking, and dishwashing) and two storage areas (pantry and tableware). Where is the best place to locate each of these activities?

The mixing center should be between the sink and stove. Ideally, you'll have all the equipment and ingredients here for making things—staples such as flour and sugar, and all the spices, flavorings, food colorings, and leavenings. The exception would be when you use an item only once, for example, a brownie mix. You could justify keeping mixes in a supply cupboard outside this efficient mixing center, because you have to reach for it only once, use it, and toss the package away. To walk to the supply cupboard every time you need the baking powder, however, is ridiculous. This mixing center may be where you make sandwiches. Is it a big hassle to gather all needed supplies, or are they all right here? Where are the plastic sandwich bags? Either move your supplies close to the place where you do the task, or move the task close to the supplies.

The cooking center, which, naturally, is centered around the stove, needs to have readily available the equipment and ingredients most often used when cooking. Think through the movements for making your favorite meal. Is everything you need within arm's reach? The stove should have its own set of salt and pepper shakers. Store the wooden spoons, spatula, and tongs in a container near the stove top if you don't have a drawer here. Notice your movements as you get out a pan. If the pans are to be stored where they will be used, they would go in a cupboard next to the stove; but if you normally put water in the pan before setting it on the burner, maybe the pans should be kept in a cupboard near the sink.

The dishwashing center should have all dishwashing supplies, hand towels, and dishcloths nearby, in a drawer if possible or in a box on a shelf if drawer space is limited. Where are your paper towels? This is where you probably clean vegetables and prepare salad. Is the cutting board nearby? And isn't this where you need to have a trash basket? You probably make a motion to put something in the trash more often than you open the refrigerator and thus placement of this necessary canister is one of the most important decisions you make. You cannot believe the number of homes in which the trash container is far, far away. Keep it close by while you are working in the kitchen. This inefficient decision is often justified by lack of space—better to pull it near you when you work or purchase a smaller one that will fit under the sink, even if it means emptying it more often. If it takes three steps to reach your present trash bucket when it could be reached in one, you are working harder than necessary. Multiply it by the number of times you use it each day and it could be as much as the length of two football fields. Who would walk that far for the trash? And this activity does not qualify as exercise; rather, such inefficiencies discourage creative cooking, turning it into real work!

You will need to define a place for **dishware and tableware storage.** According to the place for eating and washing, what will be the best spot to store the dishes? How can you set up the dishwashing movements to get them as close to the "final resting place" as possible when finished without crisscrossing back and forth? Work right to left or left to right, but try to store dishes away from the other work centers. This tableware area will vary from kitchen to kitchen. In our home, everyday dishes and glasses are in the lower cabinets so the children can set the table and empty the dishwasher without adult assistance, an arrangement that saves me twenty minutes a day. Everyday serving dishes, platters, and gravy boats don't have to be stored with the dinnerware just because they match. Keep them by the stove where they will be filled with hot vegetables or near the sink where the salad is prepared. Store items where their use begins. Try to keep highest storage spaces simple so that large things such as cake or pie covers can be lifted down in one movement. Small items are best stored lower because they can be dangerous and difficult to handle when stacked above eye level. Put shorter containers toward the front, tall ones to the back.

You will also need to designate an area for **supply storage.** You want it to be handy, but not necessarily located in the immediate work centers. This is where you will keep backup supplies and one-time items such as cake mix, soup, and canned fruits and vegetables. Because it is a one-time investment of reach for this package, you can afford to stretch and/or bend. Corner cupboards under the counter that are so hard to work with are often used for this type of storage. It will help to install a turntable or use dishpans as containers for in-and-out access. And lucky you if your carpenter built a real pantry into the layout of your kitchen.

In my kitchen, I keep recipes and cookbooks in a cabinet for secondary storage, out of work centers, but still easily accessible. Likewise, you will probably need a shelf or a mini-desk to hold supplies for telephone messages and to run the home management business from the kitchen.

After you have decided on the best place to put things, you will need to adapt the storage space with accessories—vertical partitions, turntables, bins, boxes, step-shelves, racks, and drawer dividers. These don't have to cost much money, you can sculpture many of them yourself out of boxes. Carefully consider whether the accessory is really helpful. Don't put six goblets on a turntable when twelve goblets would fit on the shelf without it. Look at your storage areas with imagination. Spices could be stored on their side in a drawer; a shoe box or bread pan could hold plastic lids or packets of seasoning mixes or flavored drinks.

EXCEPTIONS

Because of the safety needs or the physical nature of your kitchen, the "first-used" rule can be amended. Dry cereal boxes may fit only

on a tall shelf, even if it's far from the table. Or maybe you will
choose to put the dry cereals where the children cannot reach them
alone so you can monitor them. The cookie sheets will have to go
where they fit, sideways under the sink or in the stove drawer,
rather than in the mixing center. If you enjoy cooking great cre-
ations, trying new recipes, or baking often, you could justify leaving
your canisters on the countertop because of their frequent use. But,
for the most part, unless it is pretty, keep it out of sight. Put away as
much as possible. Open shelves are hard to keep looking neat and
tidy, but those things that must be left out can be pleasing to the eye
if they are balanced in a logical arrangement. The more counter
space you have, the more you can set on it before it looks cluttered.
That is a paradox, because it is the home with limited counter space
that doesn't have enough cupboards for adequate storage.

Is it safe? Household detergents are now the number-one cause of
poisoning among children age five and under. (Plants are number
two.) Plant food, pesticides, medicines, and matches must be stored
out of a child's reach. Even if you don't have young children, think
of friends with curious toddlers who may drop by for a visit. Keep
knives in a rack, out of drawers. Or use a magnetic strip, as shown
below, to keep knives away from fingers.

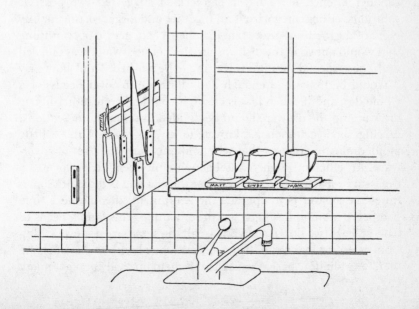

TAKE A FRESH LOOK

Think it through, watch yourself. Start by identifying work centers, where you put things, and whether there is too much to store. Are you working harder than you need to in the kitchen? In one home where I was asked to do some consulting, I watched the mother of a large family wash the dishes. She was to be admired for her devotion and care of seven children, but she was killing herself. For one thing, this manager had three categories of dishes and flatware: best, for special occasions when company came; everyday utensils; and a junky set that was used for the little children who were at home for lunch to save wear on the other things. When it was time to wash, the dishes had to be separated because half of them would not go in the dishwasher; not because they were precious but because they were soft plastic. (They would flip around in the dishwasher and had such a deep bowl that they took up too much space.) Second, as she put away the clean dishes, she sorted everything into matching piles—four or five of each thing. If any of the best silver had to be used when they ran out of the others, it needed to be put back in the china cupboard. The middle- and lower-class silver was divided and put in different trays. I was worn out watching. All the sorting and special care made it impossible for the children to do the dishes by themselves. She needed to simplify and run her kitchen more like a cafeteria. I suggested two possible solutions: either categorize it all together and forget sorting, or buy more of the medium-grade that matched. Next, get rid of everything that would not go in the dishwasher. Her counter was always loaded with these special care items waiting to be washed. Think how easy it would be if she had enough daily flatware to cover needs for a whole day, and if, when it was clean, it could all go together in one drawer. And the drawer should be divided into four large sections: serving spoons, teaspoons, knives, forks. No more of those little molded plastic dividers that will hold only one small set of silverware. An efficient kitchen has enough equipment to perform the necessary jobs, but not so much that the cleanup is difficult. Sometimes the answer is to upgrade the equipment; this mother's time and peace of mind has to be worth something. This family needs to have at least two dozen soup bowls, all the same size, for everything from cereal to ice cream. If she selects a bowl with the right shape that has a shallow base, she can stand them up easily and get many more into the dishwasher racks. For drinking, I suggested a heavy, goblet-style glass. It is easy for children to hold, they can see when they have milk or juice left, it washes well, and doesn't spill easily. Whatever type drinking utensils this family decides on, it will be easier if they have forty of them all alike. It would have cost seventy to a hundred dollars for this family to upgrade their inventory, but it would have saved Mom at least an hour a day. That would be three dollars a day for a month. I call that a bargain.

1. Create a long-term storage area for seldom used and seasonal items away from work centers.
2. Store things where they are first used.
3. Keep only as many things as you need in active work areas.
4. Study your movement patterns and define your work centers.
5. Go through cabinets and cupboards once a year to clean and sort.
6. Organize so other family members can understand and use your system easily.
7. Keep it simple and practical.

21. Drinking Cups and Problem Solving

Does the season of warm weather and unquenchable thirst breed extra drinking cups? Do they cover the kitchen counters? Is the dishwasher always full of glasses? This is not a critical issue, but management can iron out this little irritation. It's a good example to illustrate the basic problem-solving process that can be used to work out a solution to almost any problem.

1. **Recognize the issue and define it in writing:** "There are too many cups and glasses being used. The counters are a mess, it costs more to buy soap and run the dishwasher, the kitchen gets hot, it takes more time to keep the dishes done, etc." It's helpful to write out the problem, especially if it is more complicated than this example.
2. **Determine the cause.** Obviously, for health reasons, you don't want to drink from a cup someone else has used. Thus, each time a drink is needed, a clean glass is chosen.
3. **Set a goal.** Determine the ideal situation. Our ideal is to cut down the number of glasses, but we don't want to eliminate drinks as our bodies need extra liquids in hot months. Perhaps there is a way for each of the family members to use the same drinking glass several times.
4. **Brainstorm for ideas.** Ask around to find out how other people handle it. Some problems can be solved in a one-time effort and others can be improved by getting organized. Some can be solved through prevention, others through improved training and discipline for yourself and family. Solutions are different depending on circumstances such as the number and ages of people in the family, finances, space, and hours at home.
5. **Pinpoint a solution and give it a try.** Make a detailed, specific to-do list that will help you achieve your goal/ideal situation.
6. **Evaluate and modify, if necessary.** If your solution doesn't work, then you need to reevaluate and try a new effort. Perhaps the goal needs to be modified.

Now let's work through the drinking cup problem. The first resolution that pops into mind is to use disposables. It's a good solution in some homes. For many of us, however, it would be too expensive to provide eight to fifteen cups per person per day. Next thought: Devise a system for each family member to reuse either a paper cup or a glass several times. Actually, you have two choices: Mark either the cup or the place it sits.

At my home, a system of marking the spot evolved. A set of coasters is laid out in the kitchen window above the sink. Each coaster has a name on it and that person is supposed to put his or her drinking glass there after each use. To make it easier, coasters are lined up in chronological order: Dad, Mom, big sister, younger brother, etc. If you don't have a window, glasses could be lined up at the back of the sink and set on some sort of marker: lid, coaster, paper napkin, etc. My nine-year-old keeps his drinking glass behind the faucet at the back of the kitchen sink because he is too short to reach the window shelf. When it's time to turn on the dishwasher, the cups from the ledge are loaded and then as each person gets a clean one, it is put on his/her marker in the window again. Remember, even after an organized system is created, it takes training to get the family to use it.

One clever dad made a rack for paper drinking cups and installed it by the water bottle. With a large drill-bit (like the ones used to make a hole in a door for the knob), he drilled a series of holes in a narrow board just the right size for each cup to set down in the hole about two inches. This rack could be set behind the faucet or near the water cooler. Again, a name marks each hole. Some stores now carry a plastic version of this cup holder.

The other organizing possibilities are centered on a method to designate use of the same cup all the time. Much like the method used in many employee lunch rooms, a series of pegs or hooks are hung above the coffee pot and each worker provides his or her own mug. For years, at our house, we used a modified version of this system. I put a set of expandable coat hooks on the wall behind the toilet in the bathroom. Plastic rather than ceramic mugs were used for safety. Each child was assigned a different color to avoid sharing germs. With the lid down, the kids could climb on the seat and get their own drink, promoting independence and saving adult interruptions.

Remember that you can't solve a roomful of problems at once. For instance, one of my students said his problem was the rec room—it was a wreck. The room had too much furniture (three pianos, a sofa, a rocking chair, a desk and a chair, three bookcases, a sewing cabinet and chair, a drop-leaf sewing table, and an exercise bike) and too many unfinished projects (furniture to be stained, car seats to be upholstered, and a pair of slacks under construction). The desk was piled high and the open sewing machine accumulated junk. This family needed to divide the problems in the room into specific parts (books, coats, desk, magazines, mail, filing, furniture) to be worked on one at a time until the whole room was workable again.

Don't take your home problems as personal insults. Instead, learn to look for solutions. Your brain is like a computer, and it has been taking in great amounts of varied data through formal education and daily living. By feeding the problem into your computer, you can obtain a workable solution. Once you identify a problem and begin a search through your brain, ideas will begin to develop in your mind. You will notice what other people have to say about it. Just like finding a way to solve the problem of too many cups to wash, you can apply this formula to any situation.

22. Techniques for Creating More Space

I f you have gotten rid of all the excess and have made the best use of storage space but still need more room, you may find the answer in the following suggestions. A wide array of ready-made space extenders is available in stores and catalogs. Before you invest time and money, carefully consider your needs, measure the space where you plan to put it, and think through the motions of getting things out. Many of the gadgets titled "organizers" are more of a nuisance than a help. Recognize that working or living in a small space is a special challenge. It takes creative discovery—looking high and low, above, under, and in between to find a way to increase inner-space storage. Besides the ideas in *Totally Organized*, watch magazines, newspapers, and books for other ways to create new space. Take a leisurely "idea tour" through a store that specializes in kitchen accessories or a container shop. Ask the sales clerk if they offer demonstrations, workshops, or personal consulting. Your objective is to create boundaries and fences to define a place for everything and get maximum benefit from your inner storage.

Caution: Any open shelf that exposes the contents is harder to keep looking tidy than a shelf behind a curtain or doors. There is a distinct difference between shelves intended for display and those for organizing inventory. An open shelf requires more cleaning and straightening and can't hold as much without looking crowded. If you are thinking of buying or building open shelves, stop to consider if your purpose is for display or for practical storage. Display shelves will look messy if they are too full. The same applies to systems for hanging utensils on the ceiling or wall. Ask yourself how this effort to create more space will look in a month or a year.

STEP SHELVES

One friend, Margaret, went through each cupboard looking for unused "head space" and stacks. Her objective was to be able to get things out in one motion and also make it easier for her children to help. For instance, there were twelve inches of unused space above the silverware chest. By making a step shelf to fit over the chest, she could store the toaster on top of it. A variation of this idea is the vinyl-covered wire shelves that hang from an upper shelf. A step shelf is a shelf with legs that is not necessarily attached to the cupboard. It can be the same width as the original shelf or it can be shorter and not as deep. To make the step shelf, Margaret measured the desired height and width. Allowing 1 inch above the chest, she cut two narrow boards for the legs, 6 inches high and 12 inches long—the depth of the cupboards. The base was to be 20 inches long and 12 inches wide. The legs were glued to the base, it was painted, and she set it in the cupboard. In another cupboard, Margaret found 5 inches of lost space above the drinking glasses. By making a step shelf to set over the glasses, a layer of cups could be put on top, doubling the usable shelf space. In another cupboard, she created a second level for the pans so each pan and lid could be stored together to save hunting, moving, and unstacking. These step shelves can be easily changed as circumstances vary because they are not permanently attached. And you don't have to be a carpenter to make them. Margaret used pressed wood to make her shelves and had it cut at the lumberyard, figuring on graph paper how to cut the large board to best advantage. If you would rather spend the money than use the time, similar units can be purchased commercially, but they may not fit the exact dimensions of your space.

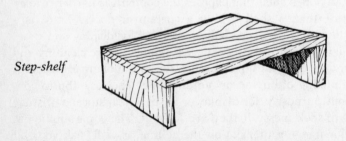

Step-shelf

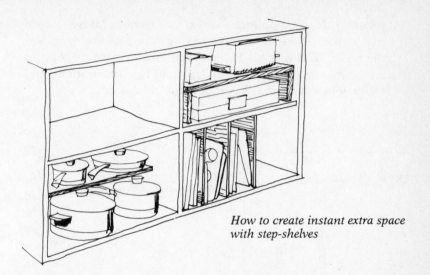

How to create instant extra space with step-shelves

Perhaps you have wasted space above your spices. A step shelf can help here, too, and it doesn't even have to be glued. Soup cans, boxes, or bricks could be used as spacers to hold up a narrow board at the back of the spice area. Apply the same principle to get two rows of paperback books on a single shelf. Either use a step shelf like the one described for spices or lay two 2 × 4 boards at the back, serving as a riser for the rear row so that you can see at least part of the back row of books. The same thing is done for people singing in the back row of a choir so the audience can see their faces.

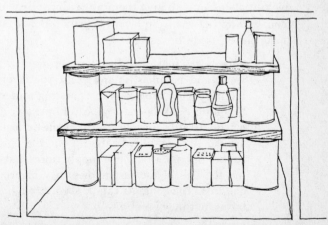

Use small step-shelves to create more room in the spice area and make items more visible.

The same principle applies for verticle side spaces. Margaret used vertical step dividers to separate baking tins, cookie sheets, and cutting board. This vertical divider could also be made by gluing a strip of U-molding on the top and bottom (see illustration), and then sliding in a piece of stiff cardboard or thin piece of wood.

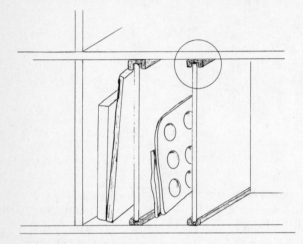

Use U-molding to alter cabinets and increase capacity.

BOXES

Boxes can be used in hundreds of places to make better use of shelves and drawers and to define boundaries. Sculpture them to exactly fit your needs and then reinforce with strong tape. Covering them with wallpaper or contact paper is not only pleasing to the eye but also seems to give them more durability and keeps insects from hiding between the layers of paper. Below are eight ways to make clever use of boxes.

1. Shoe boxes make excellent drawer dividers for socks, under-wear, and pajamas, giving each type of clothing a specific territory. They are good for separating toys to keep them from becoming junk in the toy box. To prevent spilling, make an elastic band by sewing a strip of elastic together, and snap it around the box to hold the lid on. The post office has large rubber bands, as do office supply stores. Labeling or illustrating the end of the box allows easy identification for small children. The contents can be seen through clear plastic shoe boxes, but they break easily.

2. We keep a 12×8-inch box (large enough to hold a baby book) for each child to keep his or her mementos and special pictures and certificates until they can be mounted. These boxes are shelved high enough to be out of the reach of little hands.

3. Cold-cereal boxes make terrific organizers for magazines. You can also purchase cardboard or plastic magazine holders in office supply departments.

4. Stand tall, narrow boxes on their sides in a cupboard to make a place for cookie sheets or trays.

5. Large vegetable and fruit boxes can serve as files or drawers on a shelf in any workroom. They are also great for storage and moving; be sure to label them.

6. Large, heavy boxes such as those that refrigerators or washing machines come in can be transformed into temporary closets by inserting a broom handle or pipe through the sides. Support the area under the rod holes with extra pieces of wood or cardboard. Position the rod at least four inches from the top of the box and fourteen inches from the back to allow space for the hanger. Cardboard closet boxes can also be obtained from a moving company.

7. Tiny boxes and egg cartons or ice-cube trays make individual dividers for jewelry.

8. Manufacturers are meeting our need for sturdy boxes of all sorts by producing them in decorator colors. You can buy flat, skinny boxes to store things under the bed and still keep them dust free. There are cubbyhole units (with nine squares) for shoes and accessories in the closet or for papers in the kitchen or office. A bonus feature is that they are collapsible for easy moving or storage.

BASKETS AND BINS

Plastic dishpans, mesh baskets of all sizes, and kitty-litter trays (clean, of course) have the same endless possibilities as boxes. They are durable, easy to move and clean, and can help you organize almost any room. Whether they are under the bed or on a playroom shelf, small things can be put away effortlessly. In the bathroom they can organize makeup, curlers, or bathtub toys. When a craft or sewing project is interrupted, take a minute to gather the supplies into a plastic dishpan and everything is together when it's time to start again. At times it is to your advantage to use the mesh-style baskets so you can see the contents. Stackable baskets or vegetable bins could contain several projects in the work room, or could be used for sweaters in a closet. You learn what helps and what doesn't from trial and error. One of the best investments I made was to buy four plastic trays ($15 \times 3 \times 2$ inches) to fit in my silverware drawer. Now three sets of flatware will fit in the drawer at once. Another family uses one-quart plastic buckets to stand knives, forks, and spoons in like they do in a cafeteria.

Going one step further, a drawer-filled cabinet can be created from dishpans or hard plastic storage bins available in many sizes from a school-supply house or an office- or restaurant-supply store. Two pairs of small wooden runners are nailed to the sides of the cabinet, leaving a space between the runners to hold the lip of each bin. The trick here is careful measurement to get the right size bin for your opening, but it's so much easier than making wooden drawers.

A dishpan could be hung below a shelf or cupboard to serve as a drawer in much the same way by putting a grooved strip under the

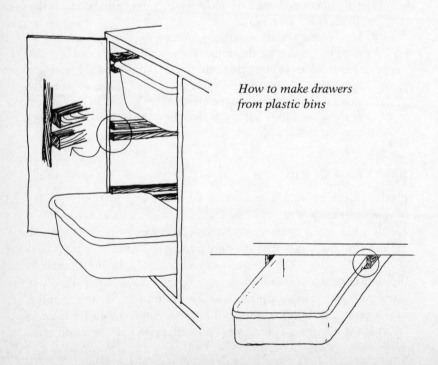

How to make drawers from plastic bins

shelf. I don't think you could put heavy items in the drawer, however. Rubbermaid sells a drawer that can be installed under a counter or shelf.

Plastic buckets from your local ice-cream stand or gallon-size cans from a cafeteria make great dividers for nails and small parts in the workshop. "If you can't find it, what's the use of having it?" says my father, who is a heating contractor. He has a whole wall of tilted shelves lined with labeled cans, dividing the many small parts he needs in his business.

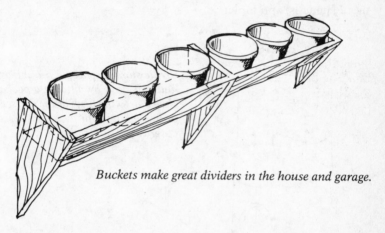

Buckets make great dividers in the house and garage.

Large trash baskets are great for collecting dirty clothes in the corner of a bedroom, storing big toys, and corraling tall things such as garden tools, baseball bats, or tennis rackets.

POLES AND BAGS

Poles can be useful for things other than plants and lights. Try a suspension pole in a room corner to solve the stuffed-animal problem. Hang the pets from small pegboard hooks that fit into the holes you have drilled up and down the pole. (Use screw-in cup hooks and you won't even need a drill.) Tie a ribbon around the neck of each toy.

Poles can be used to hang towels in the bathroom, coats by the door, or, with the right hooks, shoes in the bedroom.

Drawstring bags can be used in many other ways. When we're on vacation, we put all the coats in a bag to save hunting for them every time we get out of the car. Large bags are standard equipment for those who wash at a laundromat.

Pocket shoe bags can be hung on the back of a door to hold shampoo products in the bathroom or stocking caps and gloves at the back door. I made a smaller version for the car when we travel. It slips over the front seat, making the pockets available to the children in the back seat in which to keep their books, tapes, games, tissue, pencils, and tablet.

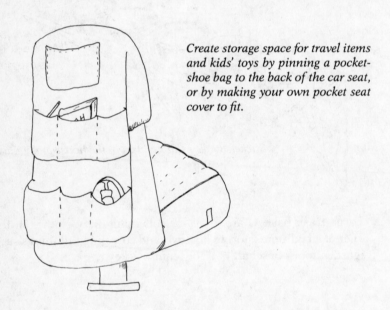

Create storage space for travel items and kids' toys by pinning a pocket-shoe bag to the back of the car seat, or by making your own pocket seat cover to fit.

PEGBOARDS, BULLETIN BOARDS, AND HOOKS

Buy a bulletin board or create your own by gluing a few pieces of cork or kitchen-carpet square to the wall. Pin up a calendar and pending papers in the kitchen or office, or make a small version in the bedroom on which to pin jewelry.

Pegboards and hooks put utensils within easy reach in work centers—office, garage, kitchen, shop, and sewing or craft areas. Pegboards can be installed behind a counter, at the side of a cupboard, or on an empty wall or on a door (if it is solid core). I wonder, though, when I see a whole wall of cooking utensils, if they are clean enough to use for food preparation. I suggest leaving out only a few gadgets in the kitchen that are used every day or so because they get dusty and look cluttered. Hang as much as you like in the workshop.

At my house, because I can't have a rod near the ironing board, I have a pegboard on the wall in the hall with large hooks on which to separate laundry and ironing that must be hung. Oversize hooks will hold bicycles and other equipment overhead in the garage. Little cup hooks hold smaller things such as coffee cups or measuring spoons. Make a decorative board with hooks on which to hang jewelry, keys, ribbons, or belts. Everyone needs a hook in their closet for the robe. You will have better luck getting kids to hang up coats and sweaters on a hook than on a hanger. If it is too hard to put an item where it belongs, they will not try. Make it easy to put things away.

SHELVES AND RODS

Many types of space extenders—hooks, rods, and narrow baskets—are now available that hang on the backs of doors. They are wonderful for those of us who are renting or have hollow-core doors. Look for these at your local hardware, discount, or department store.

I should probably explain how to hang pots and pans from the ceiling by using a ladder or commercial rack, but I will not because I hate them so, for three reasons: (1) I am short, and there is no possible way to hang pots low enough so that I can reach them yet high enough so my husband can walk into the kitchen; (2) I have never had pans I want everyone to see; and (3) to me, it makes the room look messy. I would rather live with fewer pans than hang mine from the ceiling. Copper pans are pretty, but I won't give my life to polishing them. I don't think they would stay very clean, at least not in my house. But if you want to hang your pans, go ahead. Read a current house magazine for how-to.

Tension poles are readily available in many lengths for closet, laundry center, or doorway. A spare rod on which to hang ironing or out-of-season clothes can be installed easily in an unfinished basement or attic by nailing two strips of metal (about 1 inch wide) to the ceiling joist, leaving a loop in which to slip the pipe-rod. (See illustration.) Cover the garments with a sheet to keep the dust off.

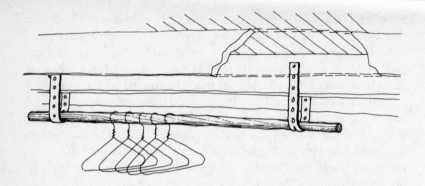

If you have the right spot, install your own rods for food wraps, aluminum foil, and tear-off plastic bags, being careful to keep them near your work centers. With a hacksaw, cut a light-weight aluminum pipe and suspend it on two U-shaped brackets. Some of the wraps and bags will tear off evenly; others may need to be cut each time with a pair of scissors. A simple idea, as I mentioned earlier, that has saved me many motions is to keep the fabric-softener sheets on a paper towel holder near the dryer. I cut a broomstick handle the right width, slipped it in the center of the roll, and now I can tear off a sheet in one motion and toss it in the clothes dryer.

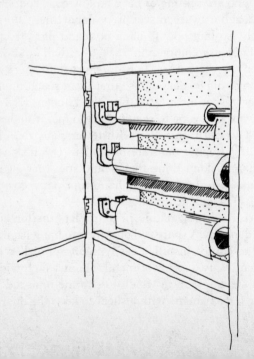

Open shelves are hard to keep looking neat (except for books) unless you arrange things as sparingly as an expensive jewelry store window. If you want to cover the open shelves, you could tack up a fabric curtain. But in work rooms and closets, shelves can multiply your storage capacity and organize the inventory. Shelves can be easily installed at the end, top, or bottom of a closet for extra storage or to hold shoes and accessories. Sometimes you can put them high above the doorways in a hall or build a narrow set of shelves behind a door. Hardware stores have a special department for do-it-yourself people. There are a few simple rules such as screwing into the studs for strength and using a level to get them parallel. You don't have to be a carpenter to put up shelving. Many of them can be removed when you redecorate or move.

BRICKS, BUCKETS, AND BOARDS

Bricks and boards are traditional for making portable bookcases or small shelves. Cinderblocks make larger divisions for hobbies, end tables, desks, or even room dividers. Spaces between shelves can be made from anything—logs, stone slabs, or boxes—if they can support the weight.

Buckets and boards go together to make large storage shelves. Five gallon buckets and boards can be stacked against a wall in the basement, garage, or bedroom. Filling the buckets with something such as sand or beans makes the shelves stable. One college couple had bucket-and-board shelves ceiling-high in their small living room to "ease the squeeze" and to prevent clutter. But before investing, compare the cost of sturdy metal shelving. It may be less expensive in your community than boards and buckets. (See chapter 17, A Place for Everything, for sample illustration.)

23. Managing Your Closet

I deally, everything in your closet is ready to wear—it fits, it's clean, and it's appropriate for the season. When you open the closet, your only thoughts are: "What do I feel like wearing today and what is proper for this occasion?" However, some of us often put ourselves through a depressing exercise. To make a selection, we review all our past purchasing mistakes, we pass over clothes we can't wear because of weight change, and we are reminded of being poor time managers because the mending, washing, and ironing are not done. To some, getting dressed is a tormenting experience.

If you want to change, set a goal that your closet will contain only proven friends. The changing of seasons is a natural time to dive into it. Target a time—perhaps a few hours on Saturday—to reorganize your closet. Take with you four large boxes or grocery sacks to sort as discussed on pages 119–120. Systematically review every piece of clothing and every accessory. Make a distinction between clothes and shoes you wear often and those you seldom wear. Ask yourself if each item is still valuable to you. How often do you wear it? We put on 20 percent of our clothes 80 percent of the time. As you are sorting, put back only favorite friends. If there is any doubt, don't put it back yet. The item may need further evaluation. Why don't you wear it? Do not fall back into the old traps: "It still has some good in it," or "I might need it someday." If you are not currently wearing an item, the reason usually falls into one of these categories:

1. It needs attention (dry cleaning, mending, pressing);
2. You do not have anything to wear with it;
3. It does not fit;
4. This is not the season for this garment;
5. You have an overabundance of clothes in this category;
6. You don't choose to wear it because it doesn't make you feel at your best—it's out of style, the wrong color, etc.

It's easy to part with some things, so put those directly into the charity box. Pass on the things you are not likely to use, and recycle them while they are still good enough for someone else, and don't take out the zippers or cut off the buttons. To do so renders the item unusable, good only for rags or fiber recycling. It isn't likely that a thrift-store shopper will buy a new zipper and stitch it into a pair of old pants.

Ideally, your closet will contain clothing for the current season only. It is nice to have a spare closet in which to store winter clothes, especially dress clothing and coats. If you do not have an extra closet, there are several options. Divide your closet into two categories, one side for storage and the other for current usage. Another possibility is to fold clothing into a cedar chest, trunk, suitcase, or box. Be sure clothing is clean and dry before storing to minimize mildew, mold, and moths.

If you are one of those people who hang on to misfits, now is the time to get them out of your closet. Get the misfits out of sight until you are that size again. If you don't separate storage area, cover them with a sheet at one end of the closet or enclose them in garment bags. Keep only those clothes that make you feel and look good. It takes courage to get rid of clothing that doesn't fit. Some think, "If I give away these clothes, I have given up hope of ever losing weight." Take another view: "I haven't been able to wear these in the last three years; they are out of style. I'll give them away, lose weight, and reward myself with a new wardrobe." Keep hope and get rid of unwearable clothes. If I can't talk you into getting rid of all misfits, at least keep just the very best of them. And don't feel obligated to wear out someone else's castoffs, either.

Now to the garments that need attention. Before you invest time and/or money in fixing or cleaning, ask yourself, "Will I wear this item even if it's fixed or cleaned. If so, set a deadline by which to have these items ready. Putting off these tasks forever is a clue that you really do not need or want these garments.

There are some clothes you do not choose to wear very often—you always seem to pick something else first. Perhaps it is not your color, the fit isn't right, or they don't make you feel your best. If you aren't brave enough to move them out today, put them in a bag for a couple of weeks and see how you feel about them later. If you haven't retrieved them, it's a sign you can do without them. I am lucky and have a double-door closet to myself. I keep dress clothes

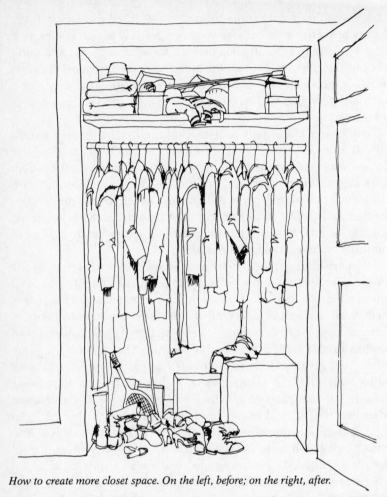

How to create more closet space. On the left, before; on the right, after.

on one side and casual items on the other. When I put clean clothing in the closet, I put them in from the outer edges. At sorting time, the garments in the middle are the ones I haven't worn, and the most likely to be sent out.

Make a list of the items you still like but that need a matchmate. Snip off a tiny swatch from a seam or take the garment shopping with you to match color and texture. Until the shopping is completed, hang those items on the dormant side of your closet. They can be transferred to the ready-to-wear section when you complete the shopping.

Watch out for, "I can wear this to work in the yard or around the

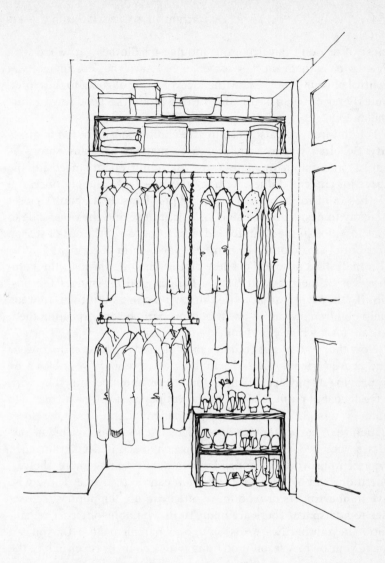

house." How many grubbies do you need? In some ways a closet is like a refrigerator. You wouldn't stuff it with orange peelings and empty pickle bottles. If something goes bad in your refrigerator, you toss it out to make room for fresh, good food. If your closet is too full, even your nice things will look wrinkled from being cramped. Keep a reasonable amount and put the others back into circulation for someone else. I get a kick out of going to a high-school play and seeing the "costumes" that come from Mom and Dad's teenage days. Saving clothing that "might be needed someday" is a luxury that most of us don't have room to indulge in. Clothes get worse with age, so pass them on. Let someone else save the "costumes." Get control of your closet. Enjoy the lovely feeling of going to the closet, quickly selecting an outfit, and putting it on. It's a good way to start the day.

For children, you also need to give careful consideration to quantity. So often we expect children to manage as many things as adults, and they cannot. Because the child doesn't need all the space for current clothes, we hang the out-of-size and out-of-season clothes in his or her closet, creating problems. In an adult's closet it's okay to designate one side for current use and the other side of the closet for storage, but for kids it's better to put the out-of-season and out-of-size clothes in another place, or in a garment bag. It eliminates the problem of these clothes passing through the laundry every time they fall from a hanger, and it removes the possibility they will put on those things you don't want them to wear. Help children manage a few things properly before expecting them to care for a whole closet full.

Now that your closet contains only clothing that is ready to wear and proven friendly, consider making more room in your closet by improving its physical features. First think about perking it up with a fresh coat of paint or some lively wallpaper. If you own your own home, you might make plans for permanent alterations in the closet structure. A carpenter that specializes in closet improvements, assesses your needs, measures how much space is needed for each type of improvement, and then sets about adding more shelves, partitions, cubbyholes, and rods. You can do the same. Those who live in apartments or who move often can use temporary accessories to add space. There are many units available for closet organization in your hardware, discount, or department store. Or, you can make your own. A second rod hung with a chain or ropes in half the closet for the shorter items can give you twenty-five percent more rod space. Step shelves at the end of a closet will give space for shoes and other accessories. A small wooden or cardboard chest with drawers or even a narrow bookcase can be set at the end of the closet or under the shorter clothing. A towel rod can be used for belts and ties or slacks. A stack of vegetable bins is handy for gym clothes, sweaters or shoes. A long board set on bricks would give a second shelf above the rod. To get control of the closet, first get rid of the unnecessary, then organize your space for optimum use.

ORGANIZING
YOUR BUDGET

24. Easy Steps to Establishing a Budget

N et worth is not necessarily determined by income. True value equals the goods, services, and savings you can accumulate. This has to do with how carefully you keep track of financial papers, whether you spend impulsively or intentionally, how wisely you shop, and how well you take care of what you have. Except for a few of the very rich, every one of us could use more money. You have two choices: increase your income or get more for your money. Other books are written on the first, my specialty is managing; and managing money means organizing it.

SPEND INTENTIONALLY

You will spend your money whether or not you have a budget. But if you have a plan, you are more likely to be satisfied with where the money goes. How many times have you made a purchase, been all excited at the moment, and then a day or two later questioned, Why did I spend my money on that? By setting goals you can eliminate regrets. When you have a purpose in mind, it is easier to sacrifice. It takes so much of your life to earn money, give careful thought to where it will go. Make a plan before you spend. So often on pay day a person is feeling good, ready for a treat, and stops at the bar or grocery store to cash the paycheck, leaving much of it there. The first impulse is an undirected splurge because new money seems as if it will go a long way. When the spree is over, there is only so much left to survive on. Compare this to the person who writes out a plan of where the paycheck is to go, then goes to the bank to cash the check, lays out the money in piles (literally or figuratively), and walks out knowing exactly how much he or she has to spend on weekend fun without robbing necessities.

The key is to write out your plan. Instead of floating ideas in your head, bring them to reality by putting them on paper. If you can't work them out on paper, they won't work in the green. You cannot hide from the facts—they will eventually catch up to you. The longer you wait, the harder it is to get control. If you don't have enough income to cover your bills, call the Consumer Credit Counseling Service in your area for personal guidance to set up a plan for getting out of debt.

If you share expenses with someone, you should both be involved in budget decisions and then honestly stick to them. Consult on special purchases beyond the basic budget and agree on how to spend discretionary income. Everyone, especially adults, should have a personal allowance for which he or she is not accountable to anyone else. This serves as a pressure vent. But the other money, designated by agreement for necessities, should not be touched unless you both agree.

DETERMINE YOUR DISCRETIONARY INCOME

A major strategy for helping to manage your money is to distinguish between what is available to be spent and what is already committed. For example, suppose your monthly take-home pay is $2,500, which sounds like a lot, but if you subtract all your fixed expenses (house payment or rent, utilities, insurance, debts, child support), you might have only $850 left for all flexible expenses (food, clothing, gas, entertainment). This figure shows a truer picture of what you can spend. Then, if you are thinking of buying something such as a camera, the question is not whether you can afford it from your $2,500, but whether you can buy it out of the $850, in which case it may take several months to save for that purchase because you still have to buy food, gas, etc. You will look at your discretionary income in a new way—you may be more careful about buying a new sofa with $75 per month payment. And if you can cut back the phone bill, or pay off one of your other debts, you can increase your available income. We live in an I-want-it-now world. To survive, you have to govern your wants. Learn to plan. Calculate your discretionary income. Step back and get an overall view of where your money goes by listing fixed and flexible expenses. Subtract the fixed total from your take-home pay and you know how much you have to work with.

WHERE DO YOU STAND?

Fixed Expenses:		Flexible Expenses:	
Insurance		*Housing*	
life	_____	heat, gas,	
health	_____	electricity,	_____
dental	_____	water	_____
car	_____	phone	_____
Savings	_____	trash removal	_____
investments	_____	repairs	_____
emergency fund	_____	*Transportation*	
travel fund	_____	gas	_____
Debts and Obligations		upkeep	_____
auto loan	_____	public	
installments	_____	transportation	
Other	_____		_____
union or		*Food and Sundries*	_____
professional		*Clothing and*	
dues	_____	*Shoes*	_____
church	_____	*Education, lessons,*	
child support	_____	*books,*	_____
alimony	_____	*Entertainment,*	
Total	_____	*recreation,*	_____
		Gifts	_____
		Medical	_____
		Total	_____

ALLOW FOR SAVINGS

Consider savings as a fixed expense and allow for two kinds. First, you need to build a cushion to take care of unplanned emergencies. It's time to start planning for them. For example, one family with an average yearly dental expense of $650 claims they have "surprises" every year. They should be putting at least $50 a month into the emergency fund to prepare for this expense. If your yearly insurance bills total $300, put $25 a month aside so that when the quarterly bill comes due, you can pay it without going hungry that month. Many financial advisors recommend 20 percent of take-home pay be designated to either catch up on past bills or to build the emergency fund. The second category of savings is to set aside money (some financial planners suggest 10 percent of take-home

pay) for investment or long-term goals to buy a house or for retire-
ment.

At first, draw a sketch of your overall financial picture. Later on,
focus on specific budget items and how to trim costs if necessary.
How will that clothing money be spent? Whose turn is it to get new
shoes? How will the money set aside for household items be spent?
And so on throughout each category.

START A WANT LIST

Every year new gadgets, toys, and tools are invented to stimulate
national consumption. Our economy is built on marketing techniques to make us want to buy. Students go to college to study
strategies on getting us to spend. All this promotion is hard on
consumers because we can't have it all. The answer to more satisfaction is to spend intentionally, not impulsively. Keep a want list.
Define your financial wants and prioritize them. As an encompass-
ing desire to have something comes upon you, write it down. It
won't be forgotten. Then when you have some discretionary money,
you can choose from the list what you want most, not just what you
happen to want today or what you see now. Writing it down frees
your mind but keeps the thought. Start a want list for each member
of the family and one for the house. Instead of the see-want-spend
method, use the see-think-plan technique. A budget doesn't have to
take all the fun out of life, it can bring long-term satisfaction. Your
goal may be a nice vacation or to fix up the house. Since you can't
have everything you need to make a choice of which you want most,
set it above other things, and be content with that decision. If you
want money for investing, you can't spend everything you get on
daily living. But once you get some money into savings or investments, it's like having someone else help you work.

SEPARATE MONEY

Physically divide your money. Some organizers with a great deal of
discipline can do this on paper. If the tally sheet shows an amount
left in one column, say household furnishings, they carry it over to
the next month. Others of us need a more physical separation of the
money because if it's there, we spend it. Here are three techniques
for separating your money.

1. Envelope method. After a skeleton budget plan is written out and the paycheck cashed, money is slipped into envelopes marked "gas," "food," "fun," "clothing," etc. What's left is left; when it's gone it's gone. This is more visual and final than abstract buying with credit cards. This is real. You can't spend money unless you have it.
2. Bank account method. Many people use a method very similar to the envelope system, except they use various bank accounts to help them separate funds. For example, one couple has a household account for current usage; a savings account for large short-term payments (insurance, emergencies, new tires, a hot water heater, dental, or medical needs). Third, they have an account for vacation and Christmas money. Fourth, they have a long-term savings account for such things as real estate, stocks and bonds, IRA, certificates.
3. Payroll deduction plans can help you set aside funds for purposes other than immediate spending.

KEEP A TALLY

Keep track of where your money goes. By keeping an expense record you can compare actual costs to the PLAN. You can pinpoint leaks and problems and revise the plan or your habits accordingly. The typical family does not know how twenty-five percent of its income is spent. We cannot assume that those expenditures were not important, but if you do not have a system of recording expenses, how can you make an evaluation for improvement? Your tally system can be more or less detailed, depending on your needs. This record could be in a bookkeeping journal, in a commercial budget book, on a spread sheet, or simply in the checkbook by being very specific as to what each check was written for.

DON'T GET STRAPPED

Long ago Indians used to torture their victims (so I am told) by tying them to four stakes with wet rawhide. As the rawhide dried it shrank, literally tearing the victim apart. Don't strap yourself down with faulty logic and sales pitches: It's tax deductible so go ahead and buy it; this money is all mine to spend as I want; it's old-fashioned to budget; consolidate your bills; education is a waste;

build up credit with credit cards; next month you'll have more money; live for today; free interest; you deserve it. Don't set up your own torture. Do not let these traps take away your freedom or cause you unnecessary pain. You can be smart with your money.

Examine your emotional involvement with spending. Some people spend to soothe depression, anger, or insecurities. Future money—for example, a tax refund that you may be expecting—looks as though it will buy more than it really will. It is like looking at the moon as it rises in an autumn sky—it is gigantic because the atmosphere magnifies the size. Before you have it, money looks like it will cover more, and credit is a convenient method of taking you into that realm of hope. We spend future money. We promise it to someone else before we have even gotten up early in the morning to go to work. Such optimism! We are counting on still having a job, no inflation, and not having any emergencies. Some people manage consumer credit to their advantage and it doesn't cause them any trouble; for others it is a millstone that will drown them. If you can't control your spending or if your consumer debt is too large, you can get rid of the cards and operate with cash.

We all have a natural cycle of wants. If you buy a new TV today, it satisfies the desire for a while. Every time you pass that new TV, you sigh, "It's so nice." But the newness fades, and in a few weeks the TV is just part of the house. A new want starts to swell inside you like a volcano building pressure. Perhaps it is a new chair you want this time. Charging such purchases makes it possible to grant your wants. You have a problem when your cycle of wants comes forth faster than your ability to pay off the past charges. It is human nature to desire more than you can afford. Part of life is learning to manage these wants. A written budget, expense records, and want lists will bring these facts into focus.

Every time you are tempted to spend when you know you shouldn't, write down three alternatives that will not cost as much. It will help you realize you do have options. Driven by desire, you can rationalize any purchase. Examine yourself. I remember a student in one of my money classes who went on and on about her smart planning. She had just consolidated all her bills (a no-no because it just makes a bigger total debt and prolonged payment time). The finance company gave her a three-month grace period before payments were to start. Listen to how she gave herself permission: "With this extra money for three months, I am going to buy some jewelry-making equipment so my thirteen-year-old daughter and I can make some pocket money. And I am going to buy a microwave because then we will eat better foods and I can lose weight." Instead of cutting back or learning from her past mistakes, she was in even deeper than before. It seemed so logical and sensible to her. But the reality of life is that you eventually have to stop spending more than you make.

One more story. A man, sharing his money problems, explained to me he was having a hard time. He was in the middle of a career change, had just accepted the care of a larger family, and had to pay alimony. Even though he was honest and sincere, he was having a hard time staying ahead of bankruptcy. Then he proceeded to tell me about a three-week trip they had just returned from to Disneyland, traveling 3,500 miles. "We really shouldn't have gone; I couldn't afford to take off work (commission salary), but I promised the kids we would go and then these problems came up." He spent that much money and lost wages to fulfill a promise to his children, all under ten years of age. I think they could have presented an alternative plan to the children and it would not have made much difference to them. The most important thing was that they have time together; it didn't so much matter where. When I was a teenager, I accompanied a family of six young children to Disneyland from Denver as assistant caregiver. We had a wonderful time, but it was a long, long ride. The next year, the father of this family asked his children, "Would you like to go back to Disneyland this year or to Elitchs [an amusement park in Denver]?" They unanimously jumped for joy to go to Elitchs. Disneyland in California was not that important to them. With this experience in mind, I wondered if the man in my first example hadn't made an expensive assumption and trapped himself into an extravagance.

While some people are hoping for their ship to come in, others build one. Be a ship builder—make your dreams come true.

25. Quick Ways to Cut Food Costs

F ood, clothing, and shelter are the three biggest items in most families' budgets. Shelter is generally a fixed cost; clothing and, in particular, food are not. By planning ahead and by shopping wisely, you can save dramatically on these costs. The next few chapters will tell you how.

So often, people buy food and then try to live on what money is left. They don't give the food allowance any limits or perimeters. How much money will you allow for food each month? Can you stay within that amount? Averages now are above $25 per week per person. But it also depends where you live and how many people you are serving. One person will find it next to impossible to live on $25 per week for food, but five people will find it easier to live on $125 per week. There is a graduated advantage for cooking for a group. The first step is to decide on a reasonable food budget. If you cut back too severely on the food budget when it isn't necessary, you'll find yourself and your children rebelling.

ISOLATE COSTS

You need to find some way to measure how much you are spending and where it goes. To say that you are spending $400 a month on food doesn't tell us enough. Your food budget needs to be divided into categories so we can take a good look at each and shave where possible. With some of our modern super stores carrying everything from motor oil to small appliances, it's hard to tell where you stand unless you separate sundries, paper, soap, personal supplies, and all other nonfood products from your food purchases.

How much does it cost you per day for food? Before you start eating dinner tonight, look over the table and mentally calculate the total for the meal ingredients: noodles, hamburger, onion, sauce, green peas, salad ingredients. Perhaps the total is $7.00 (only an estimate). How much does it cost for a typical lunch (if you eat at home or pack lunches)? How much do you spend for breakfast? Fifty years ago, a typical American breakfast consisted of cooked-grain cereal and milk. Modern advertising has convinced us to let the cereal companies cook and dry the cereal into flakes, increasing the cost ten times. A hundred pound sack of wheat, corn, rice, or oatmeal costs between $20 and $30. One hundred pounds of flaked cereal costs well over $275. We have been courted by producers and manufacturers for everything from apples to yogurt. It's time we made some of our own decisions. But first, it will help to calculate the cost of an average breakfast, lunch, and dinner. Right now my average dinner is $7.50. To serve a nice roast on Sunday will make the meal cost more than the $7.50, so we'll have to eat a less expensive meal such as homemade chicken soup to average $7.50. Become aware of which meals fall on the high or low side of your limit. Some casseroles cost more than you would think. Lasagne, to me, is an expensive meal whereas a ground beef, green bean, and potato casserole with a little cheese on top falls on the lower side. Just because you are trying to save money, don't forfeit nutrition. Curiously, the USDA now recommends less meat and more grains in the typical American diet. Luckily this recommendation also costs less. Meats can be extended with rice, noodles, wheat, or texturized vegetable protein.

The point is, if you isolate expenses, you can probably see ways to cut back. If you need to cut back, try working with the planning chart on page 172. In the beginning especially it will take at least an hour to fill it out and then keep adjusting until it is within your budget. Making these decisions before you walk into the store is the best way to change your buying habits.

One family told me that because of unemployment they had to cut their $400 a month food allowance in half. Five days a week they ate nice, typical family-style meals. They had some sort of chicken or turkey at least once. Meals included generous portions of vegetables and salad and plenty of fruit. But they did not have desserts, except on Monday, when they had an extra-fancy one. They looked forward to the Monday special. On Thursday the mother made bread and they had an old-fashioned meal of fresh bread and all the milk they could drink. On Friday, they ate beans and cornbread. This pattern kept them from feeling like they were in total poverty.

Most of the lunches were packed from home, and homemade cookies gave them a special flair. Breakfasts were either eggs in one form or another or cooked cereal, milk, and bottled fruit. Believe it or not, they did it for more than a year.

If you need to trim food costs, take a few minutes to estimate the cost of each item on your grocery list and set mini-budgets for things like crackers, salad items, and cold cereals before you go shopping. Add this up, rounding off as you go. If the total amount comes to more than your food allowance, you need to rework the menus and shopping list until it is within bounds. It is less painful to go through this process at home than to overspend at the grocery store and then try to make it up from other financial areas. Even though food is a necessity, it needs a budget boundary. Preparing a shopping list and estimating costs before you step into the supermarket is one of those miracle strategies that pays off every time you use it.

STAY OUT OF STORES

One of the prime ways to save money is to **stay out of stores.** Every time you go in for one little thing, you probably get much more. The extra you buy is not necessarily wasted, but it is often unessential. Plan your main meals at least a week at a time so you don't have to keep going back to the store. What do you normally stop for at the grocery? Milk and bread? How could you lengthen the time between stops? Have milk delivered at home. Freeze milk. Use powdered milk. If you are buying for a family, you will probably need a freezer to extend time between shopping visits. Running a freezer may cost $45 a year, but the cost is offset by keeping you out of the store.

People who cook for just one or two have special problems. It is difficult for them to save food money in the same way a large family can save. Their best weapon against high food cost is planning. In order to save waste, singles need to *correlate* meals, which cannot be done if they shop one meal at a time. Going to the store every day is as expensive as eating out. In the beginning, people cooking small quantities need to work out menus and grocery lists on paper. Learn to divide and freeze food that cannot be purchased in small portions. For example, if you buy a package of chicken parts, you could plan to make a chicken crêpe, fried chicken, and barbecued chicken. In between the chicken meals you could fix a pork chop one night and an enchilada another night. The average single spends at least fifty dollars a week on food. You have the potential of saving almost half that much. It may mean deciding ahead of time when you will "eat out" and when you will be "eating in" so that the food you purchase for today doesn't spoil in the refrigerator while you go out for a meal. In such case, you are paying for dinner twice. Learn to work with nonperishables like canned or frozen foods. Planning will help you get better nutritional balance. Preplanning will help you stay out of the stores.

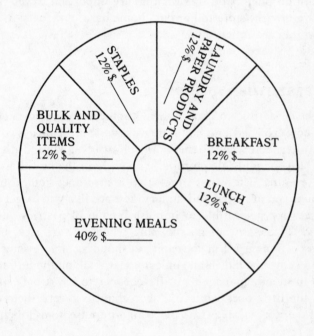

PICK A HOME-BASE STORE

Compare prices at several stores and pick one to be your "home store." One evening I took my own advice and buzzed through the three main grocery stores in my area with clipboard in hand. I compared twenty-five items I normally buy, and each item on the list was exactly the same—brand, size, and weight—so my comparisons were fair. The winning store had a lower price on twenty-one of the twenty-three items. (Two items were disqualified because I couldn't find them at all three). I am not a scientific research specialist, but it was easy to tell which store had better prices. I added up the totals as though I had purchased one of each item. The winner came out seven and a half percent below the loser and six percent less than the second best. That is difference enough to convince me which store should be my "home base"—the one where I will do the basic and everyday buying. I could save more than $300 a year right off the top. Take into consideration distance, safety, atmosphere, and services that are important to you. It pays to pick a grocery store to be your "home base" and learn it well to save on time as well as money.

THE BEST TIMES TO SHOP

Pick the best time to shop. When I complained to my neighbor about how crowded a nearby store was, she said, "I always go at one in the afternoon when 'General Hospital' is on TV and no one is there." If your schedule permits, shop early in the morning or late in the evening. The worst time to go is at dinner hour. Lines are long, and you are tired and hungry. You are likely to forget things and are very susceptible to impulse buying of pastries and convenience foods. Do not go shopping when you are sick, hungry, depressed, or angry. (But you can't put shopping off forever or you'll starve.) Leave the kids home unless you are taking them to teach a lesson in money management. It's cheaper to pay a babysitter to watch the little ones while you shop than to govern their wants. Part of the store strategy is to place high-impulse items for children at their level.

Compare national brands with generic and in-store brands. Look at prices for various sizes: large economy size is not always the best buy. Check to see if you can save money buying whole chickens, sides of beef or pork, and wheels of cheese. Cut and wrap for your needs. In many areas you can shop with a co-op, warehouse, or join a buying club. Pay attention to trends and seasonal items. When certain foods are in season, the price should be lower.

Food is associated with much of our entertainment, but concession stands have high prices to compensate for their convenience. When appropriate, take your own treats with you on drives, to the ball game or movies, or on picnics. Discourage between-meal snacks: they aren't healthy. Cut down or eliminate potato chips and other crunchy, salty, expensive snacks if you want to reduce your spending (and have a healthier diet!).

A sale is not always a bargain. Know your prices. Items are often "featured" or highlighted to grab your attention. If the sale is real and you have a cushion in the budget to build your pantry, by all means buy extras at the lower price. There is another way to save and this is to buy in quantity at specialty shops or at the closest source to the grower or manufacturer. September is a good time of year to save on fruits and vegetables at the farmer's market or fruit stand. You might cut the bread budget at bakery outlets. You can research and find places that specialize. Sometimes you shop for quality. I have a favorite place to buy egg-roll skins and corn flour tortillas because they are wonderfully fresh.

Be strong. Know what you intend to buy. An impulsive purchase is anything you buy that you had not planned on getting before you walked into the store. Store managers have elaborate instruction books; they go to national conventions every year to study the psychology of shoppers. If you are not sure what you want when you go in, you are highly susceptible to their persuasion. Managers purposely arrange things so you will pick up more than you intended. They devise ways to get your attention and to slow down your progress through the aisles. Think of the money they can make if you spend ten minutes longer in the store. The basics are strategically placed so you have to pass high impulse items first. Milk is usually located the far side or back of the shelf, not just because the cooling elements are there, but to slow you down. Shelf positioning is important; you are less likely to reach high or low than to pick something at eye level. Which soda pop is closest to the front door? Competition between suppliers is intense for priority positioning. Who decides what is placed where? In your kitchen you place things used most often in prime space. In the grocery store it is just the opposite; they put high-profit items and national brands at eye level; general necessities are placed higher or lower. End-of-the-aisle displays are designed to get your attention and remind you that you "could use more of this" or "that does look good." We have all fallen for the last-minute goodies while waiting at the check-out stand. Non-food items, which carry a higher profit than food, are strategically placed at eye level everywhere—often the same item in several places. Packaging is designed for attention. Red will grab you. Researchers have found that if they wrap a head of cauliflower in plastic, it moves from basic vegetable to impulsive splurge in the customer's subconscious. It has been estimated that sixty percent of your shopping decisions are made after you get into the store. One couple said their system for shopping was to go up and down every aisle in the store, stopping at each item to ask, "Do we need this?" It is an okay system because they don't forget much, but they are probably spending more than they should.

When you buy impulsively, you are letting someone else influence your food dollar, and you may not get your best value. Be strong. Just for fun, next time you get home from shopping take a good look at the sales receipt and put a check by the items you had not intended to buy before you walked in the store.

MAKE IT YOURSELF

There are some foods on which you can save money if you have the time to make your own. Bake your own muffins, waffles, pies, and other desserts. If you live in an area where fruits and vegetables are readily available, bottle your own fruit. Pressure-can vegetables and meats. You can also dehydrate these products. Take a class from your local extension service or ask your mother, aunt, or a mature friend to be your mentor. Usually, when you make your own, you can save money. But when it comes to food preparation, that isn't necessarily true. For example, if you make your own noodles you are saving only 45 cents. For most of us, our time is worth more than that. However, two additional variables come into the picture: preference and nutrition. I do not recommend making your own noodles to save money, but you may choose to do it because it is fun, you like them better, or you add special ingredients that make them more nutritious. Cake mixes are almost as cheap as making your own from scratch, especially chocolate cake. I can save a little money by making my own cookies; besides, I cut down the sugar by one third and boost the nutrition with soy flour, milk, nuts, and eggs. I wouldn't squeeze my own orange juice or lemon juice unless I had a citrus tree in my backyard (not possible in Colorado). When I went to work and cut back on the time I spent in the kitchen, my food bill went up 30 percent. You have to weigh the consequences and benefits for yourself.

GROW IT YOURSELF

Grow some of your own food—it's an adventure. When we first started gardening we planted everything. Now we plant only what grows best in our soil and what will save us the most money. We plant twenty tomato plants because we can harvest about ten bushels of fruit, enough to make lots of spaghetti sauce. We plant cucumber vines because we love to eat them and bottle plenty of pickles. We grow sugar peas, one hill of zucchini and a few green beans so we can enjoy them fresh, and one giant pumpkin for Halloween fun and Thanksgiving pies. It will cost us at least forty dollars a year for seeds, fertilizer, and insecticide. We enjoy the fun of harvest, and it's nice to share the bounty with neighbors and family. But if we counted the cost of water (Colorado is a dry climate) and the hours of weeding, we would be in the red. If we took that same money to the market and bought vegetables, we could probably have just as much food. But the reality is, we would not. The garden encourages us to eat the produce, which is better for us. Ask someone in your area who has grown a successful garden to teach you the tricks. Every locality has different challenges. Knowing how to grow a garden is a type of "life insurance." If you don't have your own property or can't take part in a community city garden project, buy your fresh fruits as close to the source as possible. If you are interested in large amounts of fruits and vegetables, farmer's markets are in these days. Look in your local newspaper want ads for seasonal specials.

It isn't easy to save money on food, but there are ways that it can be done if you are willing to reshape your buying habits. Go to the store only once during each pay period. Prepare good shopping lists and estimate cost before going into the store. Shop at the right place and at the right time; do some of your own baking and try growing a garden. Happy eating!

26. Lists, Menus, and Money

A young mother of twins raised her hand at a woman's club meeting and asked in all sincerity, "How can you get by without going to the store every day?" She was surprised to learn that no one else in the room had that problem. "How do you do it?" We told her to decide now what she was going to cook next week. She thought for fifteen minutes and still didn't have one thing written down; she seemed to have a mental block. I then changed tactics and instructed her to simply list seven main dinner dishes she and her family liked. It took only five minutes to make the list: spaghetti, pork chops, roast, pizza, fish patties, and fried rice. I next asked her to write down a vegetable and/or salad she would serve with each main dish. Then I suggested she make a list of ingredients she would have to buy to make these seven dinners. Our new mother was surprised that when she left, she had a shopping list for a whole week. All she needed to do was add paper and soap products, and breakfast and lunch supplies.

If meal planning is a problem for you, resolve to change and smooth out the five o'clock hassle. The cycle of food in and out of a house, and the preparation and cleanup are the biggest process in a home, and it pays to organize this area of your home life. You need to make this system fit your family. In some homes, home food preparation is only supplemental to eating out. In other homes, three meals are prepared every single day. It makes a difference whether you live alone, with another adult, or if you are serving little children. No matter where you fit, I will offer you ways to organize the food cycles to save time, money, and effort.

MENU PLANS

Before you shop, take time to plan menus so you will have all the ingredients you need without making last-minute trips to the grocery store. This rule applies whether you shop weekly, bimonthly, or once a month. At the beginning of the month (I shop that way because that's how we get paid) I start with two blank pieces of paper. On one I make a simple list of thirty main dishes that we will eat next month. On the other paper I make the shopping list—the ingredients I will need to buy for each dinner. The menu list is later posted on the refrigerator as a reminder to me of what I have on hand. Each morning I choose from the list what I am in the mood to fix considering the weather and how much time is available that day. (If I am home, I decide by ten o'clock in the morning; if I am to be gone, I make that choice the night before.) I plan some quick meals, and meals for the children if their father and I go out to eat. During the major monthly shopping trip, I buy everything that will keep and then go back midmonth for fresh salad greens and fruit. We don't have to look at the calendar to tell what day of the month it is, we know by what is on the table. We tend to eat our favorite things first and get progressively lower on the priority list. The last day we have "end-of-the-month" stew to use up all the leftover vegetables, meat, and gravy. If you are a novice at meal planning, don't try a whole month, start for just one week and work up to more later if you choose. With seasonal variations, we eat just about the same things every month. That may sound boring, but statistics show that the average family eats the same ten meals 80 percent of the time.

SIMPLE MENUS FOR A WEEK		
Meals we like	**Vegetable/Salad**	**Things I need to buy to make this meal**
Spaghetti	Green salad	Spaghetti, mushrooms, hamburger, tomato sauce, onions
Pork chops	Peas Pineapple/carrot Jell-O	Chops, peas, pineapple, carrots, Jell-O
Roast	Potatoes, gravy Broccoli	Broccoli, instant potatoes
Fish patties	Green salad Orange juice Fries	Lettuce, orange juice, frozen fries
Fried rice	Fruit Jell-O	Rice, 1 slice ham, raspberries

If you live alone—whether by choice or following an abrupt change in family—the first thing to slip is eating regular and balanced meals. There is no one to cook for, and it's not much fun eating alone. Do not give up nutrition at a time when you need energy, vitamins, and minerals to cope with stress and change. Don't make yourself susceptible to fatigue, depression, or illness. There are several options including making ways *to be with* others. Share meals back and forth with a neighbor. Invite a friend to eat lunch out once a week, or start a pot-luck dinner club. This plan-ahead strategy will help greatly. If you decide in the morning that you will have a ham omelet for dinner, you are more likely to do it. Do not wait until five-thirty to decide, or it will seem like too much of an effort. One busy college student cooked an abundant portion of something on Saturday and then ate the same thing all week. (Ugh!) He didn't have time for variety, just maintenance, while he finished his degree. This man's eighty-nine-year-old grandmother did the same thing, cooking a roast or casserole on the weekend. But, she carefully packaged most of it into small freezer bags or TV trays and labeled them. Each morning she "selected" dinner from the freezer. Modern grocery stores offer a wonderful array of individually prepared meals. I am beginning to believe it is harder to cook for one than it is for five. Nevertheless, it can be done. The key to nutrition and savings is preplanning.

In these busy times, we are looking for more ways to simplify housekeeping. New gadgets and appliances are not the only answer. Eventually we have to give in and use that old-fashioned technique—planning. With it you can go directly home from work and avoid the rush-hour congestion at the food store. You can walk right in, start food preparation, and skip that agonizing decision time. If someone else is home before you are and the dinner menu has been posted, that someone can have dinner ready when you get there. Families with special diet requirements for weight, diabetes, heart conditions, and allergies will find meal planning helps add variety to their limited food options.

SHOPPING LISTS

I will go out on the limb and say that anyone who goes to the grocery store more than once a week is wasting time. The first step is to plan your meals, the second is to prepare a good shopping list.

If you work at it, you can get very good at predicting your needs. As you begin, list these general headings on your paper: meat, produce, paper and laundry products, toiletries, etc. If you shop in more than one store, make a list for each store. A list with a moderate amount of grouping can save backtracking while shopping. Some organizers suggest drawing a map of your favorite store and preparing the list like a travellog. Draw up the shopping list in the following ways:

1. As you prepare the menu list, write out a shopping list that includes all the necessary ingredients. When shopping, if you change your mind and buy something especially tempting or on sale, just cross it out of the original menu and add the new one.
2. Check this week's grocery ads for sale items that you can work into your menus and for specials on things you use often, and, if you save coupons, go through your coupon file and pull out the ones for items on your list.
3. Take a quick inventory of cupboards, refrigerator, and freezer before you shop to spot needs and avoid overbuying. If you clean out the refrigerator before you shop, you'll know what is in there and also have more room to put new groceries away.
4. All month, keep a tablet handy in the kitchen on which to write things you run out of, or soon will need. Our list is tacked inside the pantry cupboard. My husband and children are even learning to help with the list. I trained them by responding when they mentioned they needed shampoo or deodorant, "Go put it on the list in the kitchen."
5. Put together your own shopping guide by compiling a list of typical items that you buy every month. In the old days, I kept forgetting the ketchup, mustard, and kitty litter. My monthly shopping list is tallied from the above four areas, and then, as a last check, I look at the typical standard list to see if I have forgotten anything important.

If you need to trim food costs, take time to calculate the total cost of your anticipated purchases. The last chapter includes a sample chart that shows this technique for cutting back on food costs and estimating before leaving home.

After shopping, either that day or the next, I allow time to cut up the chickens, mix meat loaf or meat balls or patties, slice or grind ham, and grate cheese so that everything is as ready to use as possible. Check for cookbooks that specialize in quick dinners and put together some of your own quick meals. Many meals can be prepared faster at home than if you went out for the same meal. It just takes forethought. When Mimi Wilson needed more time in her volunteer work with Asian refugees, she refined a cook-ahead system so that she cooks only one day a month (for five hours). Each morning she takes a packet out of the freezer and has only a few minutes' preparation at dinner hour. Mimi's ideas are in print (*Once-a-Month Cooking*, by Mimi Wilson and Mary Beth Lagerborg, available from St. Martin's Press, 175 Fifth Avenue, New York, N.Y. 10010. $6.95 plus $1.00 postage).

BUILD UP A PANTRY

The first phase of building a pantry is to **have on hand basic staples** that you can use to cook or bake when you run out of the quick foods. As long as you have flour, salt, sugar (white and brown), oil or shortening, baking powder, and baking soda you can make almost anything. With sweet spices and vanilla, herbal seasonings, meat spices like chili powder, and flavorings like soy sauce, your options are increased. It will be to your advantage to also have oatmeal, rice, and macaroni on hand. When your cupboards are stocked with the basics, you can make substitutions, maybe not always traditional. For example, if you planned to have tacos and found, after preparing the meat and beans, that you were out of taco shells, you could make do with another grain product. The taco mixture could be served on a bed of lettuce or rice, or it could be mixed with macaroni and tomato sauce and called Yankee Doodle Beef.

The second phase of building a pantry is to **keep in stock at least one extra** of anything you can't live without. That is, anything you would have to make a special trip to the store to buy should you run out: toothpaste, cat food, margarine, mayonnaise, peanut butter, razor blades, shampoo, tampons, dishwasher soap, laundry detergent, eggs, toilet tissue. Keep some canned or powdered milk in case you run out of fresh milk. Biscuit mix or crackers can be used if you run out of bread. You can build this backup supply a little at a time by getting a few extra things each time you shop, or budget a hundred dollars or so and get them all at once.

The third pantry phase is to **build a storage system,** to buy ahead and purchase products in quantity. If you are cooking for a crew, you can save by getting rice, oats, beans, raisins, nuts, popcorn, cheese, and powdered milk in bulk quantities. You can also take advantage of leader sales. Because inflation has been steady for some years, we know that if we buy several items now to use later, we can eat at yesterday's prices. Check out the group buying plans available in some cities where nonperishable items are ordered in six-month quantities. Some home managers have built such a complete supply that they shop only specials, meaning they hardly ever pay regular price. Others follow the natural law of the harvest, which means they take into their home fruit, grains, and vegetables that they bottle, dehydrate, or freeze themselves. Some would rather have the food in their home than depend on warehouses, truckers, and the local grocery store. Families in rural areas accept this as a standard lifestyle. They take in what they harvest in the fall to consume during the coming year. City dwellers have become very dependent on grocery stores, and many cannot live for more than two days on what they have in the cupboards. You must judge according to your storage space and conscience, but a good rule of thumb is to have enough food on hand so you can make it through a delayed paycheck, a surprise snowstorm, or unexpected company.

TEACH YOUR FAMILY TO
RECOGNIZE DINNER OPTIONS

Once you get the food in the house, you'll need a few more strategies to manage it. Basically, I am trying to foster independence in my husband and children. It dawned on me that because I was the one who planned the menus and did the grocery shopping, they had no idea, except for visible fast foods, what was available to fix. Unless they could open the refrigerator and "see" it, they didn't know what the dinner options were. The answer was to inform them. I solved that by updating the menu list as I was putting away the groceries. This information is put on the refrigerator door where they are sure to see it. It does not list everything in the house (for example, we always have peanut butter), only unusual things purchased this month and reminders of healthier snacks—celery and cream cheese—they wouldn't normally notice.

How do you keep your family or roommates from using ingredients you need to save for something special? Do you have one shelf from which they are free to help themselves? Are they not allowed in the kitchen at all? My philosophy is that we are a family and the food is for us to eat. When I need an item saved for a special creation, I stick a little note on it "Do not eat! Cream cheese is for cheesecake." I don't believe in locking things up or making children feel they are "stealing" food from their own house. On the other hand, I expect them to be sensitive to others. I keep a little pad of stick-on notes in the kitchen paper center, and if the last pork chop or piece of pie is for someone who missed out on dinner, the other family members usually honor that boundary when a note is attached.

27. Coupon Pros and Cons

E ver felt bad because you couldn't buy a hundred dollars worth of groceries for thirty-five dollars?

If you are willing to spend several hours a week, you can cut food costs considerably. Let's look at two styles of cutting the food bill: couponing and do-it-yourself. Everyone can save a little bit using some basic strategies from both of these categories. Your savings depend on how many people you feed and how hard you work at this endeavor. But there is a point after about the first 20 percent where you have to choose one or the other buying style for additional savings. It's like trying to travel north and south at the same time. It can't be done. If you are a do-it person, that's probably why your coupon-refund savings aren't higher.

Let us imagine an average couple doing their grocery shopping twice a week and buying whatever is wanted, with no effort to conserve. Let's give our uninformed shoppers two teachers, one an expert coupon refunder and the other a traditional home economist. This novice couple could be tutored by either of the two instructors in planning and economizing and save from ten to twenty-five percent of what is currently being spent for food. They will learn about intentional spending versus impulse buying, and they will be encouraged to make a menu sketch and shopping list.

The coupon refunder will teach them to clip and file and keep records, beginning with a small box or wallet in which to file coupons and progressing to a cabinet in which to file labels and boxes and a ledger for keeping records. Maybe they will join a coupon co-op or subscribe to a refunding newsletter. Time needs to be invested in record keeping and mailing forms before deadlines. For maximum benefit, they will need two or three hours a week to clip, file, organize, and mail. It has been proven that you can save money this way. But beware: Don't feel compelled to use coupons just because they are available; using coupons doesn't necessarily mean you are saving money. The reason the manufacturer offers coupons is to entice you to buy something you wouldn't normally buy, introduce a new product, or get you to change brands or switch stores. To spend 89 cents instead of 99 cents for something you never would have purchased means you fell for the gimmick.

The traditional home economist teacher will teach our young couple that they will save their money and reap nutritional benefits by investing about two hours a week making their own mixes and quick meals and in doing some baking. The traditional teacher will go on to mention growing a garden, canning, freezing, or dehydrating fruits and vegetables during harvest time. They will learn to buy and store grain products and staples in larger quantities for considerable savings.

The serious shopper, either traditional or couponer, invests about three hours a week in his or her savings program. The question is this: Which do you prefer and which leads to better nutrition? To some people, couponing is a fun game and they get a kick out of it. If that's your pleasure, why not? But you can't be both. You just don't see a cents-off coupon on twenty-five pounds of rice. In most parts of the country, there aren't many coupons for milk, meat, vegetables, or fruit, either. If you want to save money couponing, you have to buy the things manufacturers are promoting, which are often refined or glamour products. The reason a traditional home manager can't save much money couponing is he or she doesn't often use those fast-food and high-glamour products. The home manager has learned to economize by quantity and seasonal buying, cooking from scratch, growing a garden, and home preserving. This traditional home manager can, however, save at least 10 percent or better on paper, drinks, soap, and personal products when coupons are available for these, especially on national brands. Remember, though, that some in-store and generic brands cost less than the national products—even after the coupon savings.

Do-it-yourself people have acquired this lifestyle by habit. It does not necessarily depend on whether they stay at home or work full time but on how they learned to shop and cook. The make-it-yourself family may be spending an astounding 60 percent less than our untrained novices, depending on how far down the spectrum this saving technique is taken. For those who are serious about savings and nutrition, I maintain that you can save at least a dollar

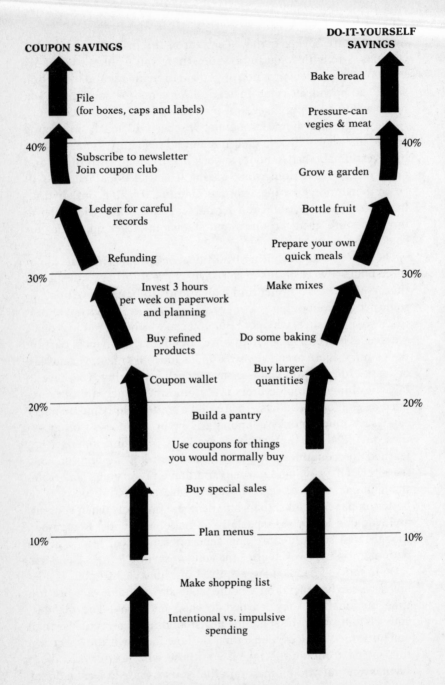

COUPON SAVINGS

DO-IT-YOURSELF SAVINGS

Bake bread

File
(for boxes, caps and labels)

Pressure-can
vegies & meat

40%
Subscribe to newsletter
Join coupon club

Grow a garden
40%

Ledger for careful
records

Bottle fruit

Refunding

Prepare your own
quick meals

30%
Invest 3 hours
per week on paperwork
and planning

Make mixes
30%

Buy refined
products

Do some baking

Coupon wallet

Buy larger
quantities

20%
Build a pantry
20%

Use coupons for things
you would normally buy

Buy special sales

Plan menus
10%
10%

Make shopping list

Intentional vs. impulsive
spending

HOW TO SAVE FOOD MONEY

a day per person on food costs by baking your own bread. Not because you can make bread cheaper than store-made, but because when you eat homemade bread (wholesome varieties), you can cut down on other foods (chips, dry cereals, meat, pastries), costing $2.50 a pound or more.

It's all up to you, whether you'd rather spend time couponing or doing more of your own food preparation. But if you aren't saving money, perhaps it's because you're halfheartedly trying to do both. Try emphasizing one method or the other to see if it makes a difference in the money you spend and the nutrition you get. Then, too, you may not have time to concentrate on either—and that's all right, too!

28. A Master Plan for the Wardrobe

H ave you ever stopped to consider how much it costs you to dress per day? A young woman doesn't hesitate to spend $150 for a dress for the prom or a New Year's eve party that she will wear only once or twice. That is $75 per wearing. But if she bought a basic suit for $150 and took good care of it, she might wear it a hundred times at a cost of $1.50 per wearing. So often, clothing purchases come under the "impulse" category. We judge our purchases by how we "feel" in that garment, which is important, but it is not the only consideration if you want to get the best value for your dollar. What type of clothing do you need most? What do you wear to work? Where do you spend most of your money? Think about your needs. Do you work in jeans and tee-shirt or in a dress suit? What do you like to do in your spare time? Make an evaluation of your spending and design a long-term plan.

TAKE INVENTORY

An important aspect of keeping your clothing and closets organized is to know what you have and what you need. It will also save you money. Go through your closet and drawers and consider your wardrobe. Make note of which jackets and shirts or blouses go with which slacks or skirts. Do you have six shirts that go with the black slacks but none to go with the blue ones? Write out your inventory. One summer, when my teenage daughters were getting ready for college, they kept saying, "We are going shopping for slacks." Yet every time they got home, they would show me lovely blouses. Pants are not as glamorous as blouses. There was such an array of blouses. They were pretty and catchy, and they were on sale more often, and every time my girls were sidetracked. I realized they were buying without direction. They consented to a closet inventory similar to the chart on page 186. We went through the closet and chest of drawers and wrote down what they had. It took less than an hour. We talked about what they would need at school and how much it would cost. Obviously, they couldn't have everything they wanted, so each item was rated from one to ten, ten being most desired. There were some cutbacks, postponements, and tradeoffs. With needs clearly identified and budget in mind, they began to shop with direction. Teens who take part in wardrobe updating can learn good budgeting strategies, and are likely to take better care of their clothes, and can have a wardrobe that truly suits their needs.

MAKE A PLAN

After the inventory, make a plan, whether you are buying for yourself or your children. When you know your needs, you can take advantage of seasonal sales. You won't be caught with a surplus of one thing and big gaps in other areas. Your decisions will be based on whether you are building a professional wardrobe or dressing a growing child. How many of each kind of clothing do you need? Your laundry schedule will also affect this decision. Should we be talking about a fifth-grade boy's school clothes and you wash denims twice a week, he would probably need only four pairs of jeans. As you inventory his clothes and he has only two pairs that fit, part of the plan would be to acquire two more. If we are inventorying a professional person's closet, and he or she sends dirty shirts to the laundry once a week, you will know that six dress shirts are not enough. Young adults tend to be captured by fad and impulse. They typically spend a lot of money on clothes and the garment industry capitalizes on that, but they can be guided into strategies that will make a more satisfying wardrobe.

I remember in one budgeting class, after going over all the ways to save money on clothing, one woman commented, "I like nice clothes, and I decided the way for me to save money is to continue allowing myself to buy the expensive things I have grown to like, but only half as many." By taking inventory and writing out a plan, she cut back on mistakes and mismatches. If she knows exactly what she needs to complement what she already has, she can be satisfied longer. Most people buy clothes on impulse: "I love this." They collect "loves" that don't necessarily go with anything else and need far more than if they bought with a plan in mind.

WARDROBE PLAN/INVENTORY

	Have Now	Wants/Needs	Rate Need (1–10)
Coats:			
Dress coats			
Casual coats			
Dress Clothes:			
Suits/dresses			
Shirts/blouses			
Slacks			
Formal Wear:			
Casual:			
Pants			
Shirts/blouses			
Skirts			
Dresses			
Shoes:			
Socks/Underclothes:			
Accessories:			

Adults usually consider clothing as an investment, and unless they gain or lose weight, an item will often last five years or more. Mature adults generally buy according to the style that they have learned to prefer and one that is complimentary to their figure. They take good care of clothing, which makes it last longer. It is a good idea, whether you are a man or a woman, to invest in a color analysis, which explains which colors are most complimentary for your skin and hair color. Sometimes the colors we like by instinct are not the best for us. My favorite color is green and for years I dressed in that color, but because I am blond and fair skinned, the green made my skin look sallow. My consultant taught me to choose clothing that helped me look healthy. With a specific palette of colors to choose from, you'll look better and, as you make purchases within that range, your wardrobe will begin to coordinate. You can mix and match and interchange items, creating new looks without additional cost.

Your plan may start with a basic all-weather blazer with a dress blouse or shirt and tie. Then build on that nucleus with more shirts or blouses, coordinating slacks and skirts. The program would include buying shoes that go nicely with several outfits. You would begin a nucleus for your casual clothing, either connected to or separate from your professional dress, and then build on that. You'll need to work in seasonal differences for summer and winter if you live in a place with temperature changes. The number needed is based on how many times a week you wear each type of clothing. You may need a separate plan for work clothes, depending on how you must dress for your profession.

With a plan in mind, you can take advantage of sales at the beginning and end of each season. No last-minute emergencies; you can shop around to find exactly what you like at the best price. If you are into a classic style, the items you buy at the end of one season will still be appropriate for next year. If you are shopping for your family, put together a list of sizes to keep with you in your planning notebook. When you see a good bargain you will know if it fits even if that person is not with you. Take this one step further and list measurements for waist, hip, pant length, etc. Tuck a tape measure in your purse and you can check the item against the measurements. Clothing sizes are not uniform. You can cut down on dollars lost on mistakes that don't fit or pieces that weren't needed by keeping a size list and having an overall plan.

I watched one mother, anticipating her children's back-to-school needs, gradually buy shorts, shirts, socks, jeans, and coats for her boys as each item was put on sale during the summer. She saved forty percent. She had a plan and knew what she was looking for. Naturally, she put the new items aside until school was ready to begin. Another time I stood in line behind an ambitious mother who bought six new dresses for her first-grader. They were on sale, yes, but other than being different colors, they were all the same pattern. That little girl is going to feel like she is wearing the same thing every day. My philosophy has been not to get a total new wardrobe at any time because it will all wear out or you will get tired of it all at once. Don't try to maintain a large wardrobe for a child or teenager in a growth spurt. In this case it is better to wash more often. I prefer a periodic update. For my school children I might buy two new sets of clothing in September, another at Christmas, and one for birthday. Even if a child should have a whole new wardrobe at the beginning of school, no one would really know because the teacher and classmates have not seen each other for three months and, anyway, in two weeks all the "new" clothes will be commonplace. Spreading out the purchases gives a periodic lift to the individual, and can save money.

Take Care. If you take good care of your clothing, it will last longer. Mend it as soon as a little tear appears or a button gets loose. Treat spots immediately, either to lengthen time between cleaning or washing, or to keep the spot from setting. Use the right temperature of water and avoid overdrying. When you wash, use a gentle cycle for sweaters and delicate fabrics, or hand wash. Even when your clothes are dirty, take care of them. Don't let them sit on the floor to be tromped on like a rag. If you want something to be nice longer, take care of it. If you use an iron, carefully select the recommended temperature. Prevent shine by using a pressing cloth on wools and corduroy. Don't put heavily soiled or greasy work clothes in the same hamper with your dress shirts. Wear an apron or change your good clothing before you cook or clean or work on the car. If you get only twenty wearings out of a shirt when you could get forty, you are wasting money. Take care of your clothing investment.

Sew Some. If you sew, sew the things you like to make best and/or the ones you can save the most money on. When we were living on my husband's teaching salary, I made his sport jackets. It took me at least forty hours to tailor each jacket. He was a good "sport" and wore them, but I began to realize that if he had a choice, he wouldn't pick the one I made. In fact, if shopping, it wasn't unusual for him to go to six stores and try on fifty coats before he found just what he wanted. My chances of making a sportcoat he liked were less than fifty to one. I decided to give up the project. With the same forty hours, I could make all the pajamas and polo shirts we would need for a whole year and save even more money. When my children were young and I was home more, sewing was my pleasure. Now, cheap labor in foreign countries has brought clothing prices down. I am out more and can shop for ready-made clothing and often pay less than I would to purchase fabric and notions. However, I still save money by making skirts and often my own dressy blouses. (They last longer and fit better.)

Near New. Not everything has to be new. My neighbor, who cleans swimming pools as a side job in the spring, buys his jeans and tee-shirts at the thrift store because the cleaning solution ruins them so quickly. When my daughters were hired to fry hamburgers, I took them to the thrift store to find black or white pants, whichever was required for their job. They would rather spend their money on school clothes than for a "required" work uniform. We were choosy, and the girls looked nice even when our investment was minimal.

Hand-me-downs can be great extenders for the family clothing dollar. In our day these are socially acceptable in many circles and most kids put up with them as a part of life. The home manager who is willing to give these clothes some special attention in the beginning can save a great deal of money (50 to 75 percent) and still keep the family looking nice. Children's attitudes toward their clothes are largely based on yours, and yours will be good if you have a master plan. Be choosy is the first, all-important rule. Learn to manage or you will soon be overrun with seconds. When going through a stack of clothing, whether it has been given to you or you are at a rummage sale, ask yourself the following questions: Does it fit my child's taste? Will it go with his or her other clothing? Do I need something to match it and, if so, how much time or money will I have to invest to find it? If you chose to keep it, fix it up immediately. Be prepared to replace a zipper, secure buttons, soak in water with a powdered-bleach solution or use several shots of spot remover. By learning how to do a few simple alterations, the "almost" right can be perfect. Take time to fix the garment and the "used" clues will be eliminated. And when you receive a compliment, there's no need to mention where it came from. Just say thanks and smile, giving yourself credit for a good job.

Keep them moving. With the ins and outs of hand-me-downs, there should be more outs than ins. We tend to become emotionally attached to our possessions, and it is hard to let go. Passing them on to be used by others decreases the pain of parting. Sharing with others or giving to a charity offers you many rewards: savings of natural resources, money, space, and time, plus you get that good, warm feeling of being generous—not to mention a little tax credit. Again, to smooth out the process of passing it on, set aside a spot (corner, box, shelf) to collect items to be moved out until you are passing a recycle center or until your neighbor holds a garage sale or until you get a call from your favorite charity. Gradually remove things from the mainstream of living when you notice they are no longer needed or useful.

ORGANIZING YOUR HOUSEHOLD PAPERS

29. Managing the Paper Chase

Paper is a hard thing to organize. It is not like food, which is stored in one or two specific rooms. There are many different types of paper with various values. Paper comes to us from everywhere—church, work, school, and play. Some of it is legally or financially important. Part of it has sentimental value. Some is needed for reference. An organized home will have several mini-systems to facilitate paper control. This chapter will give suggestions for organizing each of these mini-systems: financial, legal, kitchen/recipes, keepsakes, newspapers, magazines, reminders, and business. Basically, you need to make a distinct place for each different kind of paper. Incoming paper needs to be categorized and put where it belongs as soon as possible or it can overtake you. As soon as you can, invest in some good, sturdy office supplies that will help facilitate the paperwork: tape dispenser, three-hole punch, stapler (not the ninety-nine-cent variety), paper clips, file folders, pencil sharpener, etc.

FINANCIAL

Setting up a personal-business financial filing system takes surprisingly little time and, once it's in place, it takes just a few minutes a month to keep up to date. The most important principle here is to get all your personal financial papers together. It might be a cupboard in the kitchen, a dresser drawer, an expandable folder, or a shoe box. If you are lucky, you may have a desk or even a file cabinet, but they are not essential. If you leave important things on the coffee table or behind the toaster and expect them to be there a month later, they might not be. When you start looking and can't find them, you will get angry. It will be difficult to pay the bills, balance the checkbook, or prepare your income tax return. You will run the risk of making costly mistakes. If you do nothing more than gather these papers together, you will be better off.

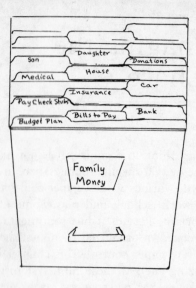

The next organizational step in is to refine your paper system by subdividing your personal papers into smaller categories so you can find them even faster. You will have four kinds of papers:

1. **Irreplaceable or hard-to-replace papers** that should be kept in a safe-deposit box, vault, or safe. Make photocopies to keep in your home files. A brochure entitled "Keeping Family/Household Records; What to Discard," (#638F) put out by the United States Department of Agriculture, recommends that important, hard-to-replace papers such as birth and marriage certificates, stocks, and bonds (see chart on page 195) be kept in a safe-deposit box at a bank. You need to remember that a safe-deposit box is sealed upon the owner's death if the estate is valued at more than $300,000, and that nothing in it can be released until the IRS has inventoried the box and often not until the estate is settled. Other options may be a good home-safe or a commercial vault.

2. **Action papers** (pending papers) that you are still working with and that you will need to act upon soon such as your budget plan and bills to be paid. Designate the first file folder in your financial file for pending papers or use a slot in your stacking trays or vertical dividers to keep action papers handy (as shown on page 201). Slip in such papers as bills, mail order and credit card invoices, statements, and premiums. When the

necessary action is completed, file the paper in the appropriate topic folder as explained in the next paragraph.

3. **Papers on hold** that you need to keep for future reference or proof. Do not mix "action" and "holding" papers together. Some people use a set of twelve file folders, one for each month, in which to gather data on accounts paid until the year is over and the tax return is filed. Then they throw out the information that does not pertain to any entry on the tax form, and use the monthly folders again for the next year. Another method is to file these money papers according to subject. If you are just beginning, start with the twenty-two categories for the "holding" file listed in the chart on page 196. Write one heading at the top of each file folder, sort your non-pending financial papers into them, and see how it works for you.

4. **Dead storage** is for active file papers over three years old. Keep copies of income tax returns and related information that substantiates entries on the tax-return for seven years.

The reward comes whenever you need to look for important papers (especially at tax time) and everything that you need is there. You can cut the work down from days to just hours and it only requires a few minutes each month. After you finish filling out your tax return, make a copy for yourself, wrap all related receipts, canceled checks that prove entries, etc., with a large rubber band and put everything in a large manilla envelope. Label the envelope clearly and store it at the back of your other "papers on hold" for three years. Hopefully you will not need to refer to it again until next year, but should you be audited, you will be glad to have the right papers all together. After three years, move the packet to "dead storage" in an out-of-the-way place until seven years have gone by.

Home Filing Checklist

Safe Deposit Box

Birth certificates	Deeds
Citizenship papers	Titles to automobiles
Marriage certificates	Household inventory
Adoption papers	Veteran's papers
Divorce decrees	Bonds and stock certificates
Death certificates	Important contracts

Home Filing Checklist *(cont.)*

Action Papers
  Budget plan
  Bills to be paid
  Letters to be answered

Papers on Hold (Personal
    Financial File)
  Paid-bill receipts
  Current bank statements
  Current canceled checks
  Paycheck stubs
  Car license and car tax data
  Log of car service and
    repairs
  Medical: paid-bills, mileage,
    prescription drugs, dental,
    eye care, etc.
  Health benefit information
  Credit card information
    (with account numbers)
  Donation records: charity,
    church, public TV or radio
  Employment records,
    resumé
  Insurance policies
  Copies of wills
  Family health records
  Folder for each child to hold
    pending papers about
    summer camp, receipts for
    school yearbooks or
    athletic passes,
    achievement progress in
    scouts, education
    information, transcripts,
    etc.

Appliance manuals and
    warranties
Receipts of items under
    warranty
Household improvements
    (deductible from equity-
    profit at the time of sale)
Inventory of safe-deposit
    box
Loan statements and
    payment books
Memberships, licenses
    requiring yearly renewal
    (such as dog licenses)
Income tax working papers

Dead Storage
All active file papers over
    three years old

Items to Discard
Salary statements (after
    checking on W-2 form at
    year end)
Canceled checks for cash or
    nondeductible expenses or
    nonwarranty items
Expired warranties
Coupons after expiration
    date
Other records no longer
    needed

GUARANTEES, WARRANTIES, AND
SALES RECEIPTS FOR VALUABLE ITEMS

At my house, we found we needed more than one file folder to contain the instruction manuals and receipts for items under warranty. We purchased an expandable folder with alphabetical tabs and placed it in the financial file drawer because the sealed sides of the folder keep the smaller pieces of paper from getting lost. Sales receipts are stapled to accompanying data and filed under a logical topic (lawnmower is behind the letter L, blow dryer goes under B, etc.). We have to be on guard to capture that receipt or it will be misplaced or tossed out. Basic principles of organization apply here because we had to first designate a place and second be very strict about getting the right papers to the right spot. Besides guarantees and proofs of purchase, we put operating instructions in the expandable file folder for all our appliances and machinery—lawn mower, hot-water heater, dishwasher, disposal. This is where you will find instructions for setting our various digital watches. We keep the serial numbers for the computer, vacuum, bicycles, and other equipment in this file. When something goes wrong with an item or it is stolen, we know where to look for any related information. For the past five years, we have saved at least $300 each year on replacements and repairs by keeping track of these receipts and service orders. Just think how much income we would have to make before we had $300 to spend. Subtract taxes, FICA, and work-related expenses and you can see that we would have to earn almost

$600 before we could go out and purchase those items again. Thus, to save money in this way is worth much more than gross income, and all it takes is a little time to get organized and self-control to keep track of those little pieces of paper.

HOME INVENTORY

Many home managers neglect to compile a household inventory to be put in their safe-deposit box. If there is a fire or burglary in your home, this record will help you remember what has to be replaced and how much each item was worth. An inventory also must show that you need to increase your insurance because your possessions are worth more than you thought. The best way to go about compiling a household inventory is to start with a sheet of paper for each room in the house or apartment. (A verbal description dictated into a tape-recorder may be faster than writing if you are in a hurry.) Start at one point in the room and go all the way around, listing *everything*. Don't forget cameras, watches, bicycles, tools, slide and movie projectors, car, TVs, and stereos. For each item, list what it is, how much it cost, when it was purchased, the model number, brand name, and a general description. Taking pictures of the rooms and your household possessions will make identification or replacement easier. Arrange expensive collections, silver, and jewelry separately and take closeup pictures. Keep one copy of your inventory at home and put a second in your safe-deposit box or give it to a trusted family member or friend.

As suggested by Pat Dorff, make a quick inventory of your wallet by laying the contents (credit cards, etc.) out on a quick-copy machine and take a picture. Then turn them over and copy the other side. You will be glad to have such information available if your wallet is lost or stolen.

HANDLING THE MAIL

How do you handle the mail? Open it first, then handle it only once if possible. By refining a distribution system, you can easily know where each piece of mail will go and thus cut down on the paper shuffle.

When you open a piece of mail that is a bill and that doesn't require immediate action, put it in the action file for pending bills. Always open bills. There may be some items that need immediate attention or someone else may have used your phone or credit card. Put magazines in the place you have agreed upon.

Newsletters from church, professional organizations, schools, clubs, etc. need to be processed as soon as possible. As discussed in chapter 3, a calendar will help you eliminate much of this paper if you write down meetings, appointments, and commitments as they come to your attention. Include details of who, where, when, what you need to take, and directions for getting there. Toss out the paper if you dare. If not, put it in your pending box (wait-and-see) until the uncertainty is past.

Naturally, there are some pieces of mail you can toss out without hesitation—things you have no interest in, you won't need, or that can easily be replaced. Get it out of your life immediately so you don't have to deal with it again.

Some of the incoming mail will be addressed to other household members. Do you leave it on the stereo? Ask each individual where his or her incoming mail should go. Where will they see it? Some may want it on their bed or desk, or perhaps they have an "in" box.

The hardest pieces of mail to deal with are those that need to be reviewed by several people. This is the kind of clutter that stays on the table for days until someone takes control and can get everyone to say they have read it and make a decision. This is where you need a more sophisticated form of inner communication. Some families take care of such business at dinner or breakfast. Others have a formal family planning meeting.

Another option is to use a variety of written messages to advance the paper race. As each interested person finishes with a letter, magazine, or newsletter, a simple notation is made in the corner, "finished, B.Mc," and it is passed on to the next person. If business offices use memos to save time and reinforce a message, why not use this strategy at home? Self-sticking notes are fun and effective. Attach one: "Bob, you may find this article interesting," or, "I can't go to this meeting at school, can you?" (Initial and note date). Newsletters from work, church, and school keep circulating because no one is sure if everyone has read it. Notes can prevent this. Another technique is to use the refrigerator or a bulletin board by the phone for pending items and immediate reminders. The kitchen seems to be a favorite spot. If it works, use it.

Handling the mail is more than bringing it in from the mailbox. It involves everything from junk to legally binding documents. It pays to set up a simple program for sorting, delivery, and taking action.

PERSONAL PAPERS

In addition to all the above paper centers, I need a system for cycling the paper I use as home manager and also for my professional career. After I sort the mail to all the above places, I take my mail to my desk and finish. Experiment and find an efficient system that works for you. I like a set of stackable trays, labeled as shown below (vertical dividers will also work). One of the secrets is to label each slot and divide your papers into two categories: (1) wait-and-see and (2) needs-action. So often these papers are tossed together in the same basket and action papers get hidden under unimportant items. (Papers you want to keep for future reference should be filed in long-term storage, as explained in the next chapter.)

Action: Papers that you need to act on soon—business correspondence, letters to answer, tickets to buy, registrations, appointments to make, etc. You need to set aside a regular time to take care of paperwork. I answer mail once a week, clearing out this box on Monday. Any matter that needs immediate attention I leave on the top of my desk to be resolved today. The to-do list can expedite this.

Pending: This is the wait-and-see box. Things you can't throw away yet—carbons for catalog orders that haven't yet arrived, the notice for a seminar you may want to attend, letters, tickets, wedding invitations (after date is put on calendar), etc. You ought to go through this at least once a month. Most items will then be thrown out, and some will be filed in long-term storage.

Catalogs: These are the catalogs that come in the mail that you may want to order from, but you haven't yet decided, or don't yet have money. If you don't usually buy, don't save them. But if you just like to dream through them in a spare moment, give those catalogs a place. Go through the box or shelf every couple of months and weed it out.

To read: Things you want to read when you have time. Grab one before leaving for a waiting room or the airport.

To be copied: Information you need to have copied next time you go to the print shop. Not everyone will need this tray.

To be filed: Paper to be filed in the cabinet during the next session or when you have a minute or two.

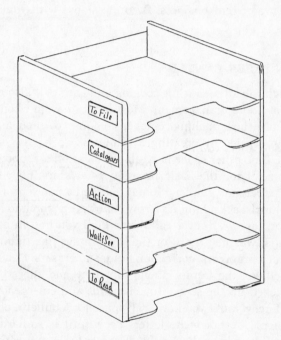

One woman said, "I didn't truly feel like an adult until I had my own desk." She was right, a desk gives a feeling of identity. If there is much paper in your life, whether from family, volunteer job, or business, you need a place to centralize it. A wooden door positioned on two file cabinets gives a terrific work surface. Like other work areas, give thought to how you arrange supplies and equipment for a natural motion flow. The top of the desk is "prime," and things placed there should be used often. Keep do-dads, novelties, and souvenirs at a minimum. A clean desk is a sign of style rather than control, but it certainly helps to keep the center surface free from everything except your immediate activity. Just like the kitchen, working one job on top of another just makes a bigger mess and opens the project to confusion. You will want to personalize your area so you can lay your hand on information when it is needed and use equipment such as the calculator and typewriter with natural ease.

Designate a specific time to take care of paperwork. One woman does it every Sunday evening. Businesspeople know they have to make regular appointments with themselves to go through mail and take care of that business. Be professional with your private life.

KITCHEN PAPER CENTER

Even though the kitchen is for cooking and eating, it also becomes the heart of home management. Most homes have a phone in the kitchen. If it is the launching center from home to school and work, make things easier by creating a mini-desk to be the center of operations. If no other space is available, clear off a cupboard shelf and organize it for the basic necessities—scissors, pencils, tape, glue, note paper, and stapler. I found I needed a marker for putting names on lunch sacks. I put up a row of hooks on which to hang the scissors and tape. A drawer caddy, the kind you find in hardware departments, was just right for the little things like thumb tacks, chalk, paper reinforcers, correction fluid, and erasers. I made room on the shelf for the family phone directory and the city phone books. I tacked up the school lunch menus and emergency phone numbers. Lucky you if you have wall space for a bulletin board.

Some people do not write letters because it is so hard to find everything. If you do not have another center for letter writing, keep a simple supply of stamps, notes, stationery and envelopes in the kitchen.

BUSINESS AT HOME

If you take any of your office work home with you or collect professional materials, you need a corner, file drawer or desk to be their "home." Your needs will depend on the amount of paper involved. Operators of home-based businesses will find it almost mandatory to physically divide home from business whether with a partition, curtain, or walls. The divider is a clue to signal when you are "on" or "off" duty, and it helps separate supplies and equipment. One of the hardest adjustments for those who work out of their home is turning their back on the opposite environment and not to be haunted by the dirty dishes when at work, or vice-versa. Train yourself to think of it as though you are switching the TV dial from one channel to another. Depending on the type of business they run, some people claim it helps to have two separate phone lines—work and personal. One man said he turns on the answering machine so phone interruptions do not invade his private time.

We live in an era of information, and much of it is on paper. If your business or profession requires a great amount of paper and your success depends on being able to find it, you need a good filing system. You don't have to have expensive file cabinets, but you need a top-notch system and you need self-discipline to keep it up. Don't let the paper pile up; keep it moving. Categorize it and cross-reference if necessary so you can find it. (More about "how" in the next chapter.)

FAMILY ADDRESS FILE

Create for yourself a mini-file for addresses and phone number. As with other things, it doesn't matter so much which system you choose as that you have a program. I have two different systems. A pop-open directory is by the phone in the kitchen for the numbers used most often by my family. This mini-desk also has a spot for the school directory and the city phone book. I keep addresses in a 3x5 file box at my desk where I write letters. (People who have worked in an office atmosphere will probably prefer a rolodex address file, but for me it takes up too much space.) Each card has one family name and address and is put in the box in alphabetical order. There is room on the card for address changes and notes on dates of correspondence.

In an effort to simplify, one family combined the phone and address files into one rolo-dex and used colored cards for a quick visual identification. White cards are for family friends. Yellow cards are for stores, businesses or repair shops, often having the business card stapled to it. Phone numbers for the children's play-mates are written on blue cards. Color coding made it easier to find the listing.

KEEPSAKES

What did you do with the photos from the last birthday party? The best place for them is in an album, but if you don't have time to arrange them, label a box for each member of your family and line them up on a shelf. Take a second to label and date the pictures and then slip them into the appropriate boxes. One mother said her twins were angry but then delighted with her when she presented them with a big box on their eighteenth birthday and told them to create their own babybooks. Whenever they did something cute or got a tooth or a shot, she wrote a quick note and slipped it in their keepsake box. I think that mother deserves a lot of credit for keeping it together and having everything dated. She had an organized system—of sorts. She kept the yearly school pictures, certificates, and notes of accomplishment. When the children were emotionally attached to a special project like the topographical map they made out of salt-dough clay, she took a picture for memory's sake because eventually they would have to part with it. The same with finger-painting and chalk drawings.

Ideally, a person should update scrapbooks once a year, but the years seem to slip by without getting to it. One father said he files the family pictures he hasn't mounted yet and/or the leftover photos chronologically, starting a new file folder each January. (Store negatives and photos in separate locations.)

NEWSPAPERS

Where does the newspaper go when you bring it in? After you have read it? Do you have reason to keep them? One family takes the paper to the breakfast nook. Family members read it during the break times throughout the day. After dinner it goes directly to the trash. At another home, the manager neatly stacks the papers on the bottom shelf of the lamp table until trash day. The secret is to keep newspapers moving.

MAGAZINES

Now we are getting into a difficult area. We pay for our magazines and subconsciously think that if they are in color they are more valuable. We start reading a new issue, turn down the pages of articles we would like to come back to, and then set the magazine down. Most of us never get back to it. The magazine is put in a pile that we will "get to someday." If we ever do go back to it, we have to go through it again and reread the articles to see if they are worth keeping for future reference. This backtracking is much slower than the rate at which the new ones arrive. We get behind but, having hope, we save them. The question is, If you had those articles all clipped and filed, would you use them? If the answer is yes, then I suggest you set up a good filing system and work on it at least two hours a week until you are caught up. (Details in the next chapter.) But if you have gotten by without that material so far, maybe you really don't need it. Then I would recommend the clean sweep approach. Get rid of all the old stuff and start fresh. You might even cut down the number of magazines you take.

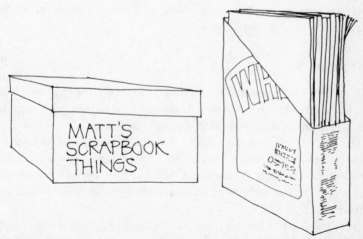

Agree on a place for new magazines so those who are interested can review them while they are still current. For some, magazines go on the living room coffee table; for others they go in the bathroom or on a nightstand. Have a program of cycling out old magazines. One plan is to take out an old one when a new one arrives. If you like to save recipes, ideas, or articles, signal their importance with a pencil or turn down the corner of the page or, even better, clip them out immediately. Put it in the pile to be filed or, better yet, file it while it's in hand. Don't let old magazines stay around too long. If the magazines are any good when you finish, send them to school for the kids to use or take them to your favorite waiting room (barber, doctor, vet).

What about the magazines you use for your job or hobby? Is it better for you to leave them whole or cut them apart and file according to subject? Most magazine companies put out an index at the end of the year, in which case get a binder to hold issues and the index together. Cold cereal boxes make good containers for magazines or, if you have money for this project, you can buy plastic magazine boxes at office supply centers. Certain children's magazines that we have subscribed to over the years have seasonal stories and projects, and they are easier to use if I categorize them by month rather than by year. This means that all the June magazines from 1964 to now are together in one box. When I am looking for children's crafts for Father's Day, I check the June–July box. The object is to create a way to keep information from magazines and *find it*. Otherwise, it is of no value to you. It only takes up space and gets in your way. File articles by topic or, if you opt not to cut up the magazines, file by year or season.

RECIPES

You either collect recipes or you don't. If you do, it's fun to go from stacked-and-piled to organized. It is one of the easiest home territories to organize, and the rewards are immediate.

The first step is to make a major division between recipes that are favorite, tried 'n' true, and those that look good and you want to try when you have time. The second step is to file recipes so you can find what you want quickly and easily. This will simplify life for the busy person.

Get a file box at least 5 × 7 or larger in which to put the recipes you have tried and liked, and that you want to keep. These are the ones worth keeping handy and preserving. Buy a pack of cards and a set of dividers to fit the box. You can glue or staple a recipe (handwritten note, clipping from the newspaper or magazine) to these larger cards without recopying. Often there is even room to include the picture so you know what it is supposed to look like. Attaching it to a card signals its importance and gives it substance to outlive splashes and smudges. You may even go so far as to cover it with clear contact paper. On the card, always write the date and where or from whom the recipe came. Only one recipe to a card. This will probably be the smaller of your two files.

For those recipes that fall into the "interesting" category, start a one-step system. Decide on something that will hold a regular 8½ × 11-inch piece of paper: a three-ring notebook or an expandable file folder or traditional file-folders (in which case you need a box, drawer, or vertical stand to hold the folders). You can easily drop new recipes into any of these. Use dividers to define general categories: salads, beverages, breads, sauces, main dishes, vegetables, cookies, desserts, miscellaneous.

Now, with your two mini-file systems, just open that recipe drawer, pick out one, and make the big decision: Is it tried 'n' liked or hope-to-use? Then slip it behind a topic heading and go on to the next. No need to recopy. A stapler will be helpful to attach small papers to something larger so they don't get lost. You may take time to go through all your recipes now or you might do ten a day or spend one hour each week. But from now on, file each new recipe as you get it so you don't get further behind. Remember to reevaluate whether you still want to keep a particular recipe. Some people collect recipes as a hobby and actually treasure them, others collect them just because they don't have time to weed through the stack and make decisions.

Suppose your favorite recipe for applesauce cake is in a book. Just make a note of such and slip the note in your file as a memory jogger when going through the dessert file. After you have tried a recipe, even if it is printed in a book, jot a note next to the recipe as to whether or not you liked it, how many servings it actually made, and any future suggestions.

As a reminder to try a new recipe, put it with your grocery list to prompt you to buy the ingredients. If you don't use it within several weeks, perhaps you'll never use that recipe, so consider tossing it out. Otherwise, put it in your reference file.

Several years ago I made a New Year's resolution to recopy a few favorite recipes from cookbooks so I could move most of the cookbooks to secondary storage. Throughout the year, each time I pulled out a book to use an old favorite recipe, I took time right then to copy it. Surprisingly, I kept that resolution, but even more of a surprise was that I used only about fifty recipes and I cleared off a whole shelf in the process. Now I have those books I refer to often, my tried 'n' true box, and my notebook with hope-to recipes on one shelf in the cupboard and the others are available, should I still want them, but out of everyday traffic. Another part of the strategy to simplify was to keep only one recipe of each variety of food. By this stage in my life I have established my favorites, so why keep ten recipes for banana bread? Thus, I kept only one recipe for brownies, one for chocolate chip cookies, one for lasagne, dinner rolls, etc. I have reaped the reward of simplifying this little corner of my house for several years.

30. File It and Find It!

W hen I was installed as PTA president at the elementary school, I was handed a big box. There were newsletters from the county PTSA, magazines from the national PTA, instructions for putting on a book fair, receipts from the carnival, and a thousand advertisements for various fund-raisers. The first thing I did was get out a handful of file folders and start separating the information into categories. I put all the advertisements in a folder at the back and labeled a folder for each current project and activity at the front. Much of the material that I inherited was outdated, and I tossed it out. It took about an hour to give order to that box, but from that time on I could find the by-laws or budget in a minute.

DIVIDE AND SUBDIVIDE

Start a filing system for the paper you want to keep permanently. The first step is to divide your papers into major categories. You don't want your counted-cross-stitch patterns mixed in with your grandmother's life story and the insurance policies. Just having it separated by major subjects is an important step. Then, if you have need for more efficiency, subdivide those categories by using file-folders with subject headings. For further refinement you can cross-reference and index your material.

Your hobby, business, volunteer, and church reponsibilities all affect what type of paper you keep. Filing is just a title for "standing paper on end" instead of stacking it in space-consuming piles. Give order to your paper. The first step is to separate it into large general categories. Even if it just stays in a labeled box or drawer or part of a drawer, it is better than being scattered all over the house. Later, you can refine and divide those papers into subheadings with file folders if you choose. A file cabinet is wonderful, but not necessary. Buy folders at a stationery supply center or discount paper store or ask a business friend to save used folders.

LESS IS MORE

Let the trash basket be your best friend. Ask yourself, If I get rid of this and should need it again, what would happen? Could I get it? Do I already have similar information? Will it pay for the space it takes? Give careful thought to what you are saving. Some organizers suggest putting an "x" at the top of a paper each time it is used. When it's time to clean out the files you can tell what material has been used and which has not. Do most of your eliminating before you put it into storage.

If your paper was in such a mess that you couldn't find what you wanted before you started, and you haven't yet used it, would you use it even if it were filed? How often will you really need it? The first time I tried to start a filing system when my children were little, I had a room in the basement stacked with magazines of every kind. New material came in the front door faster than I could process it into the files. I spent hours rereading magazines to discern the material worth saving. I finally realized I needed a fresh start. In all the years I had collected Christmas ideas from magazines, I had used only one. Rather, the ideas I used came from my friends, adult education classes, and the craft store. The Sunday School lesson book always had more than I had time to teach the children, so I never needed extra. The magazines were interesting, uplifting, or entertaining at the time, but I didn't need to keep that information forever. I got brave and took it all to the dump. What a relief. From then on, I kept less than one item per week and filed it immediately.

FILE

If you are ready for the next step, subdivide your materials into subjects and put it into file folders. Write the title at the top of the folder and alphabetize. As you pick up one paper to be filed, determine the subject title and write it at the top of the paper for easy refiling. To save rereading articles, write the subject on the page the first time you read the magazine article. Some material is easy to categorize—like arts and crafts—because it deals with concrete objects. You run into problems when you try to separate abstract concepts like "goals," "positive attitude," and "happiness." If you file an article under one you may forget where you put it a few

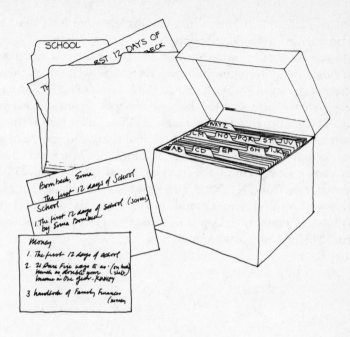

months later. Cross-referencing will help. Should you want to file the article, "The First 12 Days of School," will it go behind "school," "money," or "author" (Erma Bombeck)? In a few months, you may not remember which subject you filed it under and you will have to hunt for the article. If you have more than fifty file folders in one general category, you will probably need to use a cross-reference index with your filing system, which will also solve the problem of the lost article. As each article is slipped behind a subject in the file folder, write it down on a 4 × 6 index card, indicating on the right side which subject it is filed under. If there is a possibility of it going under another subject, title, or author, make another card. Keep all the cards in alphabetical order in a small index box. You can make more than one entry on a card (see the illustration).

Use notes on slips of paper as memory joggers between subjects and for books or items too large for the file. Suppose you have a file for teddy bear patterns and pictures. But you also have a book with some bear patterns in it. Slip a note in the folder that says "See stuffed animal book by Cheri Williams on shelf in office." You can also cross-reference between folders with notes in respective folders. The stuffed animal file may have a note in it that reads, "Also see file for bears and puppets."

If you have other areas of your life under control and you are seriously ready to refine your paper systems, write to St. Martin's Press for a copy of Pat Dorff's book, *File . . . Don't Pile!*™ She has the best system I have seen for the serious paper organizer. Last year I set a personal goal to reorganize all my files. I used Pat's system and I am very happy with my ability to find things, to put them away, and to maneuver the mountains of information that have become my career. Order Pat's book from St. Martin Press, Inc., 175 Fifth Avenue, New York, NY 10010, $6.95 plus $1.50 shipping. The starter kit with colored folders and index pages is available from Willowtree Press, Inc., Dept LK, 8108 33rd Place, N., Minneapolis, MN 55427, $9.50, postage paid.

ORGANIZING KIDS

31. Getting Your Kids to Work at Home: the Dos and Don'ts

Moms and dads assume kids should help with household chores, children feel they should help, but why isn't it happening? There are two reasons: (1) children don't work for the same reasons as adults—i.e., out of guilt or commitment—and (2) parents forget to use basic management strategies at home. This chapter contains a list of suggestions that will increase your chances of getting your kids to help. As a general rule, children will not "notice" when things need to be done. They need to be trained. Most of them have not matured to the point where they work for intrinsic (inner) reasons. An organized system of instruction with parental support will greatly increase your chances of getting your kids to work at home. Child power is a terrific resource, especially for busy parents. There are five advantages for the child who learns to work at home:

1. A child's conscience tells him or her "you ought to help out"; therefore, helping at home satisfies the conscience and removes guilt feelings for not doing his or her fair share. In a recent survey I found that 97 percent of the kids honestly feel they should work at home.

2. Working at home helps prepare a child for adult life. Skills are learned that will be helpful in maintaining everyday necessities and allowing the young adult to concentrate on other things when alone in the big world. Knowledge of skills gives freedom. Consider the advantages of the young person who has a choice of five meals he or she can fix in an hour's time. Think of the time and money saved when they know how to care for their own clothing. It amazes me that parents will spend between $16,000 and $40,000 to send a child through college to prepare him or her for a career, but that they do not take the time to teach them skills for basic home survival. Only the very, very wealthy will not have to wash dishes, cook, dust,

vacuum, wash clothes, or change oil in the car. Both boys and girls should learn these skills. Skills foster independence. Children who have learned responsibility through nurturing are better off than those who learn independence from neglect, and a loving parent can create these learning opportunities.

3. Children learn to appreciate work done for them when they take part in it.
4. Children feel like they belong when they have something to do. Children need to be needed.
5. Working together can increase the child's time with a parent. The average adult time spent with a child over ten in our country is 14½ minutes a day—not counting watching TV together. Twelve of those minutes are for instruction or reprimands. Children need our presence, and working together can be valuable.

There are at least four advantages to the parent when the kids help out:

1. Part of the workload is lifted. In the beginning, it takes as much time for you to train and supervise as if you did the work yourself, but the payoff does come, eventually, and the child can work independently.
2. The anger of being used is removed.
3. There is more time for fun things, including doing things with the child and doing things for yourself.
4. You feel successful if your child is helpful. Your success as a parent is not dependent on the choices your child makes, but when he or she does make good choices, it makes you feel better.

One time when I was doing a TV interview for the book Sue Monson and I wrote, *401 Ways to Get Your Kids to Work at Home,* a woman in the audience jumped up and challenged, "I work! I don't have time for all those games. I don't have time to make chore charts." If you work, if you are busy, you need to stop and take a few minutes to organize other members of the household. You can't possibly do it all yourself. Step back and take a good look. Take time to sharpen the saw—don't keep trying to cut down the forest alone. If you take a few minutes to organize your helpers and to create a system to move the work along, you can turn part of the load over to them, and you won't have to work so hard. There are a few basic dos and don'ts for getting kids to help.

Don't expect young children to do things by themselves. Just because the child is old enough to bend over and pick up something, parents assume the child can do it over and over again on command. This is not true. To pick up and keep at it takes a high level of maturity. Young children need adult presence when they work, even until age six, seven, or eight.

Do not expect the child to manage too many things. We put all of a child's toys, books, clothes, a bed with fancy bedspread, two blankets, and two sheets into the room; toss in a brother or sister; and expect them to keep control. For their size and maturity, it is like me telling you to go clean K-Mart, and you have exactly one hour to do it. K-Mart has many managers to keep track of their inventory. Cut down the quantity of items to a manageable number for the age and maturity of your child. Rotate some things if necessary. Arrange the room to make it as easy as possible for the child to pick up and clean. Consider hooks instead of hangers, and a low clothes rod; divide toys, putting them in bags, shoe boxes, or dishpans. When children are having trouble keeping a room neat, it is a sign they need adult guidance to clean and organize and to cut back the quantity of things to take care of.

Do let the young child help when he is willing. If the child wants to help, find a way. If not, substitute a way the child can feel helpful. (Yes, often it does take longer.) For example, if he or she wants to help wash the dishes, get rid of the dangerous knives and glasses, put a rug under the sink, pull up a stool, and let your child feel like he or she is doing adult things.

Make it as easy as possible for the child to do the job. Consider the physical arrangement of equipment and supplies. For example, in the McCullough home, all drinking glasses and dinnerware are below the counter in the cupboard right next to the dishwasher so the children can empty the dishwasher and set the table without adult assistance. A short broom may be helpful for the child. Prepare a maid-basket for the child to carry safe cleaning products to the work area. (Fill squirt bottles only one-quarter full for more control of how much solution the kids use.) Put up a few labels or signs to show where items belong or to give simple work instructions. If it's okay for the manager of a shoe store to label the shelves in the stockroom, why not in your home business?

Don't give one child authority over another unnecessarily. It seems to work in the movies, but in real life it just causes resentment and opens the way for arguments. Usually, because of their immaturity, children with authority use it incorrectly; they use power and force rather than love and patience. Unnecessary authority can cause lifelong family resentments. Do not make an older child responsible for a younger child's messes; it is not fair. Assume those for yourself.

Offer incentives to help children reach work goals. Success in reaching those goals builds an inner reward system. Eventually, maybe, they will keep their room clean because they like the room better that way. That is an intrinsic reward and requires maturity. Don't be afraid to express appreciation. Many of us speak out only when a job is unfinished. The average ratio of positive to negative expressions to a child over ten in the U.S. home is one to twenty-two. You can easily beat this national average. Sometimes it requires a behavior strategy for yourself. Promise yourself a hot fudge sundae if you can say fifty nice things to your kids today.

Do write down the chore assignment. Do not leave it to the child's memory, opening the avenue to misunderstanding. Use some sort of chore chart (as explained in the next chapter). Rotate assignments for fairness and experience. Writing out specifications for cleaning, as discussed on pages 91–93, can help the worker know exactly what constitutes a daily or weekly cleaning.

Do give advance warning of work times, especially with teenagers. Give notice, when possible, of upcoming work periods and keep them short and successful. Children who know what is expected of them at home have the opportunity to plan and organize their time and energies—the beginnings of being a responsible adult. Hold family meetings and let your children be a part of the decisions that affect them. Learning to talk things out and solve mechanical or relationship problems within the security of a family is a wonderful beginning for negotiating skills needed in the worldly market place.

Don't make work sessions too long. Kids are more likely to work energetically if they know there is an end. We all hesitate to enter a tunnel when we can't see the end for fear of not getting out. A twenty-item pickup has an end, likewise setting the timer for fifteen minutes. You might state "two hours work in the yard" or offer a

written list and promise that when everything is crossed off, the day is theirs. Don't add to the list. Kids catch on quickly, and this tactic will squelch the child's motivation.

Never redo a child's work if you have approved it. They will think you do not value their efforts and they won't try so hard next time. Inspect work, not every time, but occasionally. Your children will know when you think a job is important and when it's just to keep them busy. If you value their efforts, check it occasionally. You are checking not only to see if they followed through, but also to be able to express appreciation. Kids will work harder for approval than to avoid punishment, so be sure to issue plenty of kind words. These are the same types of guidelines you would be taught if you were teaching management training in a business office.

Teach your children how to do the job. Don't assume it will be totally learned by watching. Show, teach, train. Suppose we are going to teach an eight-year-old boy how to clean the bathroom. We need to be conscious of: (1) breaking the job down into learnable parts; (2) teaching the proper method; and (3) the physical arrangement of the equipment and supplies. We won't give him responsibility for the whole room at first. Let's try three tasks: scouring the sink, polishing the chrome, and shaking the rug. In thinking of the supplies: Is the cleanser where he can get it? What do you want him to use—a cloth or a sponge? (Hopefully not the face cloth.) Is it where he can get to it? Can he reach the sink? Maybe a step stool is needed. When it comes to teaching the proper method, you will give instructions about how much cleanser to use, and mention getting the dirt around the drain and not putting the cleanser on the chrome handles. When he shakes the rug, teach him to roll it up and carefully carry it outside so that the bits of dirt don't fall off on the way. In the beginning, new training takes lots of show and tell. Go with the child every time he cleans the bathroom, gradually decreasing your physical help but continuing the encouragement until he has mastered it at least three times by himself. Encouragement and positive comments need to be made often at this stage. "The handle shines so nicely, you can even see yourself in it." You are involving not only the child's physical senses in the job, but also his emotions. In this case, good emotions are shaping work attitudes: "It looks so nice. I can do it, and I like it better this way." But remember, even as an adult, it is easier to cook crêpes for the first time after you have seen someone else cook them. (Psychologists call this modeling.) When the child gets older, such time and detail aren't needed, he or she can work alone for longer periods of time.

Keep it fair and share. It is just as unfair to expect your children to do all the housework as it is for kids to expect the parents to do it all. Occasionally, even under the guise of getting paid for it, parents overburden their children. One day, as I finished a conversation at the store, the woman concluded, "If I hang around here a little longer, my daughter [14] will have dinner ready when I get home." My heart sank. I remember when I was a teen and occasionally had to babysit all day; time dragged, and it was so boring. This mother, who was working out of need, was expecting too much of her teenage daughter. This young girl tended her five brothers and sisters four days a week, all day long. She was to supervise the kids in cleaning the house, and they were to fix dinner. Although motivated by need, Mom was also using work as an excuse to have kids do things she didn't like to do herself. Don't turn responsibility into abuse. Don't push your children into burnout before they have acquired an adult maturity to work full time.

Try to **set a regular time every day for work** to help establish consistency in getting it done. All children try to get out of work; it's part of the game. Children will balk, cry, throw tantrums, and try to escape if they think there's a chance they won't have to do something today, especially in the beginning. Some days their help will be needed more than others. Holidays, Sundays, and birthdays might be exceptions—after all, you like time off, too. Decide what you expect and then stick to it, but at the same time be flexible and understanding. As your child matures, you will need to adjust the chores, change your requirements, and include him or her in your decision making. In the beginning it will take more time to teach your children to work than if you simply did it yourself; but eventually you will reap the rewards.

Be consistent and flexible at the same time. Be firm enough to give a basic structure to your life, but don't expect perfection. "Perfect can be the enemy of good." Do not expect that your children will do their chores or clean their bedrooms to perfection every day. You are not building a robot; you want children who can think and plan and care. You probably do not have every bit of your life caught up every day. As in your own life, perhaps visiting a sick friend is more important today than painting the porch. Guide them in making good choices. Then teach them how to make it up or recover from that postponement. That is flexibility, putting people above things.

Be consistent in what you say and always follow through. Should you tell a child to take out the trash, you have to be willing to insist and to issue punishment if necessary. Don't say something unless you mean it. After the system is organized, after you have followed all these wonderful guidelines, your children may still put off or try to "get out" of work. Don't fall into the highs and lows between fanaticism and leniency. Children want to know exactly what to expect. Be consistent in follow-up, expecting a little help from every child every day. Be flexible by being understanding and willing to make adjustments when appropriate.

32. Chore Charts: the Master Tactic

The majority of parents tell their children which jobs to do. This puts the parent in the telling position and the child in the doing category. If the parent doesn't tell, the child doesn't do. Trying to get your kids to work with the "telling-system" is like putting only one gallon of gas in the car at a time. You can't get very far before you have to do it again. What you need is a system to facilitate work. Like filling the gas tank to full, you can get a lot more distance from an effort. No matter what the age, the written word can help carry the message. Age, however, greatly affects your expectations and tactics. With children, you must tailor expectation to the age and to the child.

Basically, when discussing work at home, I like to divide children into three categories: preschool, middle years from five to twelve, and teens. The main objective in parenting a preschool child is to build confidence, teach obedience, and begin personal responsibility for grooming and property. By the time a child is ready to start school, he or she is also ready to take on a regular, daily household task. Not a big job, but enough to teach consistency. As they grow through the elementary years, you can teach various household skills, increasing ability and responsibility. Your best workers are between the ages of five and twelve. When children become teenagers, you need to change your expectations and training strategies. During the teenage years, a child is aggressively preparing for adult life by learning important social, physical, and career skills. Homework from school assignments begins to demand more and more time. You don't want the child to abandon all responsibility at home, but at the same time it may no longer be appropriate to expect him or her to vacuum the living room every day. It's a time for the children to learn priorities, to set one "have-to" above the other. Instead of feeling like a failure when my teens didn't make their bed every day, I learned to recognize the things they did do to help—babysitting, cooking, or running errands. Their ability to help when it is time to clean the house for a special occasion, keep up the yard, fix the car, or nail on the roofing is wonderful. Once I changed my expectations and training strategies to meet their stage of life, my grade as Mother went back up to B+.

PRESCHOOLERS

The preschooler should learn a basic routine of everyday neatness (making the bed and picking up toys) and of everyday personal grooming (bathing, brushing teeth, and combing hair). You can reinforce these basic habits with charts or a simple finger exercise that will aid consistency. Preschoolers cannot work alone. Young parents, sincere in their desire to teach responsibility, often ask how they can get a three-year-old to clean the bedroom. You can't. You must go with the child and help. Telling or threatening is not enough. Little children make bigger messes than they can clean up; cleaning up is an advanced skill. Young children are easily overwhelmed. Don't feel disheartened if they still need help even into the ninth year with the bedroom cleanup. When preschoolers want to help, encourage them by finding ways to let them feel helpful even though it may mean the job takes longer. If they want to scrub the floor with you, get them a little bucket and brush. The reward for this patience will come when the children are older and you want them to work.

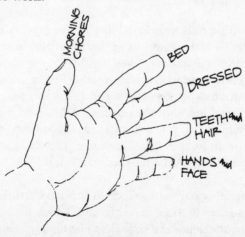

Finger play for chores. Teach young children to take on their own responsibilities with a simple reminder system on their fingers. Instead of demanding "Is your bed made?" the parent can ask "What do you have left to do this morning?" and the child can answer "I still have to make my bed and brush my teeth." You have put the responsibility where it belongs. What makes this work? The parent teaches the child a sequence of key words or phrases, one for each finger. Each day, the child runs through the list on his fingers, and does each task. When he is finished, he is ready to go to school or play.

To begin this in your home, list the tasks that need to be done every day. Pick a noun as the key word to represent each job. Arrange them in sequential order. Brushing teeth and washing would come before dressing, to prevent splashes on clean clothes. The sequence at the McCullough home is as follows: (1) hands and face, (2) teeth and hair, (3) dressed (including shoes and socks), (4) bed (including room pickup, (5) morning chore or, for the youngest children, toy pickup. (Each number coincides with a finger.) We don't include eating breakfast on the list because our children don't have any problem in that area. You must use the same set of words for all children in the family or you will get mixed up. Added responsibility can be attached to the symbol word as the child matures, but don't try to change the key words. For instance, under the third category—bed—a four-year-old may not be asked to vacuum his bedroom, but by the time he is seven vacuuming might be included.

When the child needs a reminder, the parent says, "What have you finished so far?" After going over the sequence of words on his fingers, the child will answer, "Well, I've swept the stairs and made my bed, but I still have to brush my teeth." She has been the one to recognize what must be done and she is on the way to self-rule. This memory device of learning the morning routine on fingers can be started as young as two years or as late as seven years, and will last a lifetime. The most important point is that the child learns to answer the questions "Am I finished yet?" and "What must I still do?"

I started teaching our youngest child this personal responsibility at age two and a half. After dressing him, I took his hand in mine and pointed to one finger at a time (like playing piggy-wiggy). "Now, Mattie, let's see what you have to do. Hands and face?" (He nods yes whether he had done it or not.) "Teeth and hair? No? Let's do that now." When he was finished brushing, I started again. "Dressed? Yes, and your shoes are on too! Good! Bed?" (Nods yes) "No, I'll help you. Toys? We'll pick up your books after we have made the bed." Taking him by the hand, I lead him through each activity. Naturally he was too young in the beginning to make his bed, but he stood next to me while I did it. In a year or so, he was climbing up at the head of the bed and I tossed the quilts to him. He would smooth out the covers and slither out. Then he would put the pillow on and cover it up. When we were finished, I gave him a hug and told him he could play because all his chores were finished. He left feeling grown up and successful. A bonus for me was fewer interruptions because all his needs were taken care of first. I would have eventually had to do all those things anyway, but putting them into a routine that we practiced over and over, day after day helped. I can't claim that by the time he was ten that he never left the house without brushing his teeth, but at least this early training helped. After this basic hygiene and chore are taken care of, a child is free from parental promptings. He feels rewarded for his accomplishment because he is ready for whatever opportunity arises. He can go for a ride to the store or play with a friend. Once the basic responsibilities are established, parents can be more than just reminders. They can be leaders instead of herders.

When the child gets a little older, try a "star chart" to reinforce the daily routine. Such a progress chart is especially helpful at the

STAR CHART

NANCY

Morning Routine
before 10 A.M.

	M	T	W	TH	F	S	S
Teeth	★				★		
Hair	★	★	★	★	★		
Bed	★	★	★		★		
Dressed	★	★	★	★	★		
Toys	★		★		★		

beginning of summer, when kids are tempted to let down totally without the structure of school routine. A chart that assigns jobs is very helpful, but this chart also gives a place to check off or even attach a star or a smiley-face as an intrinsic reward: "I've done something." The child's self-esteem rises because he or she has a sense of control over the little tasks of his or her own life.

GRADE-SCHOOL CHILDREN

About the time children start school, they are ready for some short regular household chores, but they need an organized pattern. A chore chart is the answer. It is a fantastic tool for pulling the parent away from telling, making the chart the regulator and getting some of the emotion out of the situation. It creates a feeling of fairness and indicates what is expected. A chore chart is simple to make; it takes about fifteen minutes. As you are looking for chores to assign, choose areas of the home that need daily care, chores that children can master, and chores that require less than ten minutes of their time. At my house, morning chores are the minimum maintenance for the main living area. Evening chores center on dinner preparation (set table, take out trash, sweep kitchen floor, empty dishwasher). Assign the chore so the child can take care of it independently without waiting for someone else to do another part of it first. Suppose I assigned Bob and Tim to do dishes—Bob to wash and Tim to dry. Tim cannot do his part until Bob has washed, opening up the door for arguments. Whenever possible, make assignments so one child does not have to depend on another.

Many years ago I designed a simple vertical chore chart to assign jobs to my children. The kids seemed to like it because they knew ahead of time exactly what their chore would be and that everyone would eventually have the same tasks. The chore chart has two rows of pockets; the first one for morning and the second for evening. Every Monday morning the chores are rotated. Although every child gets a chance in each area, the expectations change according to the age, keeping the requirements within the child's ability. For example: When the five-year-old cleans the bathroom, he only scours the sink, shakes the rug, and puts away the combs and toothbrushes. When the fifteen-year-old cleans the bathroom, she is expected to clean the bathtub, the toilet, and the floor, also.

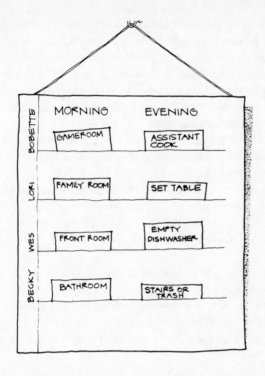

This system stimulated independence because the children did not have to "wait" for me to organize the day. They knew what their assignments were for the whole week and could take care of them even when I was not home. It also made it easy for my husband to step in and follow through when it was his turn to be "on duty." Can you visualize the advantages of the written program over a verbal system to the working and/or single parent? The "show" can go on without you having to be there to direct every motion. Sometimes the child will feel like the distribution of chores is more fair if the adult's jobs are also shown on the chart.

There are hundreds of possibilities for the chore charts to fit varying family circumstances. For a one- or two-child family, where the children have equal ability, perhaps a circular chore chart would be best. Naturally you will not expect them to do all ten jobs the McCullough kids do, because there are fewer of them; but then your child should get to do more then empty the trash and wash dishes. This chart will rotate jobs and give variety and create a sense of fairness. To adapt the chart to fit the quantity of work and number of workers, simply make a different number of pie-shaped divisions on the chart. Two circles, one smaller than the other, are cut from heavy paper. Use a thumbtack or brad in the center so the circles can be turned separately. Put it where it can be easily seen—probably in the kitchen. An example of a circular chart is shown with dishwashing assignments on page 73.

After you have decided on a system, your children will need to be trained. Make the learning time pleasant. Use lots of specific praise and positive reinforcement. Explain the job, divide the work into small portions, even write down the basic daily and weekly requirements for the room and post them. In the beginning, complete the job together, acknowledging the child's efforts. Gradually withdraw your help until the child can succeed alone, but continue the kind words.

Set a time for work. Having a regular daily work time helps establish consistency in getting it done. Some days it is only a light pickup, other days it is a thorough cleaning, but require your child to put in a little time at home every day. Guide your child into good work habits by setting time limits. Chores must be completed

before 8:00 A.M. on school days and 10:00 A.M on Saturday, is one family's rule. Another one says grooming and chores must be finished before TV, school, or other projects. For years my rule was that morning chores be done before school. They did them most of the time. If your kids do not do their work, what will happen? I do not like the suggestion that you go get the child at school. I do not believe that getting a child out of school will teach the intended lesson. Neither do I feel it is a good idea to stand at the door waiting for the children to come home and then pounce on them with your list of things to do. To children, school is work and they need some recovery time. If you are after them all the time, they will begin to avoid you. Define "on" times and "off" times for training your housework apprentices. At my house, 5:00 P.M. is "on" time, and I insist they get everything caught up before dinner or any other privilege. Before school was "on" time for elementary kids. Saturday morning was an "on" time. If you are always "on," trying to get them to do their work and do it right, then you don't have time to have fun with them or build relationships or help in other ways.

Should I call a child back to redo a job? Yes, if there has been a specific rule infraction or the child has tried to slip by with a halfway job. But remember: If you are always calling your child from play or interrupting an activity, you may one day wonder why your child doesn't stick to one project for more than a few minutes. One mother found it worked, especially in the summer, to keep a list of things that needed attention and brought it forth at the next work time, giving the children some "free time" between work sessions.

TEENAGE CHILDREN

Be ready for changes. I remember the day my eighth-grade daughter decided to curl her hair (always straight before). And I said to myself, Which is more important, the chore or her learning personal care? Later my children began leaving for school as early as 5:45 A.M. What would happen to them if I insisted they empty the dishwasher before leaving? We learned to allow for new phases, and had to change our policy. From then on, children who did not, or could not, do their morning chore before school simply did it at 5:00 P.M. with the evening chore. Later, when those older children got jobs at McDonalds and Wendy's, more changes were made. We switched to a two-hour, Saturday morning cleaning schedule, where they thoroughly cleaned their own bedrooms and assigned-chore room, leaving the weekdays to concentrate on school home-work. It is important to adjust the jobs, change the requirements, and include the children in the decision-making process as they mature. This is the direction I felt best for my family. Another family insisted the child get up ten minutes earlier every morning and still do daily chores. Many teens will get discouraged if the burden is too heavy. I remember one set of parents who did not allow their children to take part in activities outside of home or church and gave them monumental yard and household chores to do at home. They will probably turn out to be responsible adults because they have learned to work hard. But my philosophy is that when children are young it is important for them to learn how to do chores at home and to build a reasonable amount of consistency. When they get older, the lesson is in juggling personal and home chores and practicing priority decisions. Yes, parents need to monitor a child's tendency to use school or work as an excuse not to do anything at all. At the same time, they need more space for learning new skills and preparing for adult life.

If I judged my success by whether or not my teenagers had their rooms clean every day or whether they did a daily chore, I would flunk. But when they were older, they served the family in ways other than setting the table every day as they did when they were nine years old. At this time, our sixteen-year-old son attends two schools (high school and vocational school). He has double the homework and half the time in which to do it. He does not do a daily ten-minute household chore now as he once did when he was in grade school, but he washes dishes once a week, keeps his room quite well, and picks up his younger sister at school every day. He supervises (the old name was babysit) about once a week and helps occasionally with yard and car projects. What more can I expect? Should I make him do his own washing and ironing? Every parent must judge for himself. As I have thought it out, this young man is not wasting his time. He is not sloppy or abusive. If he gets good grades, he may earn a scholarship. So, I don't mind ironing his shirts for a while.

33. Kid's Bedrooms: Organize and Conquer!

The first thing to do to help the child organize the bedroom is to evaluate the reasons for the problem. Take thirty minutes, sit down on the floor of your child's bedroom, and brainstorm causes and possible solutions. Take paper and pencil. Think and think. Look at the room from the child's point of view (that's why you are sitting on the floor). Look for ways to (1) cut down the number of items to a manageable number for the age and maturity of the child; (2) arrange the room to make it as easy as possible for the child to pick up and clean; and (3) make a definite place for everything in the room. We know children like a clean bedroom, because as soon as it is clean, they want to play there. Although they like the good feeling of living in a tidy atmosphere, they are too immature to organize the room so it is easy to keep clean. Adult assistance is needed to organize, teach, motivate, and insist that a minimal level of cleanliness is maintained.

Cut down the quantity. Consider the structure and physical limitations of the room. Is there too much in the room? If four boys are sharing one room, it is obvious that each cannot have as many things as a single child. The parents need to give extra help when several children share a room. Can some part of the child's belongings be stored elsewhere? Even better, does he need all of these things? Maybe getting rid of part of them would simplify his life. It is sometimes easier for parents to keep their bedroom in order because they have other places to store treasures and equipment, but the child may be keeping all of his belongings in his bedroom. The answer may be to help the child store part of his things and discard others. After they have been out of sight for a while, the child may realize he or she really doesn't need them and they could be disposed of at a garage sale or given to Santa's Workshop. Asking yourself these questions can be very enlightening, as one mother whose twenty-three-year-old daughter had an atrocious-looking bedroom discovered. She had enough stuff crammed in her bedroom to fill a house: wedding gifts from a broken marriage and all the equipment for a new baby. Once the problem was identified, they worked together to box most of the things and store them for a time.

Check the room arrangement. While you are sitting on the floor, look for ways the room could be arranged to make it easier for a little person to manage. What about the bed? Are the sheets, blankets, and bedspread the ones adults think cute or pretty but that are hard for a child to make up neatly? Perhaps a bedspread with cording or a design marking the side edges of the bed is better. Some children have a washable quilt that can easily be pulled up rather than having a top sheet and bedspread with it. The child can make it by just crawling up to the head of the bed, pulling up the cover, smoothing it, and slithering out. Some kids go through a stage where they like to have a sleeping bag rolled out on top of the mattress. If you have enough room, pull the bed away from the wall for easier bed making. As you are looking for ways to make the room arrangement easier, ask yourself if the child can hang up his own coat and robe. If not, maybe hooks would be easier than hangers. You will probably want a wastebasket and some kind of clothes hamper in the room. Shoe boxes in the drawers make terrific dividers to separate socks, underwear, belts, and pajamas. As you sit on the floor evaluating, you will come up with some good ideas, but don't forget to ask for the child's opinion, too.

Create a place for everything. A child needs adult help doing this. Go through the following list and check items that still need a resting place. Obviously, the two-year-old's bedroom will not look the same as the seventh grader's, and the child in a room by himself will have more flexibility than children sharing a room. Make these suggestions fit your circumstances.

- Is there a place to sleep that the child can manage?
- Is there a place to hang clean clothes? Normally, this would be a closet, Is the rod low enough? If you don't want to alter the closet permanently, hang a broomstick from the higher rod with a chain (or buy a tension pole). The younger child can pull

clean clothes off the hangers, but it is a more advanced skill to put them back on the hanger. At this age, they are usually wearing clothes for one day and then putting them in the laundry, but what about the robe, coats, and sweaters that don't need washing every time? Perhaps hooks would be best. Some children don't need a closet because everything they wear can be folded.

- Is there a place for out-of-season clothes and clothes not yet grown into? So often, because the child doesn't need all the closet space for current clothes, we hang the out-of-size and out-of-season clothes in the closet, too, but this can create managing problems. Try storing these extra clothes in sturdy boxes in the top of the closet or some other area such as the laundry room.

- Is there a place for shoes and boots? Will their place be under the bed? Is there an unused space at the end of the closet that could be fitted with little shelves?

- Is there a place for dirty clothes? You would be surprised how many adults expect children to carry their dirty clothes to a central clothes hamper in the bathroom or downstairs to the wash area every time they undress. Try putting a container like a hamper, large wastebasket, or box decorated with wallpaper conveniently *in* the room or closet. Putting a lid on the hamper decreases the chances of its use by eighty percent. No lid, please.

- Is there a place for folded clean clothes? Usually the child has drawers for clean clothing. What about hats and gloves? Perhaps you could use a dishpan on the closet shelf or hooks by the back door. Some families have a special tradition of putting the pajamas away under the bed pillow or in a zip-up stuffed animal. Help the child remember the system of organization by labeling the shelves and drawers. If you have many children in your family, organize every chest-of-drawers the same way: top drawer, treasures; second drawer, pajamas, undies, and socks; third drawer, pants and shirts; and fourth drawer, junk. One more tip: Make it an annual tradition to clean out the drawers by using wrapping paper from the child's birthday gifts to line the drawers. The excitement of Christmas can motivate children to clean closets and drawers. "Let's make room for new gifts. Can we give some of these to a family in need?"

There comes a time when building a relationship with your child is more important than a clean bedroom.

- Is there a place for trash?
- Is there a place for books? Perhaps the answer is a headboard with a bookcase, a set of brick-and-board shelves, or shelves in the closet. If you want your child to read for pleasure, have a place for books in the bedroom.
- Is there a table or desk? It is especially important, after the child has entered middle school or junior high, to have a place to do homework; however, it could be done in another designated area in your home. I have pondered the remark made by one father when he described his daughter's turnabout toward doing her homework. "We gave her grandpa's desk with all the drawers and cubbyholes. She just loved to be there, loved to organize everything just so." The way you arrange things can make it easier to succeed at school.
- Is there a place to put school books and pending homework?
- Is there a place to keep finished papers and reports? Maybe a real file cabinet or just a box in the closet is the solution.

- Is there a place to keep toys? Toy boxes are the worst for storage. Every time the children want a toy, they dump out the whole box and make a big mess. Games and puzzles with many pieces seldom get back together after being dumped in a toy box. Consider separating the games, building blocks, and puzzles into net bags like the ones grapefruit come in, or boxes. Put a large rubber band or elastic band around the box in case it should be dropped, so everything doesn't come out. Hooks in the closet, a pegged mug rack, pegboard, or game tree (like coat tree but with hooks all the way down the pole) can hold these toy bags. For stuffed animals, a suspension pole could be set in the corner, holes drilled for hooks, and each animal, with a ribbon around its neck, hung from the pole. Or hang a long, two-inch-diameter wooden dowel from a plant hook in the ceiling. Screw cup hooks into the wood on which to hang toys. Secure a fishing net between two walls in a corner of the room as a hammock for dolls and animals.

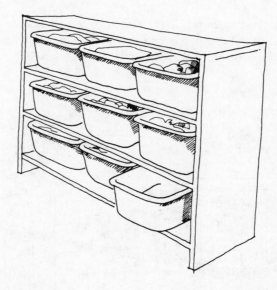

Children play better with toys that are divided into small containers rather than dumped all together in a large toy box.

- Is there a place for display? Little things that are important to the child need a place, especially if there are younger siblings who might ruin them. A simple knickknack shelf or a corner shelf might be the solution. If there are more items than will fit neatly, rotate them. A bulletin board or clothesline along a wall could be used to display posters or art papers and reports. There are pictures and mementos that are nice to put in a scrapbook to be shown to future generations. Guide the child in knowing what to keep. Old blurred, or dark pictures have no value. Label pictures with names and dates for easy identification.
- Are there other organizing tools? A mirror, calendar, pencil holder, and pin cushion help a child get organized.

Even though this is quite a long list, you will find it helpful in keeping things to a minimum so the child can manage them. Don't let hobbies and collections get out of hand. It may be necessary to reevaluate your holiday and birthday giving or have a discussion with generous grandparents.

Set limits. The places you have created to put things can carry an automatic limit. A dishpan or box for school papers is a limit. When the box is full, the child goes through the papers, keeping only the

favorites. After storing things for a while, some of the initial emotional attachment is gone and it is easier for the child to discard them. A bulletin board and knickknack shelf are limiting. When they are full, some of the papers or hobby items need to be stored. Another important limit to consider is clothing. How often do you wash? Every other day? Once a week? Count the number of days between washings, add a couple, and that could be the limit on how many clothes are out. So often we keep two or three times that many clothes in the closet or chest and it complicates efforts to keep the room clean. Involve your child in learning to manage a few things well. Limits also need to be set for toys. Think about a rotation system, leaving some of the toys out on the toy shelves for a week or two and then rotating them with different ones that have been stored elsewhere. Young children find old toys carry the freshness of new toys after they have been out of sight for a time. With fewer children per family, toys that last longer, cuter things available, and with prosperous grandparents, the number of toys per child has increased. Kids have more toys, and parents live in smaller quarters. Add those two together and without management you have a mess. After a hard planning session, stand back and evaluate where toys are used. Sometimes it is better to rearrange and store toys in the places where the children use them. If you find yourself picking up a mountain every day, your children may be playing a game called "dump everything" instead of playing with them as they were designed. It is time to cut back the available inventory and rotate.

Add something new from time to time to spark interest. Give a new set of bed sheets or a bucket of paint for a birthday present. Just changing the furniture around when cleaning gives a feeling of newness and motivates the child to keep it clean for a few days. The child's bedroom doesn't have to have everything new or look like a magazine picture, but a change gives a boost to the child.

Do not throw away a child's belongings without asking. One mother said she has her seven-year-old son's bedroom under control. While he is at school, she goes through his things, throws out the junk, and cleans the room. To do it *for* him is only a temporary solution. It is not teaching him the skill of managing his possessions; he needs practice at letting go of things, at making those decisions. Heaven forbid if that child hasn't changed before he gets to be an adult, and worse yet, if he should marry one of my daughters! Children must learn the delicate art of turning loose. Set limits in the child's bedroom and then guide him in making decisions about what to keep and what to eliminate. After the child is five or six, include him in throw-out decisions.

34. The Messy Bedroom: Solving a Special Problem

A messy bedroom for several days signals a need for parental help in cleaning and organizing. Most children have trouble keeping their bedrooms tidy long after Mom and Dad think they should do it by themselves. At about five or six years of age, when children start school and become involved with friends, they start collecting more things and they begin having trouble keeping the room clean. At this time, there is a great need for parental consistency. The parent need not insist that the child's room get forty-nine points on a fifty-point inspection every day; that isn't fair. Besides, very few adults live that way. Help the child do a little minimum maintenance (pickup, make bed, take care of paper and clothing) every day, and give the room a good cleaning with vacuuming and dusting, once a week, maybe on Friday afternoon or Saturday morning. This tidy atmosphere is good for the child's self-image. It says, "I am neat," and it pleases Mom and Dad. This attitude doesn't bind the child to always having to keep everything put away. There is much more to life than a clean house, but a tidy atmosphere frees one to do other things, especially fun, creative things.

Help the child learn a cleaning system, and divide the cleaning into small categories so that he can *see* progress. Have them start with the biggest thing first—the bed. After it is made, both parent and child can see progress—a measurable improvement. One possibility is to have the child pick up all clothes, then paper, then toys. Another program is to pick things up by color: everything red, then yellow, then green, and blue. Take the attitude that this is the child's room and he or she is the manager, and the parent is the "consultant" when cleaning. Don't be afraid to ask "What would you like me to do?" but leave the child in charge. (It's okay to refuse to work if the child is not working, however.) What you are after is independence, a young person who can see for himself or herself what needs to be done. Continue guiding the child with the cleaning. It is more rewarding to do a complete pickup *before* digging into the other cleaning procedures like dusting, going through the closet, or straightening drawers. The theory is to work from outside to inside areas. Encouragement and positive statements are the major reasons for the parent being with the child during cleaning periods. Point out progress by comparing with the beginning mess, but don't turn the room into a moral issue. Convert them into appreciating and desiring neatness without a lot of blame and putdowns.

Don't be after the child—"Go clean your room; go clean that room"—or the child will become insensitive to your instructions. If you say to do something, you must be willing to take the time to see that it is done. If the child is holding back, try gently easing into the job by asking him or her to pick up twenty things. This small bite may be more acceptable, the end is within reach. As parent, you can hope that motivation to do a little more will be kindled by the time the first quota is reached. If not, at least the room is a little better. One little boy put ten things away during each commercial break during Saturday morning cartoons so he didn't have to give up any TV time.

The two-point method of putting clothes in a hamper can be lots of fun and can motivate your children to pick up. If the garment goes into the hamper when tossed, you get two points. Instead of starting Lecture Number 38 about clothes all over the floor, just pick up a sock, toss it in the hamper, and announce, "I get two points." Most children join in very quickly and want points, too, and try to make the basket. From then on, the parent keeps score as the child picks up the clothes. (Sometimes this game works on husbands.)

When a child says, "I don't have to clean my room, I like it this way, and it is mine." Firmly answer, "This room belongs to your parents. We will gladly let you use it, but we have the right to set the cleanliness level." It is better to help the child organize the bedroom and periodically help clean it so the child learns to like order and gains the skills to keep it that way. If the parent cleans the room for the child all of the time, the child will learn to like it clean, but expect someone else to do it. If we leave the care of the room totally to the child without teaching skills, he or she may decide not to clean it and learn to accept it messy—which is hard on the child's self-image and future spouse or roommates. We know children enjoy cleanliness because as soon as an area is clean, they rush there to work or play. The challenge is teaching the persistence to keep it tidy.

What about the child who is very, very messy? It might help to know that only one child in five is born neat; the rest have to be taught. It will take patience and, even though it sounds discouraging, you may have to stick with helping the child clean for many years, not just weeks. When trouble comes, consider if you can ease the problem by asking yourself these questions: Is this an organizational problem? Are there more things in the room than the child can manage? Is the child lacking in skill? Is this a relationship problem? Am I giving positive verbal rewards? Maybe it is the adult attention the child is seeking, and this is the child's way of getting it. Carefully look for the possible cause of the problem because it could be that the room is only a symptom of other problems. During their teens, most children go through a stage when they rebel about keeping up the bedroom. At this time the relationship is more important than the bedroom, and you need to back off the room issue and rebuild the relationship. If they have kept their rooms fairly neat during previous years, chances are they will return to neatness.

BEDROOM INSPECTION CHART

0-5	Bed made	_____
0-5	Under bed clear	_____
0-5	Drawers neat (2 checked)	_____
0-5	Drawers and closet door closed	_____
0-5	Closet floor straight	_____
0-5	Clothes neatly hung up	_____
0-5	Desk top and nightstand tidy	_____
0-5	Room dusted	_____
0-5	Floor picked up	_____
0-5	Floor vacuumed or swept	_____
50 possible points		_____ your score

For children six and over, we found it helpful to draw up an inspection chart (see page 241), listing what we expected to be done in the room and putting a rating on each category. At the time I initiated this check sheet it helped my children understand what I was looking for. I required that they pass by forty-five points out of a possible fifty by noon on Saturday. (Then I saw to it that they succeeded by offering help if they wanted it.) After the room was clean, there was a family activity or personal free time as an incentive. To keep it fair, the children had the right to inspect my bedroom. We used this device for only six weeks, and occasionally as a reminder, but it taught a lesson. One father said he made "under bed" worth fifteen points to overcome his daughter's weakness to stash everything there.

Children have different levels of motivation for keeping a room clean. As parents, we hope that when they have their own homes, the inner motivation will increase because it is *theirs*. For now, you can help them organize their bedrooms and succeed in keeping them clean. If it comes to a clash, remember: The child's membership in your family is more important then a clean bedroom. If you can, give them the skills of housekeeping now so that when or if they want to, they can employ them. If they absolutely refuse, close the door. This problem is even more difficult with stepchildren because you don't have the same recognized authority. You can get most children to keep an acceptable level of housekeeping by using these strategies. Learning to keep the bedroom neat can be a giant time-saving habit, redeemable throughout life, but it takes patience and training from the parent.

35. How to Motivate with Incentives

I n the eighteen years or so that children live in your home, they will need lots of "carrots" to keep things interesting. Children need outside incentives to reach goals until they have the level of maturity to do something because they want to and because of the inner rewards they feel. You probably don't wash dishes because your spouse offers you a banana split. You do it because it needs to be done. You have also learned what happens if you don't do the dishes—it is harder later. Thus you motivate yourself for intrinsic (inner) reasons. Your object is to get your children to the point where they will make a bed, pick up a coat, and put away their dirty dishes. Rewards and consequences are stimuli from outside to be used while the child is developing the mature, intrinsic motivation and self-discipline from within. Working for rewards is a way children develop the habit of accomplishing goals. Don't use them every day or they become a bribery or payoff, but incentives can be used occasionally to perk up interest, when trying to change a behavior, at the onset of something new, or when the situation is slightly threatening. You will be doing lots of things with yor kids over the years. Get a double benefit from some of them by turning them into motivators.

The following is a brief collection of rewards and incentives. You have to keep working to find the right blend of rewards and incentives to keep your child motivated. Each child has his own secret combination; you have only to find the right set of numbers to unlock it.

A basic rule: Whenever possible, create a program that rewards the desirable action rather than emphasizing the wrong behavior. For example, one new stepfather explained his chore system of subtracting points from a beginning of one hundred for everything the children did not perform. The theory was okay; he was trying very hard, but we discussed reversing the plan so that points were added for each accomplishment. The children's response was wonderful. They were challenged to build a high score. (When I give a successful example, you must not assume that the tactic worked for ten years; like most others, it worked for a few weeks. But it helped program good work habits and draw attention to the desired outcome.)

POSITIVE REINFORCEMENT

Studies have proven that pointing out what's wrong doesn't bring about a change or even move as quickly toward the desired goal as does giving positive comments about the correct aspect of the job. A negative comment reinforces the wrong performance. A positive comment builds confidence and the desire to do better, to reap even more approval. You can never say too many nice things to your children. On the other hand, so often we become pressured and in our hurry trim the frills of appreciation. We begin to issue commands and make quick statements about what is wrong or unfinished. Remember that the negative, positive, conditional, or unconditional approval you give can determine how successfully the child will master a certain task.

Evaluation should be immediate. Do you remember studying many hours for a test and anxiously wondering about your score but not finding out the results until several weeks later? The child strives for recognition; the sooner it is given, the better. I do not suggest that you follow the child all day and comment on every little thing that is done. But toss out appreciation and recognition here and there when you think of it. If you are slow to remember, buy a golf counter and wear it on your wrist. Count the number of times you say nice things. See if you can increase your positive expressions, which in turn will do amazing things to your children. There is always something good that can be said; even if you can't compliment the job, you can express thanks for the effort. If the job does not pass inspection, criticize the job, not the child. Verbal rewards should be generously given to your apprentices. Children want attention, and if they do not get it from doing good things, they will do naughty things to get attention.

PRIVILEGES

Work before fun gives incentive to get it done. That's the reason for the family routine "chores done and bed made before TV or play." Anything the child wants to do can be an incentive, but remember, not every privilege should hang on a mountain of work because motivation can be squelched. There are parents who use the next pending privilege to bleed the turnip. Keep the incentive simple and reasonable. The objective in the beginning is to help this child succeed and, in the end, success is the greatest motivator.

Privileges depend on the age of the child. Time with parent is a wonderful reward—"When you are finished picking up the clothes on the floor, I will read you a story." Roller skating, swimming, a trip to the store with parent, or allowing a friend to spend the night—you have to know what will motivate your child.

LOVE NOTES

Love notes can be a lot of fun once you start looking for ways to write your appreciation. At the elementary school, the children get "Happy Grams" and "Glad Grams," which are sent home to tell the parents of good behavior or accomplishment. Use paper and pencil to note recognition at home once in a while. You may want to design your own certificates, ribbons, or coupons. Everyone loves to receive certificates. Get ideas from coloring books or newspaper ads. These could be awarded at family meetings, at dinner, or left propped against the bed pillow. If you are short on time, a pad of self-sticking notes gives you fifty chances to leave little messages of thanks here and there. Wouldn't it be fun to open the medicine cabinet and find a love note?

STICKERS

A fad among children now is to collect stickers. If your children like them, use them. When school is out, kids tend to feel free, free, free. One father made a simple check-off chart to use for the first three weeks after school was out to get the kids back into the habit of doing personal grooming and chores before they started to play or watch TV. The chart included bathe, make bed, eat, brush teeth, pick up bedroom, practice music, and do morning chore. When the child had everything checked off, Dad gave them a sticker if they finished before 10:00 A.M. It worked! They faithfully used the chart and sticker rewards for several weeks. School teachers make good use of stickers; parents can too. When you can find such a thing that motivates your child, it is wonderful.

FOOD

Food can be used as an immediate reward, especially to change behavior. Important principles for using this type of behavior modification are as follows: (1) work with only one behavior change at a time; (2) keep the task simple; (3) make the reward minimal; (4) be unwaveringly consistent in giving the reward only when all the desired behavior is performed. You have to be careful using food as a reward because you may teach bad eating habits, so don't go overboard. But food can be a powerful motivator. "Everybody who picks up and puts away twenty things gets a popsicle." You can't be handing out popsicles every time you want something done, but if you were ready to have a treat time, why not have a short pickup time first?

MONEY

Money can be used as an incentive but with the same cautions that are used in other areas: with moderation and simplicity, and without escalation. One new mother of a thirteen-year-old stepson said his habit of not flushing the toilet drove her crazy. They decided to motivate a better habit of charging fifty cents every time he forgot. It worked. Ideally, it would be better if he could have been rewarded when he remembered to flush, but with the evidence gone, how would you keep track? I do not recommend using the program of charging a child money for leaving things out or for "extra service" they cause. If you choose to do so, use it sparingly and keep it simple or the record keeping will defeat you.

If your child wants money for a special purchase, it can be enough motivation for her or him to try something new. When my son Wes and his friend wanted money to go bowling, I offered it to them for scrubbing the kitchen floor, a task they had never tried, but they did it and I paid them. Several years later, the friend's mother commented to me, "I am sure glad you taught my son how to scrub a floor—he does it for me all the time." I am glad it paid off for her, because my son hasn't done it since. Nonetheless, I know that he knows how.

You have to watch for the right incentives. Make life fun—for you and for the children. Kids usually work better for someone else than their parents because it seems new, different, and challenging. You can bring some of that excitement into your everyday life at home if you keep your eyes open. It needn't take a lot of time. Incentives and rewards are motivators from outside the child and can be anything the child likes—books, privileges, strokes, food, or money. A good incentive may be needed in the beginning of training or to perk up interest, but it can gradually be eliminated. Incentives start to become bribes, however, when the reward has to keep getting bigger to initiate the desired behavior. Incentives are not used all the time for everything. I do not walk around dishing out candies and ribbons and making up games all the time—that is just the frosting. Early in my parenting years, I set up a chore-chart system to make daily assignments. We have used that program for sixteen years. The initial investment was only thirty minutes. Most of home life is basic routine, and the chart carried those assignments. But we have also used incentives to teach new habits and give motivation from time to time. You will be doing lots of things over the years. With a little forethought, you can turn them into learning experiences.

LOGICAL CONSEQUENCES

No matter how exciting, how easy, fun, fair, and organized you have made the work, you must anticipate that your rules will be tested. And you should be ready by deciding how your policies will be enforced. The outside world is filled with consequences. If you don't pay the phone bill, your phone service will be disconnected. When you walk on thin ice, you will fall through. Whether you are an adult or child, if you stick a nail in an electric outlet you will get shocked. These are natural consequences. Using natural laws as discipline whenever possible is most effective. When there isn't a natural consequence or it is too dangerous, logical consequences can be structured by the parent. Examples: "If you misuse the car, you turn in your keys." "When you cause a spill, whether on purpose or by accident, you clean it up." Learning to use consequences takes effort, so think ahead. Generally there are two types of logical consequences:

1. If a privilege is misused, it is withdrawn for a short time (could be car, radio, telephone, allowance).
2. If damage is done, the consequence should be to undo the damage as much as possible.

Using logical consequences can be extremely effective and save much frustration and friction. Structuring safe consequences increases respect for rules. But the child needs to understand the association between the broken rule and the discipline. This type of discipline can keep you on the level of teacher rather than executioner. Taking time to determine the consequence may mean leaving the scene until you can logically think it through. Be sure you have a good feeling about the direction you are pursuing; you must feel that it is right for your family. Nothing works for everyone. If used with anger or for retaliation, you damage the child and your relationship. Before you act, ask yourself these questions about the consequence:

- Is it reasonable?
- Is it enforceable?
- Is it consistent with nurturing care?
- Is it too powerful?
- Is there anger, resentment, or retaliation associated with issuing this consequence?
- Is it clearly related to the offense?

You want this consequence to be a logical, rational result of the child's misjudgment, and you want the child to understand the connection between the two. Carefully think through the relationship between the behavior and the consequence. Most parents withdraw allowance or stop TV privileges for everything. If you are angry or mad, you are too likely to retaliate rather than correct. Keep it simple so the child can understand the association between the act and the consequence. Give a warning when possible: "You understand the consequence of this behavior will be . . ." And when it is over, take time to talk with the child to be sure he or she understands the connection between the action and the discipline.

I don't like rules that have no room for understanding. One parent said he would never take a book or lunch to a kid at school who forgot it because they need to learn to be responsible for themselves. This might help for a child who was continually irresponsible. But at my house, my kids are good at helping me when I'm in a spot, so when they make an occasional mistake, I don't mind helping *them* out if I can. We need to temper our reaction with understanding and reason. One teenager told me her family rule was that they never came home after 10:30 P.M. or they had to move out. "Not even for prom?" I asked. *"No."* That is why she was living here in Denver instead of at home in another state. If your rules are absolute, you may forfeit your opportunity to influence or help your children or bring them back into responsibility. Never say *never;* never say *always*.

Consequences need to be nurturing. I have never cared for the theory that if your children don't do their chores, you get them up at midnight to do them. It takes a parent with unwavering patience to pull off that kind of discipline. When I tried it, my children always got the wrong message. They did not think, "Next time I will take out the trash when Mom says." Their interpretation was of anger and hate. Good consequences teach self-control, fairness, and respect for rules. I have found it better to insist, for example, that chores be done before dinner, and then, if necessary, we postpone dinner until they are finished. In extreme cases, the child has to go to his or her room until he or she is ready to cooperate. Sometimes the child needs to sit in the corner (no longer than ten minutes) to get control of self or to think through the problem. Punishment can be too long. If it exceeds the child's tolerance it will only feed the child's sense of being unjustly treated and give rise to hostility. I recall the example of the parent who gave his son a ten-speed bike with instructions to "put it away every time." The first time the boy left it out, the father sold the bike. The boy learned hate rather than responsibility. Maturity comes in a slow progression of small steps. The parent's job is to guide the child into such responsibility. I think it would have been better to "impound" the bike for several days to withdraw the privilege and let him earn another chance. After a child has been disciplined, be sure he or she understands why and talk about possible alternatives next time. Then show that child you love him or her, not to buy forgiveness but to reassure the child that you still care for him or her.

36. Kids and Money

Y our child's future happiness depends more on *how* he or she manages money than on *how much* they have. In order to manage money, they must have some money to manage. Since there are many valuable experiences to learn before the child is old enough to earn money outside the home, how will you provide money to practice on?

1. Give it to them when they ask for it;
2. Allowances;
3. Make jobs available for which they can earn money at home.

Most families use a mixture of all three types of giving children money. Define your attitudes and positions about children and money. Do you have an overall plan? Probably, after your children are twelve, you won't want to give them all the money they want to encourage them to earn some money outside the home as part of their precareer lessons. Know that it will take some extra adult time to guide your children in good money management, but it works. The payoff comes when they can make it on their own.

PAYING JOBS AT HOME

Many parents prefer to offer jobs to their children for which they get paid. Money-making opportunities depend on where you live and the safety of your community. If you choose to have your children get their money by earning it, there are several guidelines that will make your efforts more successful.

Pay immediately. Young children can't wait for payment. Pay them as quickly as possible. They love to count up the coins as their funds increase. Even when your children get older, don't delay more than a week to settle up. If you must wait, keep some sort of written ledger that you can both see. Without the immediate payoff you risk two pitfalls: they lose incentive and/or you increase the hassle over mistakes. The child claims he or she did more than you can remember, etc. It takes maturity to wait for a paycheck. Kids love see-through banks. They like to have it where they can count it and measure progress if saving for a particular object. Guide them into keeping it in a safe place and, if there is very much, putting it in a bank account. Earnings can be paid either by the job ($1.00 for stacking the wood), or so much for every half-hour of labor. Paying by the job gives incentive to get it done quickly, and parents will not fret as much about "an hour's work for an hour's pay."

Distinguish between jobs for money and jobs that one does simply because of family membership. Being paid for making one's bed introduces a faulty premise because in the big world we generally do housekeeping without pay. Besides, when a child no longer needs money from you, he will assume he doesn't have to make his bed any more. Pay for things that you would normally do, or that you might pay someone else for. It has been my policy that if a child wants or needs to buy something and I feel it is worthy, I make a way for them to earn it. (Fold clothes, sweep garage, scrub railings, wipe windowsills, stack wood, water lawn.)

Teach them how. Even though you may be paying, you will need to take time to teach the child the specifications of the job. I remember once my son wanted to earn money and asked if he could wash the car. I told him, yes, as I would be glad to have someone else do it. He took the hose and squirted the car, then came in and asked for payment. I had assumed he knew all about the hot water and soap, scrubbing, rinsing, and wiping, but he did not. Children do not automatically know about work processes.

ALLOWANCES

The allowance system, especially in the early years, seems to be successful. The child can count on it, can begin to budget, plan, and make decisions. An allowance—perhaps so much per week or month for each year of age—would give enough money to experiment with for needs and wants. (Twenty-five cents per year of age for a seven-year-old would be $1.75.) That small amount certainly will not be all they need, but in the beginning it gives them enough to learn the value of various coins, how to make purchases, and how to evaluate them.

Pay on time. Have a specific time when allowance is given out, and be prompt in paying it. I prefer to give an allowance on Monday rather than Friday so the money that is intended for lunches is not spent the previous weekend on fun. Then, if they save some money through the week, they can have both. Have the correct currency values. To put children off—"I don't have the right change," becomes a problem and complicates your goal of teaching the child to budget. I go to the bank the first of the month, get the coins and bills I will need, put it into four envelopes, seal and put them away until each Monday when I get one out to pay allowances.

Be sensitive to the needs of your family. When our children were very young, we gave them a minimum allowance and then, for about seven years we did not. If the child wanted to buy something, we set up a special program. All of a sudden we noticed problems our children were having that an allowance would ease. For example, one teen, who had worked all summer and had learned to appreciate the independence of his own money, was having trouble making friends because of a move. Many of the other high school kids were going "out" to fast food places for lunch; eating in the school cafeteria was "square." As parents, we discussed possible solutions. It was not a good time to insist this child get an after-school job because he was already working at maximum and showing new efforts toward good grades. This boy was used to having some pocket money, and the change was driving him crazy (no money, seeking new peers, demands of homework). We decided the best thing for us to do was to give him a lunch allowance equivalent to what it would cost to eat at school. If he went out to eat several times, that was his choice, but it meant he would have to pack a lunch on alternate days. We also gave him a gas allowance for driving to and from school because it was impossible to walk or take the city bus from where we lived. Easing the pressure in this one area for a year helped him over the hump.

One of the advantages to an allowance is that the child can count on it regularly and practice budgeting and planning—two important lessons. Keeping allowances small enough so that they do not meet all growing wants as children enter teen years provides an incentive to earn more. If you have more than one child, it will help them to understand their position and a progression of privileges if you give allowance according to age. That is, a ten-year-old would get a little more than an eight-year-old. Kids need to know they are individuals, not just part of the pack where everyone is treated exactly the same, and this is one way to send that message.

Do not withhold allowance as punishment. Most children associate allowance with performing household work because that is the first thing parents withdraw as punishment when the child doesn't perform family duties. Unless you have made a contract with the child to pay for home chores, don't withhold allowance. For example, if the child doesn't carry out the trash, use a different penalty, perhaps no free play time until it's done. If you dock the child a quarter for not taking out the trash, he or she will naturally assume that the allowance is payment for such service. Action that would require allowance penalties would involve misuse of money for things like buying candy, gum, and pop (if that is against your rule), stealing or breaking someone else's property, or using the money in some manner you cannot condone. Theoretically, an allowance is to train the child to take over the management of his or her own affairs.

PROGRESSION OF RESPONSIBILITY

There is a sequence of steps when dealing with money just as there is in learning to read. The first steps are making a choice and then handling and understanding the mechanics of buying. Choosing the purchase, counting coins, facing the sales clerk, getting back change, and carrying the paper sack are primary lessons. Let them have opportunities to buy. Later, school will offer opportunities to practice more responsibility. When they carry the currency for school lunch, a field trip, or to buy a book, they are learning. There will be a few times that they lose their money. Help them find ways to carry it safely. Grandma used to tie coins in a cloth hankie or sew them in a lining. A zippered bag or sealed envelope with the child's name on it will help prevent loss as the child skips, tumbles, and

STEP-BY-STEP MONEY OVERVIEW

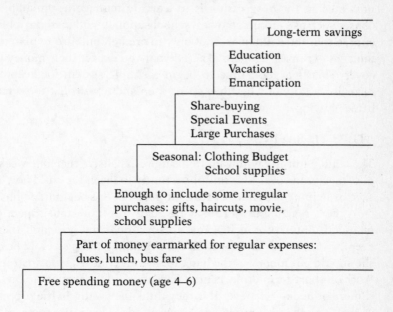

Long-term savings

Education
Vacation
Emancipation

Share-buying
Special Events
Large Purchases

Seasonal: Clothing Budget
School supplies

Enough to include some irregular
purchases: gifts, haircuts, movie,
school supplies

Part of money earmarked for regular expenses:
dues, lunch, bus fare

Free spending money (age 4–6)

runs to school. Help your child learn shopping strategies and how to evaluate purchases. For instance, your young child may decide to buy a little gadget that will break in a day. You might offer advice, but do not impose your opinion by force unless the object is dangerous or involves a request of your time that you cannot give. (No more gerbils.) The reason for having some money to spend is so the child can learn the consequences of making choices. The reason children need parents is for protection and guidance. Let them buy the dumb toy and see what happens. When the toy breaks, don't say, "I told you so," but help the child evaluate why and consider possible alternative purchases next time. When it is time for gift buying, don't just hand them a box of hankies and say, "I got this for you to give your Dad for Father's Day." Whenever possible, let child be a part of the choice and the actual purchase.

After the beginning free-spending stage, increase the money allotment to cover other expenses so the child can learn to allocate money for regular expenses such as dues, lunch or milk money, and bus fare. Children will do well to learn that all money is not for their pleasure—that there are responsibilities that go with it. The next step in the progression is to learn to manage irregular purchases such as haircuts, movies, school supplies, and birthday presents so that the child learns not only to predict, but also to plan for unusual expenses. Explain exactly what you expect their money to cover. This is a good time to begin a simple system for keeping records—a tally of what they spent it on and a want list to review before buying.

STEPS TO SAVING

The child naturally will want items more expensive than one week's allowance can cover. Use this opportuntiy to teach the child how to save by helping the child set realistic goals. In this beginning phase, help them reach short-term saving goals. An important aspect of financial maturity is being able to set a financial goal and then, keeping it in mind, save for it. In the beginning, telling a child he or she should put money in the bank to save for college is too abstract. Work on short-term projects first. Save money for vacation, to buy a camera or book—whatever it is they think they want. In the process of waiting, they often change their minds. There are some purchases (like a bicycle) where you may need to match funds. Such agreements are fine. And the child will probably take better care of the bicycle. It is a thrill to work hard for a goal and then make it.

Yes, there is a time to teach long-term saving. Children who pay for at least part of their college appreciate it more and are less likely to just glide through the four-year course. You may decide to start such an account before your child is ready to participate in its deposits. That's fine, but don't exclude the lessons from short-term goals. You could facilitate that by having two separate accounts—one earmarked for education and the other for short-term wants. Check around for the details of various accounts as some don't take out a service charge for juveniles.

As your children get older and start to work outside the home, what will be your savings requirements? Again, it's not a good idea for children to get the idea that any money they earn is just for play. There is such a thing as having too much spending money. One family insisted children save twenty-five percent of earnings for college or pay that much room and board. It depends on the child's other financial obligations. If they are working part time and paying for things such as car insurance, such demands about savings

MY MONEY

_____
month

Things I need	Things I want	Estimated plan for this month	
1. _____	1. _____		
2. _____	2. _____		
3. _____	3. _____		
4. _____	4. _____		
5. _____	5. _____		
6. _____	6. _____		

These are my purchases

Item	Want	Need	Cost

may be unfair. The important thing is that you discuss your expectations with your teen. Most parents gradually pull back in providing for wants, letting the child assume obligation for special clothing, makeup, dates, and recreation. When our first son got a full-time summer job, I went to the bank with him where he opened an account so he could cash his paycheck, deposit the agreed percent for savings, and walk away with the green that was his to spend. Before you have the money, it seems like it will buy much more than when you are actually laying it out. When the money is almost gone, with more things still to buy, there is a temptation not to save "this time." Depositing the savings money and settling other debts first was the solution for our son at that time.

PREPARE YOUR CHILD TO BE A
SUCCESSFUL WAGE EARNER

See that they learn some skills that are marketable and that build self-confidence. Prompt them to take advantage of local training sessions such as classes on babysitting, first aid, and proper care of equipment (the lawn mower or bicycle). Be aware of what the schools are offering. Encourage your children to learn skills that will prepare them for the working world. Some schools offer trade opportunities. Most high schools have classes in typing, sewing, and car maintenance. Boy Scouts and Girl Scouts have wonderful programs to make children aware of career choices and let them explore various fields. Schools also have classes in career exploration and tests to recommend aptitude. Your child will need help finding his or her first job and understanding the etiquette and performance that help one keep a job. Some parents set up a cottage business at home to teach their children how to work. Decision time: Will you provide the paying jobs, or will they earn money outside the home? It depends on your circumstances and the child's age. After about age twelve there can be opportunities to sell goods and services outside the family—things like caring for the neighbor's yard or pets during vacations, babysitting, or handling a paper route. The challenge for parents is to watch for teaching situations that prepare their children for these working opportunities. Most families go through the paper route stage. Help your child succeed Every child needs some sort of training—either delivering, collecting, or organizing. Others have tried offering goods or services. Our oldest daughter made $1,000 for a trip to Hawaii with the high school choir making and selling suckers.

It's good to have a job where regular, consistent performance is required. Baseball, swimming, and other extracurricular activities develop skills and discipline, but they don't teach personal responsibility in the same way that a job does. Kids need to learn to succeed to work.

CREATE BUDGETING EXPERIENCES

Create your own learning experiences to teach a child money management. A good time to do this is with school supplies or clothing purchases. Help them plan what they need and then shop wisely by watching sales and avoiding impulse buying. A short-term lesson in budgeting might be to plan your family vacation together, discussing the total money allotted—how much will be needed for gas, food, and lodging, and how much will be left for fun and entertainment. Then see how it unfolds during the vacation itself. Gradually give children more financial responsibility, preparing them for the time when they leave home and money management is totally theirs. One family has progressed to the point where they feel confident in giving each teen all his or her clothing and shoe allotment, school lunch money, bus fare, and allowance in one lump sum each month so the child can do his or her own budgeting.

You can create a good training experience by turning over a clothing allotment to your teens. But don't do it all at once. They will need training in shopping strategies and budgeting before you turn them loose. It's like learning to drive a car. There will be some textbook learning in the classroom, some practice driving on the range, a time when the young driver is under a permit and must be with an adult driver, and then a time when he or she has earned the right to drive alone. Just as we don't turn fourteen-year-olds loose with a car, you don't just hand them $50 a month. Yes, the young adult can have fun spending it, but if your object is to build a wardrobe and shape this person for a responsible adult life, take time to train this shopper.

Lay down the rules. What do you expect this money to cover? All clothing—including shoes, boots, swim suit, and winter coat? Or will you supplement for "special needs"? The dollar amount you give for clothing will depend on what you expect it to cover. If the allowance is not enough to allow the child unlimited spending, then teach skills for intentional spending. Young adults who enter life knowing how to set priorities—how to set one "want" above another—have a better chance of succeeding. When you lay out the rules, you also need to explain what will happen if the rules are broken.

Before the young person goes out on the "range," he or she should know what to look for. Most people buy clothes by impressions: "I love this." They collect "loves" that don't go with anything else and need far more clothes. Why do you think department stores have such large sections of clothing for the under-thirty crowd? Because they have extra money to spend, because they buy by impulse, and because they buy fads. Stores make lots of money on these impressionable shoppers. If you want your youngsters to learn to be satisfied, they must shop with direction—but that doesn't mean they can't have fun.

Go with your child, pencil and paper in hand, and help prepare an inventory of the closet and chest of drawers. This is very enlightening and will take less than thirty minutes. (Refer to the inventory chart on page 186.) Next, have the child write out a list of things he or she wants to buy. Obviously, your child can't buy everything with one month's clothing allowance. There will be some cutbacks, postponements, and tradeoffs. Money seems like it will go much farther "before" you get it. Bring these wants down to reality. Have the child rate each of his or her wants from one to ten, ten being the most desired. If I were you, before handing out the money, I would insist that my young teens prepare such an inventory/proposal. Then I would review it with them, offering suggestions but not making demands. For the first few years you will need to do this. Gradually pull back your help as your children prove their competence. You are preparing them for the total independence when they leave home and money management is completely theirs.

Youth need practice on the "driving range," learning the techniques and strategies of shopping. Perhaps you have already taught them how to evaluate fit and workmanship and to consider care instructions such as handwashing or dry cleaning. Your children will make some mistakes; we all do. That's the reason for training. When you first send them out shopping on their own, make them accountable to you, but without taking away all their freedom.

If this clothing allowance is to cover everything, some planning will be needed. What if your son wants to rent a tux or your daughter wants to buy a dress for the prom? What will happen when a winter coat costs $100? Will they need to save $10 a month toward that winter purchase? There will be no problem at all spending the allowance. The question is, will they have a reasonable wardrobe from the purchases? Think through investments. Is it logical to spend $90 on a party dress that will be worn twice? (That's $45 per wearing.) Life is tough. Guide your children in preparing a wardrobe plan. If they spend the allowance on new tennis shoes and socks this month, what will it go for next month? Teach them the tricks of seasonal shopping. They need to know the difference between a real bargain and an in-store feature. Somewhere along the line, take your child to an image consultant or enroll in a class that discusses personal color programs. Our eyes are not necessarily drawn to the colors we look best in. By establishing a color plan for the wardrobe, the consumer can gain more satisfaction from purchases.

If the child is part of the buying and accounting, he or she is likely to be more satisfied with the clothing selections. The child may take better care of the clothing and perhaps he or she will understand that tradeoffs have to be made when there is not enough money to buy everything now. When these young people enter adulthood, they can transfer these early lessons to other areas of financial planning and get more of what they want.

37. Organizing Kids for School

H elp your child get organized for school. It is a good stepping-stone for responsibility. Help the child to be a better student and improve self-concept by handling homework and small details like school notices and permission slips.

Help your children keep track of their things by **putting their name on everything** from notebooks to mittens. Put names on lunchboxes. (Personally I hate them. I would rather buy paper sacks than wash the box everyday. Besides, it's always in the way on the kitchen counter.) Permanent markers work on many surfaces; gummed address labels are convenient for others. Order fabric name labels from local fabric shops and stitch them into coats, hats, and gloves. (You can get a hundred for less than five dollars.) It takes so little time but the returns on lost, stolen, and misplaced items are tremendous.

Start the "bag habit," the sooner the better. Have the child take a backpack or tote bag to school. One kindergarten teacher made this a requirement. The children put notes to parents, finished work, permission slips, and library books in their bags to be taken home at the end of the day. At home, the bags become the "gathering point" for things to be returned to school. Success at school depends on how you organize and keep track of papers and things as well as on how much you know. Most children take school seriously and want to succeed at it. A simple vehicle such as the bag helps children get organized and increases confidence in their ability to handle the school experience. Luckily, backpacks and tote bags are in. Help your child get started on a good foot and begin reinforcing this pattern early in the year. You will need to establish an acceptable place for the bag to be kept at home.

One family made their children responsible for getting up and off to school from the beginning without parental prodding. The family tradition was to purchase an alarm clock for each child when they started first grade. If the child had difficulty getting up, the alarm clock was the bad guy, not the parent. These parents have also encouraged the child to pause at the door before leaving to ask him or herself, Do I have everything? and the children are learning personal responsibility. A helpful management technique is to identify an acceptable "launching pad," which serves as a collecting spot for lunch, gym suit, and homework.

Keep a family calendar on which you correlate activities and commitments. Encourage your child to transfer his or her school business onto the calendar—minimal days, photos, parties, field trips, practices, rehearsals, and meetings. Correlate family involvement by discussing upcoming events once a week. Children can begin this time management skill early and reap the rewards their whole life.

Children often do not have enough intrinsic motivation to do homework on their own. Parents should not take over or do the actual work for the child, but there are three basics: time, place, and support. Look over your child's papers when they are sent home and be interested in what the child is studying and how the papers are marked. Meet the teacher, go to parent-teacher conferences, review the textbooks. This is not a takeover, but responsible concern.

Create a place where learning is convenient. Provide a table or desk, good lighting, and proper supplies (paper, pen, pencil, dictionary, atlas, etc). This place may be a room designated as the "study" or it could be that everyone sits around the kitchen table or the child may have enough space in the bedroom for a quiet corner. I remember my first desk. I begged my fourth-grade teacher for homework so I could feel "grown up" and have reason to work at my desk. In the beginning it was play, but I think it started a good attitude toward school because I was having problems before then. Encourage your child to succeed at school without doing the work for him and you'll be initiating patterns of lifelong success.

Designate a time for homework. It is so hard to "find" time. It is much easier to have work periods set aside. Daily short sessions are better than one long cramming session. Keep them thirty minutes or less until the child's interest and aptitude increase. Since Friday is the day most reports are due and quizzes take place, it may be necessary to schedule some of your adult time to practice spelling words or to proof reports on Thursday evening. Cut down distractions during study time. Certainly don't rent a movie and expect the kids to do homework while you are watching it.

As parent, **be available to discuss or give support.** Do not take over. Instead of telling the child what to do, help him or her see what to do. Try the questioning technique: "What homework do you have tonight?" "When do you plan on doing it?" "Do you need a ride to the library?" "Will you need any assistance?" Don't ride your kids. There is a difference between hassling and encouraging. Homework is the child's responsibility, but a supportive parent makes the responsibility easier to carry, just as a parent's employment is easier if a child cooperates in helping with household chores. Peer influence in drug use, early dating, and other undesirable behavior is strong. If the child doesn't find satisfaction from doing a good job at school, the chance of following these influences increases as the child searches for something to give that "I belong" feeling.

Guide your child into setting weekly school goals to curtail ₂o-crastination, increase productivity, and limit forgetfulness. Mai. school assignments known well in advance are still put off until the last minute—weekly spelling or vocabulary test, Friday quizzes, term papers, and projects. Help them set priorities. For example, "I have to get _____done this week and I will start on this _____." So often, a teen's life revolves around homework and the young people are at their teachers' mercy. There are times when they have to decide which to do and which to let go. Help them weigh the consequences. Writing it out clarifies the situation so they can make a more logical decision. It may be helpful to use a chart like the one on page 265. After using these sheets for a month, Sidney, a high school sophomore, commented, "My life revolves around homework, and this chart helped me write everything down in one place and not forget it. It keeps me organized." High school students who maintain a part-time job or who participate in choir, band, athletics, or other extracurricular activities, in addition to their regular class load, need encouragement to organize their time and energy. A personal calendar might be the solution. Show them how. They can learn to fill in assignments and long-term projects and then plot a time line for getting them done. That's how business people tackle projects.

WEEK OF _____	
Things I Have to Do	**Things I Want to Do**
Monday	Tuesday
Wednesday	Thursday
Friday	Saturday/Sunday

One clever mother taught her teenagers to use a color coding system for schoolwork. Assign each class a different color (math green, English orange, chemistry yellow, etc.) Folders or notebooks, and bookcover correlate with subject. Colors gave an instant visual recognition. At the front of each notebook, the student kept an overview of the class, listing requirements, grading policy and a running tally of earned points. The young person always knew exactly where the grade stood. A good student has a good system for keeping track of handouts and notes. A good student paces homework so it can be turned in on time to get the best possible grade. Being a good student has as much to do with "paper flow as what you know."

SCHOOL PAPERS

Certain young children are attached to their schoolwork. They can't bear to throw it out after putting so much effort into it. What should you do with the paper? I set a dishpan marked "school papers" in the child's closet. When it is full, I instruct the child to go through it and keep only a few favorites. At the end of the year the child goes through the box and chooses ten favorites that we keep in a special progressive notebook. The dishpan is an effective limit. Some of my children couldn't care less, others appreciate this program. For display, I string a line across one wall of the bedroom on which to hang school art or posters with clothespins. When it is full, the child takes down an old one to make room for the new one. Another built-in limit. One family put corkboard in the hallway and created a "Hall of Fame" for display.

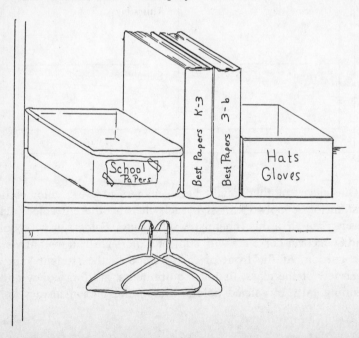

When students get into their teens they may find it beneficial to keep essays, terms papers, and book reports. For one thing, they should have a carbon copy in case the teacher loses the one they turned in. Second, over the years, many subjects like drugs and alcohol are discussed more than once and the student can build and expand the first report. Where can they keep this information? A fruit box is just the right size to hold file folders. Help the child set up a place for saving these papers and other loose reference material. As a parent, I also keep an eye open for information about Indians, dinosaurs, South America, drugs, careers, etc. It has come in handy many a night when we needed material after the library was closed. We don't want our kids to be pack-rats, just prepared. You can help them learn to manage the paper in their lives.

GETTING ORGANIZED FOR BIRTHDAYS AND HOLIDAYS

38. How To Simplify Card And Gift Giving

KEEP TRACK OF DATES

Devise a way to keep track of birthdays and anniversaries. One grandmother has a tole-painted birthday board, with all her grandchildrens' birth dates on it. If you like to send cards, you might like to buy them a month or even a year ahead. Address them all at once, and, in the corner where the stamp will go, write the date the card should be mailed. One thoughtful grandfather makes one excursion to the card shop, buys for the whole year, and then puts them in a three-ring notebook that has a pocket divider for each month. The grandchildren love to get mail, especially from Grandpa, and he always remembers! He has a system that helps him keep track.

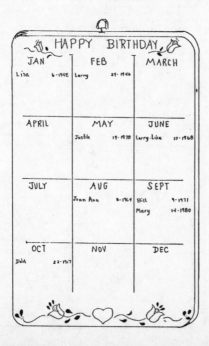

I keep a permanent list of special days in my planning notebook, and it only requires three pages. When a friend says "yesterday was my birthday," I write it down. Next year maybe I will send a note or give that person a call. As long as I'm making confessions, I do not buy cards except sympathy cards. With limited funds and so many

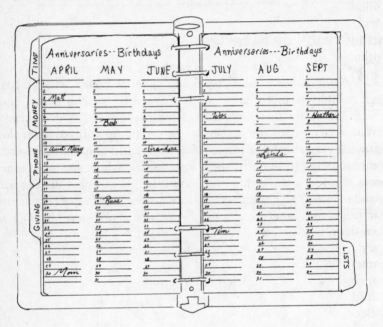

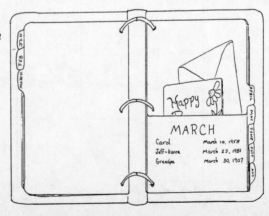

Make or buy a notebook with pocket-dividers for greeting cards.

gift-giving occasions, I need to spend the money on the gift rather than a card that will just get tossed away. We make our own cards if we have time. If not, we just cut out a motif from the wrapping paper and make a simple name tag. By the time I become a grandmother, I may do it differently. For now, I have a box of plain announcement cards on which I had printed on the front, "Mr. and Mrs. Robert McCullough." We use them with wedding gifts or for writing thank-yous; the rest of the cards we make ourselves or do without.

KEEP AN IDEA LIST

Even if you don't do anything else to prepare for Christmas from January to November, having an idea list is the biggest time- and nerve-saving secret I can offer. I suggest you nurture this art in two ways. First, gather ideas from hints others happen to drop and insights you receive all year long. The art of giving is to understand the people on your list and how they feel about things. Do they treasure handmade items and the effort that goes into them? Do they like practical, useful gifts or frivolities? It is a challenging game to watch your friends and family for hints of gifts they will appreciate. When it works, you both win. If you write down those gift ideas as they come, you won't forget them.

Secondly, ask each person (mom, dad, kids, grandma, and grandpa) for a "want list," giving a peek into their feelings and desires. It may take several tries to get adults to talk about their wishes, but keep after them. Each person is asked to be very specific by including inexpensive suggestions and some practical items as well as dream ideas. You aren't obligated to give these things, but it offers a nice range of ideas to fit the giver's budget and mood. We ask our children to begin a list the day after Thanksgiving; it's part of the tradition. It started more to keep the kids busy than as an organizational tactic. At first the children go through the dream catelog page by page and write down everything. But it's interesting to see how they narrow the fantasy. This activity also gives parents time to prepare the children should their hearts be set on something they cannot or do not want to give, letting the kids down gently and guiding their wants into other territories. We all have varying methods of handling gift giving. Keeping an idea list is handy whenever the occasion arises throughout the year and offers a starting point.

Keep in mind that every gift carries an obligation. There are times when it is not fair to give, especially extravagantly, because the receiver cannot handle the obligation that goes with the gift— not just the feeling that a gift must be given in return, but the feeling of commitment that is due the giver. Be sensitive to others and try not to make them feel uneasy, obligated, or guilty by your generosity. Keep those token gifts in line. A small gift of food does not usually carry the same amount of obligation as some other things.

Every year in her national newspaper column, Ann Landers prints a letter that goes about like this: "Dear Ann: My husband has not worked for over a year and we are just barely making ends meet. Is there a tactful way to stop exchanging Christmas presents? We can't afford to send any, and we don't want any gifts, so how can this be handled?" Her reply usually reads: "As I've suggested before, around Thanksgiving, send cards to those on your Christmas gift list saying, 'We are thankful for folks with whom we can be frank. We are not in a position to send Christmas gifts this year, and we don't expect gifts, but please accept our love and sincere good wishes for a healthy, happy, blessed holiday.' "

Now I ask you, if you received a letter like the one above from your sister asking to be relieved of a burden of exchanging gifts, what is your inclination? Since she is having a hard time, you would probably want to help; more than ever you want to be generous. But if you send something, how would she feel? Guilty. Help her maintain her dignity. If you choose to send something, food carries less obligation than other tangible items. Perhaps you can wait and send something later, maybe you can send money anonymously through her minister. Only you can decide. Be sensitive to how your generosity affects others.

DEVELOP AN OVERALL PLAN

If gift-giving is a part of your lifestyle, you will also need to organize that territory. First, decide on some overall policies, as this area of life involves both time and money.

1. How will you accommodate gifts for immediate family and close friends? Yearly occasions such as birthdays, Christmas, Mother's Day, Father's Day?
2. What will you do about occasional gifts that are given for wedding, baby, birthdays outside family, and "tickler," token, or special-occasion gifts. What about flowers for a funeral?

A major consideration is money. Will your budget allow these items? Will you "blow it" every time? Generosity is a virtue, but if it is not governed, it can be a vice. Get over the idea that the size, expense, or novelty of a gift represents the depth of your love. Set an amount that is within reason and then shop within that amount. Gift items purchased for immediate family members would logically come from the standard family budget. For example, if you purchased a new pair of slacks and sweater for your son's birthday, that would come from the family clothing allowance, even though it was a gift. I would suggest a small monthly fund for gifts outside the family, perhaps within the "entertainment" category to accommodate occasional giving. If you celebrate Christmas with a lot of gift giving, you are better off to save ahead than follow the "splurge and scrimp" method so many holiday shoppers use. It's crazy to be paying for Christmas purchases in June when you would rather be on vacation. Everyone uses a list to help them organize their Christmas giving, but many forget to set money limits. You can still have fun shopping, but you won't suffer the long, dry, out-of-money spell the rest of the winter. Don't look at this holiday, as "it only comes *once* a year" rather consider it comes *every single year.* Learn to plan for it and stay within reasonable limits. To help me stay within my circumstances, I watch for classes on various skills like flower arranging or stitching soft sculpture that allow me to make some of our gifts in my spare time. You would be surprised how much you can accomplish if you do some little project with your hands every night while watching the evening news.

A second consideration is time. How will you manage to shop for or find enough time to make the gifts? Part of your decision will depend on how often these gift-giving occasions arise. Because my husband and I have lived in the same community for such a long time, we know many people and are invited to at least twenty wedding receptions a year. Add another four or five baby showers and a dozen birthday parties that involve the children. The cost can become burdensome. The urgency to go "shopping" for each occasion always seems inopportune. I don't want to sound heartless, but out of self defense we initiated three actions. Naturally, immediate family and special friends have different consideration.

1. **Eliminate some giving.** An invitation is usually not a mandate. If you are not close to this person or don't feel a particular desire to give a gift to celebrate this occasion, don't. I am not sure where formal etiquette stands, but I do not give both a shower and wedding gift to casual friends.

2. **Give generically.** Decide on a "standard" wedding gift once, and give the same thing to each couple. Again, I don't mean to be heartless, but save yourself the process of "finding" the right gift every time. When we were living on a school teacher's income, our standard gift was a pair of pillowcases that I made from nylon tricot and trimmed with lace. Now, my "standard" gift is a copy of my book *Totally Organized*. I spent six hundred fifty hours explaining how to get control at home, what more could I give of myself? Choose a "standard" within your capabilities. People who have money but not time handle this by calling the department store where the bride has registered and order a piece of silver or china from the pattern the bride has selected. For a baby shower, I usually give a set of bibs; it's practical and no one else thinks of it. On the other hand, if you just love to shop and look around, do it. To me, shopping is not recreation. Another possibility: reduce the hassle by going together as a group and giving one major gift rather than several small ones.

Some people face a problem of "have-to" giving. Gifts that must be sent because of obligation when the feeling of love or enthusiasm is restrained. These feelings arise from (1) unsettled relationship problems; (2) not knowing the individual well enough or being around him or her often enough to know what to give; (3) he or she already has everything; (4) the person is hard to please; and (5) gift-giving is a financial burden for you. I do not know all the answers. Each person will resolve and compromise a little differently. If everyone feels the same, maybe it is time to break the tradition. Sometimes the answer is in giving generically—gift certificates, food, or magazine subscriptions. Other people make a donation to charity in honor of the receiver.

3. **Have a backup supply.** In a remote, out-of-the-way corner, keep a few gifts, buying things as you see them or when they are on sale. This can save last-minute shopping if your child receives a party invitation or you're unexpectedly invited to a shower and don't have the cash or the time to run out and buy something. By getting an item on sale, you can give something nicer than your budget would normally allow. Caution: Don't get too many gifts ahead. Styles and stages change.

The major disadvantage of buying gifts ahead is they lose their appeal. Whenever you make a purchase, there are emotions that go along with it. This applies to items you buy to stock the "gift shelf" as well as for people who are so organized they buy three Christmas gifts each month from January to October. Suppose in February you buy an absolutely beautiful sweater for your daughter for next Christmas. You tuck it away on the top shelf of your closet, and to make sure you don't forget about it, as so many of us do, you write it down in your notebook. In December, you get the sweater out to wrap it, you still think it is pretty, but an urge swells up inside you to "buy something else to go along with it." The sweater no longer seems like enough, not necessarily because of the dollar value, but because the emotional satisfaction, the emotional anticipation of seeing her receive the gift has faded. After several months, the fun, the excitement, the impulsiveness you felt at the time of purchase has diminished. Your wants have changed and so has your perception of her wants. When you understand what is happening, you can often resolve this problem. People who make this buying-ahead-system work for them usually do it with token gifts or with gifts for extended family members. For intimate relationships, they buy within the season. You might try doing most of the shopping ahead, but saving a few things to buy at the last minute so you can catch the excitement of the holiday crowds. Keeping a list of things you have already purchased may help make a logical evaluation. You need to understand the source of your hangup before you can solve it. My problem was that the earlier I started, the more I bought, and I kept escalating. For myself, the solution was to open a Christmas savings account, put in a little every month, and not start shopping until after Halloween. Giving the season a boundary helped me to cut back on regrets, mistakes, and overspending.

You need a long-range plan for your giving so it doesn't get out of hand. If you have children, consider what you will give at a particular age. Start out simple. Think about what you are starting when you hand a two-year-old ten presents. Giving to children has a crescendo affect so start small. If you give your five-year-old a bike, what will you give him when he is eight—a radio? And will he have a stereo by the time he is twelve? We all like to give our children special things—my tax man calls them "bell ringers." But in your efforts to delight, pace your giving. Don't give a child a bike until he or she is mature enough to understand and follow traffic regulations. Save that radio until later; radio programs are not targeted at children. Think about saving some desirables until the child is a teenager. Consider the child's educational and social activities at the time. Gifts can be a way to help children explore and discover their likes and aptitudes, but let a child enjoy the toys of childhood—don't toss him or her into the adult world too soon. Gifts, chosen carefully, can be good investments in a child's overall education.

SET UP A GIFT WRAP CENTER

Set up a mini-center for gift wrapping. If you have enough space, you may designate a corner and set it up permanently with all the needed supplies. Otherwise, choose a shelf on which to put your box of supplies. When it's time to wrap, pull out the box, take care of the project, and then put everything away. You have the efficiency of order but don't have to give permanent space to that occasional activity. At my home we use a combination of both systems. During the year, wrapping supplies are kept in a box in the linen closet (not used for linens because they are kept in individual bedrooms and bathroom.) I try to keep a pair of scissors and a roll of tape with it. During sales, I buy a variety of inexpensive paper that can be used for various occasions. I keep ribbons in a mesh-style dishpan. Within the family, we often use the same bows several times.

When the Christmas season arrives, I set up a more detailed system for organizing gift wraps and supplies. In the beginning, I collected them all in my bedroom, and everyone used my bed on which to wrap, always leaving a mess. My solution was to make the supplies portable so the kids could take them to their own bedrooms or set up a temporary work station at the table. I bought a plastic wastebasket large enough to contain the tall rolls of paper. A pocket apron, like the cloth nail-aprons you find at a hardware store, was attached to the front to hold little things like tape and name tags. Make a small hole in the soft plastic and insert something like a shower-curtain ring or even a piece of string to hold the apron in place. Tie a pair of scissors onto the basket—they will stay around longer.

Try making yourself a gift-wrap organizer. You'll absolutely love it. Mail order catalogues offer a cardboard version, but carefully read the size description because some of them are so small they don't hold very many large rolls of paper.

I am probably the only woman in the United States who does not buy gift-wrap paper the day after Christmas. It takes up too much space and space costs money. Second reason: Even after Christmas, I still have so many wants, that if I am lucky enough to have any money left, I do not want to spend it on a holiday 364 days away. I find that if I catch the first sale of the season on gift wrap, right around Thanksgiving, I can come within pennies of the after-Christmas sales but have a choice of all the new papers in lovely designs. The only reason I store Christmas wrapping paper is if I have some left over.

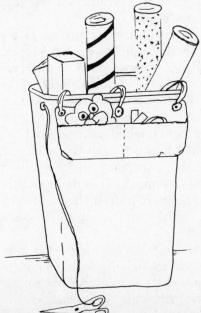

*Make your own gift wrap center
from a large waste basket.*

THE CHRISTMAS MUSHROOM

It starts out as such an innocent thing—a desire to share your love and charity and an effort to make the season "special." With those admirable goals, you can turn the holiday into a very stressful and depressing time. The name of the Christmas Mushroom comes not from a tiny plant, but from an atomic explosion, an escalation that results from trying to create a memorable holiday. A prime example of the Christmas mushroom: As a thank-you token, the wife of a junior high school principal decided to order and put on a special buffet of breads, cheeses, and cold cuts for her husband's faculty. The affair went very well. (The cost—over a hundred dollars.) Next year, the hint comes to do it again. Is she committed for life? Traditions start so innocently, but they can turn into bonds of slavery if you don't manage them. Another example: One year, in a moment when we were caught in the spell of Christmas, my husband said, "Let's buy a computer and give it to the family for Christmas." After thinking it over, we decided to wait until January to buy the family computer and eliminate any link between the holiday and such an expensive investment. Don't create a monster you can't finance. Next year, in an effort to make Christmas "special" the inclination is to do something even greater than last year. Take hold, give direction to this area of your life.

A big part of the mushroom is our giving and buying. As the gateway to spending is opened more than usual, two things happen: (1) It quickens generosity for giving to those you love and care about; and (2) it awakens your own desire for things. You begin to see all the things you can use, the things you have always wanted. Follow such a person around, and you'll see them buy more for themselves than they do as gifts. There is moral infringement here, but if your holiday budget is limited, the money may be gone before the gift list is filled. Everyone makes a shopping list for their gift buying, but many people forget to set limits, both on the amount to spend and the number of gifts to be given. Instead, they are led by impulse and excitement, which is why stores set up enticing displays and offer wonderful sales.

Another way we expand gift giving is to buy "side gifts, especially for those to whom we already give major gifts. Watch someone caught in this cycle. They buy a round of gifts at every sales promotion between October to December. When the Avon catalog comes, they order something for everyone from it. At the school book fair and at the craft sale, they buy another round of gifts. Eventually the realization comes that none of the items "count" as a primary or main gift; they are all secondary. In their enthusiasm to give, many parents magnify by giving: (1) a main gift or bell-ringer; (2) something whimsical; (3) something practical (book, socks); (4) new pajamas (so they look nice for pictures on Christmas morning; (5) a new outfit of clothing; (6) an ornament; and (7) a big stocking full of trivia. Recognizing it is the first step. Decide on two types of limits: money and quantity. Second, write out a gift list, refer to it often, using it as a guide, not to take out the fun, but so you don't lose vision.

39. Handling Major Holidays

W e all enjoy holiday festivities—parties, reunions, concerts, and programs. We look forward to giving gifts to loved ones and seeing the special light that shines in their eyes as they open our gaily wrapped offerings. We relish the traditions of preparing food and taking part in various activities centered around our families and neighborhoods. We love the special and magical spirit that is all around us. However, as the season progresses, the gifts, the extra projects we have taken on, and the things we want to do begin to crowd our everyday life. Projects, parties, and programs intended for our pleasure and entertainment can become "obligations," and the fun disappears.

Whether you celebrate Hanukkah or Christmas or both, this is the time of year to put all your management skills into practice. For most of us it involves at least six weeks of our spare time and lots of money. It is our love and excitement for this season that tempts us to go beyond reasonable commitments. We want to take part in more and more; we don't get quite enough sleep; we spend a little more than we should. If ever there was a time for planning, writing things down, making lists, and accepting our limitations, this is it.

Plan. The first step is to take a careful look at your available time. Just like money, time in the future looks like it will cover a lot more than it actually will. Bring it down to reality. To start, grab a piece of paper, a pencil, and a calendar. You will find it helpful to staple or tape several calendar pages together so that you get an instant overview of the entire holiday season (six to ten weeks). On the paper, write down all the things you want to do in order to be ready for the big day. (For simplicity, we will use Christmas as an example. But the same ideas apply to Hanukkah or any busy time, even preparing for a wedding or a move.) You may still be adding to this list for several days as you collect data. List in detail the necessary preparations—for gifts, baking, cards, pictures, craft or sewing projects, decorating, etc. Some of these activities can be delegated, and the nice thing about preplanning is that when you are organized you are better able to utilize help from others, including spouse, children, and employees. Collect activity and program dates. What day is school out? When will the company party be held? The church program? The school play? Piano recital? Craft sale? Dig deep into your memory of last year for parties, programs, and obligations that may recur. Will there be a house guest? This may mean that housecleaning will take priority over other things.

Next exercise: Put both the things to do and your commitments in the calendar squares. You'll be surprised how full it is already. Set up intermediate deadlines for projects. You've noticed how cool and collected your friends are who have to mail all their packages early in November. Set up some of your own deadlines so everything isn't backed up to Christmas Eve. This is where good management practice comes in handy. Notice the sample Christmas Planning Chart. Use this planning strategy whether you start early in November or are down to the last minute. If you were selling tickets to a theater, you could let in only as many people as you had seats. Similarly, only so many extra projects will fit comfortably on your holiday calendar. Recognize when it is full and then stop. Writing plans on the calendar will bring them into a concrete visual dimension. If you are working a full-time job, have a new baby, care for an invalid parent, or have been ill yourself, take these limitations into account.

Try to allow a time cushion for unexpected emergencies such as the dishwasher breaking down or the children getting sick. Expect some unexpected happenings; they come every year. If you have children, reserve the last few days for the extra time they will need with you and for the little details you couldn't foresee. This calendar exercise is not hard, but it is vital. It gives you a visual picture of how much you can take on without spoiling the pleasure of the holidays. Remember the third week of November will be taken up with the details of Thanksgiving preparations, and the children are home from school. Also remember that children take up more time during this busy season with rehearsals, costumes, programs, or wanting help making little gifts for teachers, family, and friends. More activity means more mess, which means more housecleaning.

All of these things multiply and complicate the season, and that is why you don't want to overschedule.

At this point, if you are realistic you may find that you can't do all the things on your list, so set priorities. Decide what has to be taken care of and which things can be postponed or skipped, using the basic "selected neglect" system. Look at each item on your calendar in terms of its priority—is this item something that *needs* to be done or is it just something you *want* to be able to complete? Keep the calendar and reassess it often. It is reassuring that we celebrate this holiday, but every detail need not be exactly the same from year to year. If things are too stressful, avoid taking on more. Recognize that you can't do everything, but if you start getting organized, you can get more done than you otherwise could.

Set a cutoff date. Several years ago at our children's school program, I sat next to a friend who was calmly enjoying the pageant. Wringing my hands, anxious to get home to finish a quilt, doll, and a down vest, this woman sat calmly taking pictures and enjoying her children. Leaning over, I asked, "What's your secret?" She answered, "I put all my mother-only projects away by December tenth if they aren't finished, and just ride the tide." Right there I vowed that I wouldn't get caught under pressure again, and I would set an early cutoff deadline like my cool friend.

The next year, remembering the lesson, I decided I would use December 15 as my cut-off date because that was the last day my children and husband were in school. I assumed that December 10 was probably a little exaggerated, since I am an organizer. I learned the hard way that the cutoff date needs to be one week *before* school is out, because, as usual, things kept coming up to delay my progress and the last week of school found me down to the wire and hoping for every minute to finish making an afgan, pajamas, and robe. I did not have any cushion for last-minute, unpredictable requests. The following is the list of things my family asked me to help them with: two gifts for husband's secretaries, one faculty-party token gift, two requests for three dozen cookies each, twelve loaves of rye bread (for children's teachers), one hundred suckers, two dozen rolls, seven secret Santa gifts, two ornaments to trade at church dinner, one French dish for pot-luck supper (I don't cook French), breakfast for fifteen teenagers, and two more batches of suckers. No wonder I lost the spirit. And yet it was my own fault. I wanted to help my family and teach the virtues of generosity, but at the same time I had other things to do—all self-imposed, but nevertheless, stressful. This example illustrates some of the most important principles of organizing Christmas, that is, managing your time by recognizing your limitations, learning to say no, and establishing a cutoff date. Every year, no matter how carefully I plan, when it gets close to the final hour I have to pack some projects away because I don't have time to finish everything I had hoped. (I refuse to give half-finished items with promises to complete it in January, because that month has enough of its own stressful surprises.)

One year after I had explained this whole theory to a newspaper reporter, she asked, "Well then, Bonnie, this year you won't have that last-minute pressure, will you?" I had to confess that I would probably always have that difficulty because "as soon as I see that I can get everything done on time, my mind latches onto another wonderul idea for something that I might just be able to work in if I push myself a little harder."

Keep up. When I put my house on "hold," for whatever reason—a writing assignment, working, canning, or holiday projects—there is a minimum amount of work that must be done each day or we sink into clutter and undoneness. What is your minimum? You can tell you have cut too much when frustration and confusion hit. Recognizing and keeping your minimum household requirements will help you enjoy outside projects without everything falling apart at home. Remember to make the dinner decision before ten o'clock. If you will be away from home during the day, that means ten the night before; if you are to be home, it means ten in the morning. For even better efficiency during this busy season, plan menus a week ahead and post them so other family members can get started on dinner if you should be delayed. Otherwise, without thinking, you may be using money to eat out (not for pleasure, but for lack of plan), money that you would rather spend on gifts. Take time every day to maintain normalcy with a five-minute pickup in every room (a little longer in the kitchen). Also keep up with the laundry and dirty dishes because falling behind will immobilize a household very quickly, leading to frustration, discouragement, and depression that blocks those holiday plans.

SAMPLE PLANNING CALENDAR

31 Halloween	Nov. 1	2 Cut out placemats	3 Music lessons	4 **Deadline—duplicate family letter**	5 Sew bias trim	6 Craft sale
7	8	9 Meeting	10 Sew napkins Music lessons	11 Shopping	12 **Deadline—complete napkins and placemats**	**13**
14	**15**	**16** **Shopping**	**17** **Music lessons**	18	19	20 **Deadline—bake fruitcake**
21	22	23	24 Bake pies Music lessons	25 Thanksgiving (no school)	26 Bake gingerbread for houses	27 Extended family party
28	29	30 **Deadline—mail packages**	Dec. 1 Music lessons	2 **Deadline—address cards**	3	4 Host buffet for teens before dance
5	6 School craft sale Deliver crafts 8:00 A.M.	7 Shopping	8 (half-day of school) Music lessons	9 Band concert	10 **Deadline—adult-only crafts and sewing completed**	11 Clean house
12 **Deadline—decorations up**	13 Decorate gingerbread houses	14 School program	15 Youth caroling Music lessons	16 **Deadline—main gift shopping finished**	17 School class parties Office party	18 Church social
19 Recital	20 No school ---------- Clean house	21 Clean house	22 Grandma arrives	23	24 Family night	25 Christmas Day
26 Boxing Day Write thank-you notes	27 Kids' break-up-gingerbread-house-party (one friend each)	28	29 Sledding party	30	31 Host New Year's Eve party	Jan. 1 Take down tree and decorations

Keep calm. As Christmas Day draws closer, recognize that the little ones will need more and more adult companionship. They are anxious, excited, and hyper, and need help dealing with those feelings. It is often said, "Christmas is for chidren," but sometimes we wish they would wait quietly on a chair and just show up serenely on Christmas morning. That will not happen, and what's more, children may misbehave, not even responding to threats that "Santa won't come." A better solution is to look for ways to let the children be a part of your preparations. Assign one to be in charge of displaying cards on the door or wall or banister—wherever you put them. Children love sealing envelopes and licking stamps. Let them take part in getting ready—decorating the tree, making gifts, baking, sending cards, cracking nuts, learning songs and stories. Try to maintain a reasonable routine for children including regular bedtimes, naps when appropriate, and sit-down meals. Make sure you and they eat nutritiously, avoiding too many sugary foods. As the final day draws nearer, build a climax by allowing more time to be with your children. Picking a compassionate service project that they can take part in will also help the time pass quickly, and it will draw their attention away from "What am I getting?" to the fun of giving. As adults we often put up our tree and decorations early because we enjoy the atmosphere but remember it increases the "waiting time" for the child. If you have young children, don't torment them by putting packages under the tree too early.

Give some thought to activities they can do at home, because you can't take them to places of entertainment all the time. We all think of letting children help make and frost cookies, but that creates such a mess that most parents do it only *once* a year. Have just as much fun without the flour mess by allowing the kids to trace around the cookie-cutter shapes on paper, thin foam sheets, or felt. Be prepared with a few other craft projects and have the supplies on hand so you can pull them out at the right moment. For starters, consider the following: Make paper chains from red, white, and green paper, or cut out snowflakes from paper napkins. Let them string popcorn, breakfast cereals, candy, cranberries, peanuts, or bits of styrofoam packing. They can make place cards, gift tags, or placemats (paper disposables are available at the grocery store), from old cards, or by tracing around cookie cutters. Make your own ink stamps. No need to carve a carrot or potato, just buy a package of Dr. Scholl's adhesive foam, in the foot department at the drug-store. Draw a simple figure or word on the paper backing, cut it out, peel it off, and stick the foam to a little block of wood. Presto, you're ready to dab the stamp on an ink pad and start decorating paper for wrap or cards. Red and green ink pads are available in office supply departments. If you don't want all these snowflakes and chains in your living room, let the children decorate their bedrooms. Put a paper tree on their wall or the back of the door. One family buys a fresh, three-foot "Charlie Brown" tree for kids to decorate themselves. Libraries and bookstores have hundreds of activity and craft books from which to glean ideas. Remember that your friends are feeling the same pressure and their children are also experiencing hyperactivity. Perhaps you can swap children.

We battle fantasies of perfect families at this time of year. The holiday season is not all happiness for anyone. Accidents happen, illness strikes, disagreements surface, kids get overtired or behave selfishly. Your children, like everyone else's will probably say on Christmas morning, "Is this all?" It doesn't make them bad, naughty, or selfish, it means they are normal. Plan something on Christmas day to help them through this letdown. Some of the problems at Christmastime can be handled by lowering expectation and accepting imperfection while others can be dealt with by planning. No season is perfect, but yours may be better because you managed with reason and logic, not impulse.

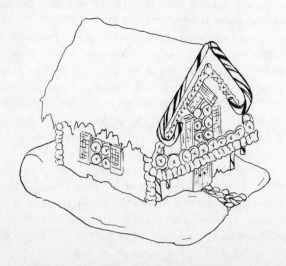

40. The Last Word

Let me tell you of an incident that happened ten years ago. My husband was the Scoutmaster of an eager bunch of Boy Scouts. With a good committee behind them, they had set up a plan for the whole year with monthly camp-outs and activities. My husband came to me distressed when it dawned on him that he had committed to a camp-out on our wedding anniversary. He asked if I would consider celebrating a day later. What could I say? But I was still a little unhappy to think that he would be in the mountains with a dozen boys and I would be home alone. Then I decided it really wasn't his choice and maybe I could do something special for him. A plan began to formulate in my head. As soon as my husband left for work the morning of our anniversary, I started to make his most favorite thing in the world—cherry pies. When they were finished, I opened the windows and cooked cabbage so he would not detect the smell. I wrapped a pie in foil and slipped it under the car seat. As I packed his dinner for the camp-out, I tucked in a note: "Happy Anniversary. Though we can't share it together, you'll find a surprise under the front seat of the car, but you must not get it out until after the Scouts have gone to their tents. Love you always." What a hit. Somehow everyone in camp found out about my anniversary surprise and sent home a "Scouter's Wife Award."

After reading that story you might assume that I do things like that all the time. Do not make assumptions. You need to know that I did that once, a long time ago. I do not even make pies for my husband's birthday because his mother usually offers. This is my point, so do not miss it: When we hear of, or read about an example that is intended to give us hope or offer suggestions, in our minds we add assumptions. From the vignette, you might assume that I make pies or cutesy little surprises all the time. After reading this book, you may have all sorts of crazy notions. You may even be comparing yourself to a "perfectly organized person" who exists only in an imaginary world. I certainly hope my readers do not have the impression that I am perfect. Not long ago the PTA president at

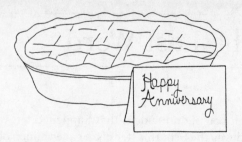

our school said, "I find it hard to believe, Bonnie, that you are the same person that writes those columns in the newspaper." For one thing, I purposely try to be very low-key in my own circles, but second, this woman is making assumptions. Maybe she thinks I should have the PTA account books balanced every day. Perhaps she assumes that my kids always do their chores, that dinner is always ready at five-thirty, that I am never rushed or behind, or that I do not get discouraged. Like everyone else in the world, I must cope with have-tos and the demands of the outside world, and still find time for my own wants. Every year I have to adjust to new problems and reshuffle my priorities. I have a little sign on my front door— YOU DON'T HAVE TO BE CAUGHT UP TO BE IN CONTROL—because people are disappointed when they find my house does not always rate a ten. If you were to drive down my street or to walk into every house in our neighborhood, you probably couldn't tell which one was mine. The clue comes when you add up how many things we get to do. I am not a superwoman. But I will forcefully tell you that my capacity is much, much greater than it was twenty years ago. There are so many things I have been able to do, even while working and raising a family, that I could not have done if I had not redirected my work patterns and organized my home. When we look at another's successes, we tend to assume it was easy. We do not see what they have given up to reach those accomplishments. There is a heap of work in living. I have spent tremendous amounts of time studying home management. I have spent thousands of hours sharing this information through both writing and teaching. But it does not take away the fact that next week I will have to put in 28 hours of housekeeping at my home. It's not just a question of how much you know, the questions are: Do you use it? Does it help you?

To be organized is not synonymous with meticulous. To be organized means you do things for a good reason at the best time and in

290

the easiest way. To be organized does not mean that you never get lost. It means you know how to find your way back. It doesn't mean that you never get behind, rather that you can stick to it until you have recovered. Setting up organizational systems in your home for paper, people, food, money, and things is like laying down a sprinkling system for your yard. Initially, it takes time and money to install that sprinkling system, but after it is down, all you have to do is turn a dial. The same applies to the programs you can develop at your home. Then you need to be alert because adjustments need to be made as you make transitions from one phase of life to the next.

No one teacher can give you all the answers you need because homes and cities and climates and individuals are too different. Using the problem-solving process will help you to find your own answers. You will also want to continue your search for help from other books, magazines, teachers, family, and friends as you refine your special systems. Each organizer has a little different perspective and a unique way of explaining things. However, you will often find similar principles coming forth from New York, Denver, and Los Angeles at the same time because what works, works; truth is truth.

Life is like sailing on the sea of calm and stormy water. The captain of a ship cannot control the storms, but he/she can direct the ship safely through most. You cannot control some of life's problems. But you can be the captain, direct the crew, give instructions, and see that the supplies are on board. You can listen to the forecast; prepare yourself; watch for signs, and when the storm comes, tighten the hatches and steer. A captain knows how to steer into the waves at the right angle and not destroy the ship. You know how to use MM to keep from sinking. You have learned not to complicate your house with too much "stuff." You have ideas for keeping up with the laundry and the dishes, or organizing paper and managing money, husband, and kids. The information is yours. May you be able to manage your home as a good captain and may you not only get where you want to go but also enjoy the trip.

> You Don't Have to Be Caught Up
> to Be in Control

Index